Bloom's Modern Critical Views

Bloom's Modern Critical Views

Bloom's Modern Critical Views

LEO TOLSTOY

Edited and with an introduction by
Harold Bloom
Sterling Professor of the Humanities
Yale University

CHELSEA HOUSE
P U B L I S H E R S
A Haights Cross Communications Company

Philadelphia

Library of Congress Cataloging-in-Publication Data

Leo Tolstoy / edited and with an introduction by Harold Bloom.
    p. cm. -- (Bloom's modern critical views)
Includes bibliographical references and index.
  ISBN 0-7910-7444-7
  1. Tolstoy, Leo, graf, 1828–1910--Criticism and interpretation. I.
Bloom, Harold. II. Series.
  PG3411.L416 2003
  891.73'3--dc21
                                2002155991

Chelsea House Publishers
1974 Sproul Road, Suite 400
Broomall, PA 19008-0914

http://www.chelseahouse.com

Contributing Editor: Janyce Marson

Cover designed by Terry Mallon

Cover photo by ©Bettmann/CORBIS

Layout by EJB Publishing Services

Contents

Editor's Note

My Introduction centers upon Tolstoy's superb, late short novel, *Hadji Murad*.

R. P. Blackmur somberly concludes that human life could not sustain Anna Karenina's "intensity," while Isaiah Berlin sees Tolstoy's as Enlightenment's martyr, sacrificing everything for the truth.

John Bayley finds that Tolstoy's answer to *What is Art?* is his own *Anna Karenina*.

Anna A. Tavis contrasts the different anarchisms of Tolstoy and Joyce, after which Amy Mandelker centers upon Anna Karenina's self-presentation as aesthetic object.

Caryl Emerson, in the first of two essays here, juxtaposes Tolstoy and Dostoevsky, using Bakhtin as a corrective to George Steiner.

W. Gareth Jones explores the varied epic narratives of *War and Peace*, while Martin Bidney searches the great book for its epiphanies.

Felicia Gordon analyzes some of the ironies of adultery in *Anna Karenina*, and in Theodore Fontane's *Effi Briest*.

The spiritual battle between Tolstoy's vision of death and Dostoevsky's passion for immortality is outlined by A. Galkin, after which Vladimir Golstein rather harshly finds Anna Karenina a victim of the Peter Pan Syndrome: Not to Grow Up.

In a final essay, Caryl Emerson returns to meditate upon Pushkin's comfort with the ethics of language as opposed to Tolstoy's dark intimation that the peasants had the truth, with their immemorial proverbs and their freedom from reading.

Introduction

With God he has very suspicious relations; they sometimes
remind me of the relation of "two bears in one den."
—MAXIM GORKY, *Reminiscences of Tolstoy*

T olstoy, while at work upon his sublime short novel, *Hadji Murad*, wrote
an essay on Shakespeare in which he judged *King Lear*, *Hamlet* and *Macbeth*
to be "empty and offensive." Reading one of his few authentic rivals, Tolstoy
"felt an overpowering repugnance, a boundless tedium." Homer and the
Bible were equals he could recognize, but Shakespeare unnerved him. The
customary explanation is that Tolstoy was morally offended by Shakespeare,
but the truth is likely to be darker. *Hadji Murad* has a mimetic force difficult
to match elsewhere. To find representations of the human that compel us to
see reality differently, or to see aspects of reality we otherwise could not see
at all, we can turn to only a few authors: the Yahwist or "J" writer (who made
the original narratives in what are now Genesis, Exodus, Numbers), Homer
and Dante, Chaucer and Shakespeare, Cervantes and Tolstoy and Proust. Of
all these, Tolstoy most resembles "J." The art of Tolstoy's narratives never
seems art, and the narratives themselves move with an authority that admits
no reservations on the reader's side. Gorky wrote of Tolstoy that: "He talks
most of God, of peasants, and of woman. Of literature rarely and little, as
though literature were something alien to him." The *Reminiscences of Tolstoy*
is continually astonishing, but perhaps most memorable when Gorky
describes Tolstoy playing cards:

> How strange that he is so fond of playing cards. He plays
> seriously, passionately. His hands become nervous when he takes
> the cards up, exactly as he were holding live birds instead of
> inanimate pieces of cardboard.

1

That is the author of *Hadji Murad*, rather than of *What is Art?* Tolstoy holds Hadji Murad in his hands, as if indeed he held the man, and not a fiction. I read Tolstoy only in translation, and believe that I miss an immense value, but what remains in *Hadji Murad* overwhelms me afresh at every rereading. Tolstoy finished the novella in September 1902, shortly after his seventy-fourth birthday. Perhaps the story was his profound study of his own nostalgias, his return to his own youth, when he had participated as a volunteer in the Caucasian campaign (1851), at the age of twenty-three, and when he wrote *The Cossacks* (1858, published 1863).

Everything outward in *Hadji Murad* is historical, and Tolstoy evidently was precise and faithful in adhering to documented fact, and yet the inward story is a phantasmagoria so powerful as to devour and replace whatever we might yearn to call reality. Hadji Murad, like every other major figure in the narrative, was both a historical personage, and a living legend in Tolstoy's time, yet he is Tolstoy's vitalistic vision at its most personal, persuasive, and poignant, being a vision of the end. That is to say, *Hadji Murad* is a supreme instance of what the heroic Chernyshevsky, critic and martyr, praised as Tolstoy's prime gifts: purity of moral feeling, and the soul's dialectic, its antithetical discourse with itself.

Perhaps *Hadji Murad* can also be read as the return in Tolstoy of the pure storyteller, who tells his story as a contest against death, so as to defer change, of which the final form must be death. Tolstoy's ruinous meditations upon the power of death ensue from his awesome sense of life, a vitality as intense as his own Hadji Murad's. His crisis in the mid-1870s, when he wrote *Anna Karenina*, as set forth in his *Confession* (1882), supposedly turned upon a dread of nihilism, a conviction that no meaning of any life could be preserved once it ceased. But Tolstoy's famous refusal to divide life from literature, which could lead to the absurdity of his "Shakespeare" essay, led also to *Hadji Murad*. Consider the opening of the novella (I give the Aylmer Maude translation):

> I was returning home by the fields. It was mid-summer, the hay harvest was over and they were just beginning to reap the rye. At that season of the year there is a delightful variety of flowers— red, white, and pink scented tufty clover; milkwhite ox-eye daisies with their bright yellow centres and pleasant spicy smell; yellow honey-scented rape blossoms; tall campanulas with white and lilac bells, tulip-shaped; creeping vetch; yellow, red, and pink scabious; faintly scented, neatly arranged purple plantains with blossoms slightly tinged with pink; cornflowers, the newly

opened blossoms bright blue in the sunshine but growing paler and redder towards evening or when growing old; and delicate almond-scented dodder flowers that withered quickly. I gathered myself a large nosegay and was going home when I noticed in a ditch, in full bloom, a beautiful thistle plant of the crimson variety, which in our neighborhood they call "Tartar" and carefully avoid when mowing—or, if they do happen to cut it down, throw out from among the grass for fear of pricking their hands. Thinking to pick this thistle and put it in the centre of my nosegay, I climbed down into the ditch, and after driving away a velvety humble-bee that had penetrated deep into one of the flowers and had there fallen sweetly asleep, I set to work to pluck the flower. But this proved a very difficult task. Not only did the stalk prick on every side—even through the handkerchief I had wrapped round my hand—but it was so tough that I had to struggle with it for nearly five minutes, breaking the fibres one by one; and when I had at last plucked it, the stalk was all frayed and the flower itself no longer seemed so fresh and beautiful. Moreover, owing to its coarseness and stiffness, it did not seem in place among the delicate blossoms of my nosegay. I threw it away feeling sorry to have vainly destroyed a flower that looked beautiful in its proper place.

It does not matter at all that the thistle is so obviously a synecdoche for Hadji Murad himself. What is at work here is the authority of Tolstoy's own recalcitrance. Like the thistle, Tolstoy's stance is firm, rooted in the black-earth fields. "What reality!" we think, as we stare at Tolstoy's fictive cosmos. If in Balzac every janitor is a genius, in Tolstoy every object resists inanimate status, be it the "Tartar" thistle or the low ottoman that rebels against Peter Ivanovich at the beginning of *The Death of Ivan Ilych*:

Peter Ivanovich sighed still more deeply and despondently, and Praskovya Fedorovna pressed his arm gratefully. When they reached the drawing-room, upholstered in pink cretonne and lighted by a dim lamp, they sat down at the table—she on a sofa and Peter Ivanovich on a low pouffle, the springs of which yielded spasmodically under his weight. Praskovya Fedorovna had been on the point of warning him to take another seat, but felt that such a warning was out of keeping with her present condition and so changed her mind. As he sat down on the pouffle Peter Ivanovich recalled how Ivan Ilych had arranged this room and had consulted him regarding this pink cretonne with green leaves. The whole room was full of furniture and knick-knacks, and on her way to the sofa the lace of the widow's black shawl caught on the carved edge of the table. Peter Ivanovich rose to detach it, and the springs of the pouffle, relieved of his weight, rose also and gave him a push. The widow began detaching her shawl herself, and Peter Ivanovich again sat down, suppressing the rebellious springs of the pouffle under him. But the widow had not quite freed herself and Peter Ivanovich got up again, and again the pouffle rebelled and even creaked. When this was all over, she took out a clean cambric handkerchief and began to weep. The episode with the shawl and the struggle with the pouffle had cooled Peter Ivanovich's emotions and he sat there with a sullen look on his face. This awkward situation was interrupted by Sokolov, Ivan Ilych's butler, who came to report that the plot in the cemetery that Praskovya Fedorovna had chosen would cost two hundred roubles. She stopped weeping and, looking at Peter Ivanovich with the air of a victim, remarked in French that it was very hard for her. Peter Ivanovich made a silent gesture signifying his full conviction that it must indeed be so.

It has been remarked that the pouffle or ottoman here is more memorable, has more vitality, than the personages have in most other authors' fiction. Of *Hadji Murad* I am moved to say that everything in it—people, horses, landscapes—exuberantly is rammed with life. Isaak Babel, whose *Odessa Tales* are my own favorite among all modern short stories, reread *Hadji Murad* in 1937, and recorded his happy shock at his renewed sense of Tolstoy's vitalistic force:

Here the electric charge went from the earth, through the hands, straight to the paper, with no insulation at all, quite mercilessly stripping off all outer layers with a sense of truth....

Tolstoy, who moralized both abominably and magnificently, has little original to say concerning the pragmatics of literary representation. What might be called his theory of such representation is outrageous enough to be interesting:

The art of the future will thus be completely distinct, both in subject matter and in form, from what is now called art. The only subject matter of the art of the future will be either feelings drawing men toward union, or such as already unite them; and the forms of art will be such as will be open to everyone. And therefore, the ideal of excellence in the future will not be the exclusiveness of feeling, accessible only to some, but, on the contrary, its universality. And not bulkiness, obscurity, and complexity of form, as is now esteemed, but, on the contrary, brevity, clearness, and simplicity of expression. Only when art has attained to that, will art neither divert nor deprave men as it does now, calling on them to expend their best strength on it, but be what it should be—a vehicle wherewith to transmit religious, Christian perception from the realm of reason and intellect into that of feeling, and really drawing people in actual life nearer to that perfection and unity indicated to them by their religious perception.

In the age of Proust and *Finnegans Wake*, of *Gravity's Rainbow* and "An Ordinary Evening in New Haven," Tolstoy's "art of the future" is still, thankfully, far in the unapparent. Yet there is a strength in Tolstoy's own attempts to write his art of the future that makes us hesitate, partly because Tolstoy seems at moments to have found his way back to an art that never quite was, even in the remote past, and yet something in us wants it to have existed. There is, in a tale like "How Much Land Does a Man Need?" (1886), a balance between ethos and pathos that caused James Joyce to call it the finest story he had ever read. I myself give that tribute to *Hadji Murad*, but the tale is a dreadfully impressive nightmare, and yet a vision of reality, irresistible in its Biblical irony. I say "Biblical irony" with precise intention, because Tolstoy's ironies seem to me neither Classical (saying one thing while meaning another) nor Romantic (playing upon contrasts between expectation and fulfillment). Rather, they resemble the ironies of the Yahwist, and turn always upon the incongruous clash between incommensurate orders of reality, human and divine, eros and the spirit. It is not accidental that Tolstoy was obsessed with the Biblical story of Joseph and his brothers, because in some sense much of Tolstoy's greatest art is a transumption of that story. To read the tale of Joseph as Tolstoy read it may be a way of seeing what Tolstoy valued in literary representation, and may help us to appreciate more fully the greatness, almost beyond the reach of art, of *Hadji Murad*.

II

It is hardly invidious to say that *Hadji Murad* is the story that Hemingway always wished to write, but could not accomplish. If we could imagine an early twentieth-century story written by the author of the *Iliad*, then it would be *Hadji Murad*. Like Homer, Tolstoy neither loves battle nor hates it; both epic poets simply accept it as the condition of life. The world of *Hadji Murad*, whatever precise relation it has to the actuality that Tolstoy experienced as a young soldier in the Caucasus, is a scene where battle is the norm, and open warfare is morally preferable to societal treachery, whether the society be Russian or Tartar, the realm of czar Nicholas or the Imam Shamil. Overt battle is also nobler than the sad impingements of societal depravity upon those who fight, with the superb exception of Hadji Murad himself and his little band of followers, devoted to the death. In such a fictive cosmos, Hadji Murad the man combines in himself all the positive attributes divided in the *Iliad* between Achilles and Hector, while being free of the negative qualities of both heroes. Indeed, of all natural men of heroic eminence in Western literature, Hadji Murad is the most impressive.

How does Tolstoy so shape his representation of Hadji Murad as to arouse none of our proper skepticism (or his own) of the potential heroism of the natural man? No sensitive reader of Tolstoy's story would dismiss Hadji Murad as we are compelled to dismiss the fisherman in *The Old Man and the Sea* or Colonel Cantwell in *Across the River and Into the Trees*. Hemingway's natural vitalists are neither natural nor vital enough, and their sacred innocence is too close to ignorance. Hadji Murad is shrewder as well as more courageous than anyone else in his story. He dies in battle, knowing he must, because he has no alternative. But he dies without Achilles' rage against mortality, or Hector's collapse into passivity. He can die with absolute dignity because he knows that he is not only the best of the Tartars, but superior also in horsemanship, daring, fighting skill, and charismatic leadership to any of the Russians. Famous for all his exploits, his last stand will be not less famous, and yet he need not comfort himself with such a realization. Perhaps his heroic completeness is implicit comfort enough.

Of the two chief Homeric heroes, Achilles excels in force and Odysseus in craft, but Hadji Murad is foremost in both qualities. Like Achilles, Hadji Murad has chosen immortal fame, and yet, like Odysseus, he wishes to return home, to rescue his women and his son. Unlike Odysseus, he fails, and yet Tolstoy's art makes it impossible to judge Hadji Murad's last exploit as a failure. The hero, in every phase leading up to his hopeless break-out and final battle, remains elemental, a force like wind, a kind of pure flame. That force and purity are not less elemental in the Tartar hero's dying:

> all these images passed through his mind without evoking any feeling within him—neither pity nor anger nor any kind of desire: everything seemed so insignificant in comparison with what was beginning, or had already begun, within him.

Elemental dying, strong process as it is, goes on simultaneously with the last spasm of Hadji Murad's sublime vitality:

> Yet his strong body continued the thing that he had commenced. Gathering together his last strength he rose from behind the bank, fired his pistol at a man who was just running towards him, and hit him. The man fell. Then Hadji Murad got quite out of the ditch, and limping heavily went dagger in hand straight at the foe.
> Some shots cracked and he reeled and fell. Several militiamen with triumphant shrieks rushed towards the fallen body. But the body that seemed to be dead suddenly moved. First the uncovered, bleeding, shaven head rose; then the body with hands holding to the trunk of a tree. He seemed so terrible, that those who were running towards him stopped short. But suddenly a shudder passed through him, he staggered away from the tree and fell on his face, stretched out at full length like a thistle that had been mown down, and he moved no more.
> He did not move, but still he felt.
> When Hadji Aga, who was the first to reach him, struck him on the head with a large dagger, it seemed to Hadji Murad that someone was striking him with a hammer and he could not understand who was doing it or why. That was his last consciousness of any connection with his body. He felt nothing more and his enemies kicked and hacked at what had no longer anything in common with him.

The synecdoche of the mown-down thistle, called "the Tartar" in the novella's first paragraph, reminds us of Tolstoy's original tribute: "But what energy and tenacity! With what determination it defended itself, and how dearly it sold its life!" Hadji Murad also "stood firm and did not surrender to man" and marvelously demonstrated the vitality that will not submit. But why does this archaic heroism so captivate Tolstoy and, through Tolstoy, the readers of the story? Gorky said of Tolstoy: "He always greatly exalted immortality on the other side of this life, but he preferred it on this side." We should also recall Gorky's memory that Tolstoy liked to remark of *War and Peace*: "without false modesty, it is like the *Iliad*." *Hadji Murad* is even more like the *Iliad*; uncannily so, because its hero is Homeric to the highest degree, and yet something beyond even Homer, which remains to be explored.

It is totally persuasive that Hadji Murad is virtually without flaw, granted his context and his tradition. Tolstoy, as an artist, intends to transume the whole of the heroic concept, from all archaic sources, and in his Hadji Murad he fulfills that intention. The archaic hero falls somewhere between man and a god, but Hadji Murad is only a man. While the archaic hero of epic has as his special excellence what J. M. Redfield calls "not integration but potency," Hadji Murad is wholly integrated. What Redfield calls "the ambiguity of the hero" does not apply at all to Hadji Murad, whose elemental force, unlike that of Achilles, has in it none of the latency of the savage beast. Without in any way moralizing his hero, Tolstoy removes from him the childlike element that never abandons Achilles.

After Hadji Murad is dead, and even as his killers rejoice, Tolstoy renders his hero the tribute of a true threnody:

> The nightingales, that had hushed their songs while the firing lasted, now started their trills once more: first one quite close, then others in the distance.

We can remember the universal adage, that if nature could write, it would be Tolstoy. His art itself is nature, and deserves that Shakespearean praise, despite his jealous dismissal of Shakespeare. He could not rival Shakespeare, but he came near to being Homer's equal.

R. P. BLACKMUR

The Dialectic of Incarnation:
Tolstoi's Anna Karenina

If there is one notion which represents what Tolstoi is up to in his novels—
emphatically in *Anna Karenina* and *War and Peace*—it is this. He exposes his
created men and women to the "terrible ambiguity of an immediate
experience" (Jung's phrase in his *Psychology and Religion*), and then, by the
mimetic power of his imagination, expresses their reactions and responses to
that experience. Some reactions are merely protective and make false
responses; some reactions are so deep as to amount to a change in the phase
of being and make honest responses. The reactions are mechanical or
instinctive, the responses personal or spiritual. But both the reactions and the
responses have to do with that force greater than ourselves, outside
ourselves, and working on ourselves, which whether we call it God or Nature
is the force of life, what is shaped or misshaped, construed or misconstrued,
in the process of living. Both each individual life and also that life in
fellowship which we call society are so to speak partial incarnations of that
force; but neither is ever complete; thus the great human struggle, for the
individual or for the society, is so to react and so to respond to "the terrible
ambiguity of an immediate experience" as to approach the conditions of
rebirth, the change of heart, or even the fresh start. Tragedy comes about
from the failure to apprehend the character or the direction of that force,
either by an exaggeration of the self alone or of the self in society. That is

From *Eleven Essays in the European Novel* by R. P. Blackmur. © 1964 by R. P. Blackmur.

why in Tolstoi the peasants, the simple family people, and the good-natured wastrels furnish the background and the foils for the tragedy, for these move according to the momentum of things, and although they are by no means complete incarnations of the force behind the momentum are yet in an equal, rough relation to it. The others, the tragic figures, move rather, by their own mighty effort, in relation, reaction, response to that force, some with its momentum, some against it; some falsifying it in themselves, some falsifying it in society, but each a special incarnation of it; some cutting their losses; some consolidating their gains; some balancing, some teetering, in a permanent labor of rebirth. There is thus at work in the novels of Tolstoi a kind of dialectic of incarnation: the bodying forth in aesthetic form by contrasted human spirits of "the terrible ambiguity of an immediate experience" through their reactions and responses to it. It is this dialectic which gives buoyancy and sanity to Tolstoi's novels.

Let us see how this happens in *Anna Karenina*—how it happens not only in the name and tale of the heroine but also and in relation to the tale of Levin; and how these gain some of their significance through being told against the background of Stiva and Dolly Oblonsky's unhappy marriage. That unhappy marriage is the image of society in momentum, that momentum which only requires the right face to be put upon it to be tolerable, which is true neither for the illicit affair of Anna and Vronsky nor for the profoundly lawful affair of Levin and Kitty. Stiva and Dolly are too near the actual manner of things, are too wholly undifferentiated from the course of society and of individuals, ever to feel the need or the pang of rebirth. All they want is for things to be as they are. Stiva, as the old nurse tells him when Dolly has caught him in an affair with a governess, Stiva has only to do his part; and Dolly has only, now and always, to return to her part. Anna and Levin are very different. Each, in a separate and opposed way, can be satisfied with nothing less than a full incarnation, a rebirth into the force which at crisis they feel moves them. Anna craves to transmute what moves her from underneath—*all* that can be meant by libido, not sex alone—into personal, individual, independent love; she will be stronger than society because she is the strength of society, but only so in her death at the hands of society. Levin craves to transmute himself upwards, through society, into an individual example of the love of God; he, too, will be stronger than society because he finds the will of God enacted in the natural order of things of which society is a part, but he will only do so as long as God is with him in his life. What separates both Anna and Levin from the ruck of rebels is that they make their rebellions, and construct their idylls, through a direct confrontation and apprehension of immediate experience. There is nothing arbitrary about their intentions, only their decisions; there is nothing exclusive or obsessed about their perceptions, only their actions. They think and know in the same world as Stiva and Dolly, and indeed they had to or they could never have been in love with such eminently natural creatures as Vronsky and Kitty. They live in the going concern of society, and they are aside from it only to represent it the better.

This is the world, the society, which is for the most part understood through its manners; and that is how Tolstoi begins his novel, by showing his people through the motion of their manners, first those of Stiva and Dolly, then those of the others. By the end of the First Part of the novel, we know very well the manner of life of each person and could extend it to suit any further accident of life: we know the probable critical point in the temperament of each which rises or descends to some old or new form of action or inaction, and we know it by the kind of manners each exhibits and by how far into the being of each the manners seem to penetrate: into all that is on the surface of Stiva, into all there is anywhere for Dolly, into a layer of permanent irritation for Levin, into a layer of perpetual possibility for Anna, into the radiant sweep of things not yet her own for Kitty, and into the animal vitality of things for Vronsky (who is at the beginning, and always, less a man than a sensual force inhabiting a man).

> For all this the comedy of Stiva's manners and Dolly's manners coming to terms with each other, not *they* but their manners, stands. Stiva deals with the ambiguities, Dolly with the intolerable things of marriage by manners. Stiva brings the huge pear of his own zest, but he can also weep. Dolly has a temper, but she can also weep. For both, tears are a kind of manners; and thus a reconciliation is effected. We see in this couple how it is that manners dictate the roles by which we escape acknowledging reality.

We begin with the same *kind* of manners Jane Austen mastered, the manners that pass for things otherwise only potentially present. But in Tolstoi we know at once that the manners are of something whose potency is pressing into the actual situation, something yet to be revealed in the words of the book, or at any rate to be carried into the open of our consciousness by them. Manners are a flowing stream; they are on the surface of what is swept along, hardly more by themselves but a wayward intimation of what is swept. In Jane Austen, even in *Emma*, the shape—the very water-shapes—of the stream of manners is itself pretty much the subject. In Tolstoi the stream will gradually take on the subject, will become united with it, as a brook takes on the brown of wood-earth and peat: as the Mississippi pushes its mud-color burden twenty miles to sea. Indeed the process begins, in *Anna Karenina*, in the first half-dozen pages, with the old nurse's remark to Stiva: Go, do your part. She tells us real things are at stake in this play of manners, things to be dealt with even the more because they are not acknowledged. And so it is with each personage as he turns up, except perhaps for Vronsky. There are hints of something pushing through.

For Dolly, there are the children, a noise in the hall and a clatter, in the nursery, the *unattended* children; and they hint that Dolly's manners, temper and all, are only a part—of what? For Stiva, there is the moment of extreme aloofness after dinner in the restaurant, that aloofness among intimates for which he knew what to do: to make conversation with some *aide-de-camp*, or some actress, with someone not at the center but approaching the center; and so we are aware that the aloofness is from something. For Anna, there is, as an exercise in manners, her *first taking note* of her hypocrisy in dealing with her husband. For Kitty there are such things, still in the play of manners, as her recognition in Anna of something uncanny and her excitement at the utterance, not the substance, of Levin's declaration of love for her. Only for Vronsky there is nothing, as if his manners were so vital or his life so lacking that they were equal to his need.

But for Levin, the other half of Vronsky, there is enough to make up for all the rest. He is, in his unmannerliness, in his steady breach of the expected manner, an effort at declaring what the manners are about; but he is only one effort, one declaration, which can by no means minimize or defeat the others should they come to make their declarations. Levin's very breaches of manners are organized into manners themselves, as organized as the fools and the plain-spoken men in Shakespeare. He is a foil, a contrast, a light to Anna, Stiva, Karenin, Kitty, and Vronsky; and he is a successful foil by the accident of the condition of his temperament, by what he misses or ignores of what they all see. Stiva was right: Levin had no idea of girls as girls; he had no idea how good a fresh roll might smell and taste even after dinner—and indeed there is something vulgar in Levin when he sees a wife as a dinner, vulgar in the bad sense. But he is vulgar in the good sense when, thinking of Kitty, he tells Stiva it is not love but the force outside him which has taken possession of him. It is as if he had found a concrete parallel to the perception which had come to him in reading a sentence from Tyndall: "The connection between all the forces of nature is felt instinctively." Better still is his deep human illumination of the relativity of morals when under the impact of his rejection by Kitty in presumed favor of Vronsky, he comes to a new and compassionate judgment of that intellectual wastrel and revolutionary libertine his brother Nikolay. He thinks of him, and sees how the good force is corrupted. No doubt it is in this passage that we see through Levin's vision of his brother the death and life that are to come in the book. The shift from scorn to compassion, under the pressure of his own brooked love, seems a true act of imitation—of mimesis—which Aristotle tells us is a fundamental delight to man's mind, no matter whether the object of imitation is ugly or beautiful or monstrous.

But this is perhaps to get ahead of the story, when what we want is to become part of the momentum of the story to which the manners of the characters point. The instances of perception isolated above are all pretty mechanical; they do not yet occur organically, by the psychic drive of what has already been formed; they merely illustrate how the characters are being gotten hold of by the story: by the little or big things manners cannot quite either cover up or handle. Mainly, so far, it is a story told of how the people do cover up and do handle. We are on our most familiar living ground. For manners are the medium in which the struggle between the institutions of society and the needs of individuals is conducted. Viable dramatic manners exist so long as the struggle has not become too one-sided, so long as no total credit is given either to one side or the other. When in imagination or dogma the institutions are seen to triumph the manners become hollow, cold, and cruel. When the needs of the individual triumph the manners tend to disappear, so that life *together* becomes impossible. In either case we get a monstrous egoism, incapable either of choice or comparison, an exercise in moral suicide and sterile fancy.

No such case is reached in this novel. Far from breaking down in either direction, we find, even at the worst, at Anna's death or at Levin's access of life, everywhere but at the last retreat of Vronsky to a death in which he does not believe, that the great part of human behavior is viable in manners. It is through manners that the needs and possibilities of each person are seen in shifting conflict with the available or relevant institutions, including the twilight institutions—the illicit, amorphous institutions—which stand at the edges of the institutions of broad day. Stiva, Anna, and Vronsky depend on the twilight institutions of marriage and general social conduct which encroach on the edges of the broad day institutions upon which Dolly, Kitty, and Levin depend. Karenin, at Petersburg, belongs to something else again; he has composed his dissatisfactions in a manner which contains its own rebelliousness: his jeering, desiccated conformity. But it is only the public aspect of the struggle which is between the broad day and the twilight. In actuality the struggle is conducted in the medium of manners between individuals trying from their different needs to shape institutions into some tolerable relation to their own partial apprehensions of reality. Here again it is Levin who has the first illumination; he knows there can be no victory and that there must be a balance. Himself a disbeliever in institutions, and therefore the more apprehensive of their force, he resents the maimed and maiming complaints of his brother Nicolay against the need of institutions: the forever need of make-shift. But best of all are the brother and sister Oblonsky, Stiva and Anna of the voided marriages: the one whose manners will last him forever, the other whose manners will be less and less good to her where they lead her, until at last she creates a fatal manner of her own. Stiva rises always into good nature. Anna is herself a form of nature. Both have something more than sincerity and both, because of the twilight of their actions, have something less than honesty. Think of Stiva at waking reaching for his dressing gown and finding, because he is not in his wife's bedroom, uncertainty instead. Think of Anna, away from home and because of that looking down the stairs at Vronsky and seeing possibility.

What Stiva finds, what Anna sees, is the momentum their manners had been about; and if we look at the gap between Part One and Part Two we see that the momentum is what carries us across the gap. Everybody has been left in an unfinished situation (Anna, Vronsky, Levin, the Oblonskys) or in a "finished" situation (Kitty) which must change. Thus there is both anticipation (uncertain but selected) and expectation (certain but unknown) but we cannot know which is which and cannot determine what is authentic until it has transpired. The business of the novel is how to find out and body forth what has already happened. We know only that for each of these people and for all of them together there must be more of the same thing, with the difference that they will know it better.

The emergence of this sort of knowledge depends on plot, but not upon the mechanical plot, not upon the plot of the "well-made" novel, or at least not primarily, but upon the organic, self-perpetuating, self-reproducing plot (reproducing whether by cycle, by scission, by parallel) which, as Aristotle says, is the soul of action. Surely it is not too much to say that the soul of action is momentum, and that, therefore, plot is the articulation of momentum. Only, in our stage of culture, we do not know ahead of time, we have only means of tentative guessing, what is the significance of plot conceived as the soul of action. We are not in the position of putting these people into relation with some received or religious or predicted concept of significance—as Sophocles, Vergil, Dante were. We are working the other way round: we have to find out in the process of the experience itself. We are about the great business of the novel, to create out of manners and action motive, and out of the conflict of the created motive with the momentum to find the significance: an image of the theoretic form of the soul.

To accomplish this art of psychology, this art of the psyche, this driving form and drifting form (as the stars drift) is perhaps the characteristic task of the novel in a society like that of the nineteenth century: a society without a fixed order of belief, without a fixed field of knowledge, without a fixed hierarchy; a society where experience must be explored for its significance as well as its content, and where experience may be created as well as referred. This is the society where all existing orders are held to be corruptions of basic order; or, to put it differently, where, in terms of the confronted and awakened imagination, the creation of order has itself become a great adventure. This is what Anna and Levin have, great personal adventures in the creation of order: an order is the desperate requirement each has for the experience each bodies forth.

Let us look at a few examples in the Second Part of the relation between manners and momentum and of the force under the momentum breaking through. There is the gradual spread of the scandal of Anna and Vronsky from rumor to declaration to conflagration. At first Anna uses the manners of the fashionable set to promote her relations with Vronsky, then she *breaches* manners to solidify them, and at last—with her husband, with society, with Vronsky—she throws manners away, and the force which has been there all along takes over although she does not as yet wholly know it. When asked at Betsy's party what she thinks of repairing the mistakes of love after marriage, she answers: "'I think,' said Anna, playing with the glove she had taken off, 'I think ... of so many men, so many minds, certainly so many hearts, so many kinds of love.'" After that party her husband, home to read, finds himself uneasy at the situation there tacitly (by manners) acknowledged between Anna and Vronsky. They have breached the formal role of the husband of a pretty wife, and he must speak to her in order to correct their estimate of the situation. As he thinks and walks the floor we see there is something more. When one set of manners impeaches another set—when the twilight assaults the broad day—an ambiguity appears. He who had always worked with reflections of life, and had shrunk away from life itself as something irrational and incomprehensible, now found himself "standing face to face with life." He had walked a bridge over the chasm of life and now the bridge was broken. Thus he is forced outside his official manners, is forced to think of Anna's *own* life for the first time. The plans he makes are all official, to communicate a firm decision and to exact obedience. But when Anna appears, glowing, a conflagration on a dark night, he found he was assaulting an impenetrable barrier and was reduced to begging. She had closed the door into herself, and he knew it would remain closed. As for Anna, his assault found her armored with an impenetrable falsehood and was strengthened, Tolstoi says, by an *unseen force*. His very speaking confirmed the new force and focussed it on Vronsky. In attempting to deceive him she makes the mistake of being natural, candid, light-hearted, qualities which in the circumstance are effects of the unseen force. In the new life between Karenin and Anna, Anna could lie awake feeling the brilliance of her own eyes, but Karenin found himself powerless because the spirit of evil and deceit which possessed her possessed him too. He could only implore and jeer.

When Anna and Vronsky perfect their new life in adultery they find they have murdered the first stage of their love. "Shame at their spiritual nakedness crushed her and infected him." Without the aid, rather the enmity, of decorum, manners, institutions, they cannot cope with the now visible force that binds *and* splits them. Being what they are—that is, being by Tolstoi condemned to full and direct experience—they cannot let the force pass. Vronsky tries to cover up with kisses. Anna tries, and puts off trying, to join together the shame, rapture, and horror of "stepping into a new life." She tries for and cannot find an order in thought. But in her dreams, when she was not protecting herself from her thoughts, she sees the hideous nakedness of her position. She dreams of two husbands, two Alexeys, two happinesses, and the dream weighed like a nightmare because it dramatized the impossibility of the only solution. As for Vronsky there is what happened when he went to see his mare, Frou Frou, the day before the race. The mare's excitement infected Vronsky. "He felt that his heart was throbbing, and that he, too, like the mare, longed to move, to bite; it was both dreadful and delicious." Swift never did this better; and Tolstoi does it without bitterness, though the scene is one which contains most of the occasions for human bitterness. What Vronsky wanted was Anna like the horse. But like the horse, Anna must be used in reckless pastime, or not at all. Take away the pastime, and the recklessness becomes uncontrollable and all the beautiful anarchy in the animal—all the unknown order under orders known—is lost. So, as with Anna, Vronsky failed to keep pace with Frou Frou and broke her back.

While Anna and Vronsky are bodying forth reality, Kitty is being cured of one reality by immersion in another. She is away, taking the waters. Tolstoi gives the tale of her cure lightly and ironically, but it is nevertheless accomplished by very hazardous means, and furnishes interesting analogies to what happened to Vronsky, Anna, Karenin, and in a way, also, to Levin who is immersing himself in the idyll of the simple life on his estate. Almost

Kitty becomes a "pietist," a professional doer of good, a conspicuous instrument of false charity: a filler-up of the void of life with the "manners" of sincerity, virtue, and faith in the phase where life is left out. One hardly knows whether it is Mme. Stahl or Mlle. Varenka who better represents the negation of vitality. Both are unconscious charlatans of charity: the one for occupation, the other for duty. Kitty is taken in by both, and being a creature of vital impulse, herself tries the role of charlatan of charity from her heart. She has reached a moment of conversion, but not to recognition of life or God, rather to puerile substitutes for them, when she is rescued by the sick man Petrov's hysterical "love" for her combined with the return of her father full of health and humor and buoyancy. Petrov's "love" she recognizes, though she does not put it into words: "one of those things which one knows but which one can never speak of even to oneself so terrible and shameful would it be to be mistaken." Through her father, through the contagion of life he spreads, she sees Mme. Stahl's short legs and hears the feeble laughter of Varenka. And in the little crisis of these recognitions, she is converted *back* to life.

The figure of Varenka remains only as a threat, the threat of something the opposite of reality. This is the threat of public life, of life in public: the threat of turning the heart into an institution: the situation so desired by Karenin, in which one no longer feels what one ignores; when without conscious hypocrisy or deceit one ignores both the nature and the springs of human action, when all natural piety is transformed into the artifact of piety. There is no sympathy in it, much less mimesis, only empty histrionics: the vanities of spiritual ill-health mistaken for the pangs of vocation.

In all this Tolstoi never leaves us in the dark. It is only Kitty, the little Princess, who is led astray into thinking here is a career, or a new life, with these creatures who take no part in the momentum which sweeps them along. It takes only the lyric stagger of her "lover" Petrov, repeated to show it was doubly meant, a stagger for disease and a stagger for love, and the genuine momentum of her father the old Prince to pull her back into the stream. If we the readers remember in what language Tolstoi introduced Verenka we should ourselves never have been deceived. A creature without youth, nineteen or thirty, "she was like a fine flower, already past its bloom and without fragrance, though the petals were still unwithered." She is one of those who have nothing to suppress, no matter what the situation.

It may be, of course, that Tolstoi wrote all this to express his instinctive hatred of professional bad health: the bad health that keeps on living and makes of the open air a morass. These people also however make a parallel to the true purpose of the book: they cover up the encroaching reality of death much as Dolly and Karenin cover up what is for them the vanishing reality of life. The difference is that the sick and the charlatans succeed: they are equal to what they admit of their condition, and so take power over the living (nobody can so dominate a situation as the confirmed invalid); while Dolly and Karenin are never equal to their situation and still struggle with it, however pitifully or pretentiously, and lose power over others as over themselves with each successive act. The difference may be small from another perspective, but from Tolstoi's perspective it is radical. That is why the figure of Nikolay Levin passes, a small harsh whirlwind, across the scene: the very whirlwind of a man preparing and building into the reality of his death: tall, with stooping figure, huge hands, a coat too short for him, with black, simple, and yet terrible eyes: this figure shouting at the doctor and threatening him with his stick.

Tolstoi has many skills in the dialectic of incarnation. Here is one where the incarnation is of raw force itself, but it must be thought of in its setting. Consider how he surrounds the affair of Anna and Vronksy—the seduction, pregnancy and declaration—on the one side with the true idyll of Levin in the spring and on the other side the false idyll of Kitty at the watering place. It is across Vronsky and Anna that Kitty and Levin reach. At the very center lies Frou Frou, the mare, with her broken back, struggling up on her forelegs, then falling: all because Vronsky could not keep pace with her. Vronsky kicked her with his heel in the stomach. "She did not stir, but thrusting her nose into the ground, she simply stared at her master with her speaking eyes."

Vronsky's unpardonable act was no accident; neither was it done by intention. It was rather that, at a moment of high arbitrary human skill, at a moment of death-risk and momentary glory, the center of all eyes and the heart of an almost universal act of mimetic participation—at that moment something like fate broke the rhythm. Yet Vronsky was right: "for the first time in his life he knew the bitterest sort of misfortune, misfortune beyond remedy, and caused by his own fault." What is beyond remedy is beyond judgment: is its own justice; and if it is nevertheless caused by Vronsky's own fault, it is because the fault is universal. It is the fault that inheres in Kitty and Levin, in Dolly and Stiva, Anna and Vronsky alike: the fault of not keeping pace. This does not seem hard to understand in its general symbolic reach, that it may happen or that it may not that a breach of pace may be fatal. It is a harsher act of imagination to grasp the actuality of the absolute intimacy *and* the absolute inadequacy—the deliciousness *and* the dread—in human relationship; precisely what must be grasped if that phase has been reached.

But what is even more terrifying about Tolstoi's honesty—or let us say what is more astonishing about his genius—is that he could have broken the back of a mare in the midst of the crisis in the passion of Anna and Vronsky without either adding or diminishing *human* significance but rather deepening the reality. It is as if in this image he had gotten into the conditions of life from which the conditions we know of emerge: into conditions purer and conditions more intolerable: into an order which includes all human disorders.

These are affairs, as Tolstoi like Dante knew, of which the sane mind makes no report except in symbol, however they may remain thereafter the very growth of the mind. So it was with Vronsky. His friend Yashvin the rake understood it best, "overtook him with his cap, and led him home, and half an hour later Vronsky had regained his self-possession." The death of Frou Frou had become a part of him, no longer separately recognized.

Like the death of Frou Frou, so it is with the passions that inhabit our heroes. The passion of the force will pass but not the force, and if the passion has not wrecked the hero (as it does Karenin) the force will be stronger after the passion has passed than before. That is why the notion of purification is attached to the passion of tragic action. Society, nature, and the individual in society and nature, have three common arrangements to take care of the situation when genuine passion has passed. There is the arrangement for outlets in the demi-monde or twilight world. There is the arrangement for the cultivation of passion for its own sake, which suits those afraid of being *otherwise* occupied. And there is the arrangement that when the passion passes those who have been joined in it will find themselves insuperably bound—unless a fresh passion of the force supervene. Both for Anna and for Levin, with their different aspirations, none of these arrangements is enough. Or rather, for Levin none of them will do at all, and for Anna they will all do in their turns. But both need the identification of force with love, the one outside society and nature, the other through society and nature. Anna needs to become herself standing for everybody, Levin needs to become everybody in order to find himself represented. That is why both Anna and Levin are subject to fearful jealousies. Their rebirth into new life is never complete and the identification of force with love is never complete. Thus the force remains free, capable of assuming all possible forms. That is why Anna dreads in Vronsky and Levin in Kitty the positive enactment of what is at constant potential in themselves. Their jealousy is that they crave each other's possibilities, and hence each is bound to muster out of the force that moves them a new burst of passion in the hope that this time the new birth will take place but in the hidden certainty that it will not.

Vronsky, even more than Anna, as their love becomes more of a scandal, is deprived of the social phases of "force" and is required to envisage it as if naked, and an enemy. The worm of ambition in him which had been covered in the first stages of love is now uncovered by the scandal of love. He understands perfectly what his friend the successful general means when he says, "Women are the chief stumbling-block in a man's career. It's hard to love a woman and do anything." He understands but he answers softly that the general has never loved, and he understands even better when the general returns it, "We make an immense thing of love, but they are always *terre à terre.*" It is what he understands, and keeps out of sight, that gives him a hard expression when Anna tells him she is pregnant. He is thinking of all that is lost, and of the duel that must come. Anna does not understand that and gives up all hope that his love will be enough for her, though in the same breath of her mind she tells him that it will be. She sees he has already been thinking and will not tell her all he thought. She is, she tells him, proud, proud, proud—but she cannot say what she is proud of; and Vronsky if he had spoken must have said the same thing. They get at so differently what lies between them that they wholly misunderstand each other, but never for a second do they fail to grasp the force that compels the misunderstanding.

As for what happens to Karenin there is no better image than the lawyer whom he consults about a divorce: he plucks four moths out of the air, as if he were the law engorging the individual. Unlike Anna and Vronsky, who are deprived of them, Karenin is more and more taken over by the brutality of the social phases of "force." He makes one final effort to reverse himself—as do Anna and Vronsky—when Anna, in childbirth, thinks herself dying. Then all three reverse and renounce their roles, and do so in deep analogy to Levin and Kitty at the true death of Levin's brother Nikolay where they gain great access to their true roles. It is the image of death—the attractive and repulsive force of death—which takes over each of them. There is something in the rhythm of death which for Vronsky, Anna, and Karenin elicits a supreme failing effort to keep pace, as there is for Levin in his brother's death. For each, it is as far as they can go in their opposed directions.

Indeed it is Anna's literally incomplete death-scene which is the death in which rebirth takes place. She makes a histrionic mimesis of death because of the two women within her. Thinking, in her last spasm of social guilt, to kill one, actually she kills the other. No, not, by thinking does she do this, unless it is something outside the mind that thinks. Rather she, the whole of her, takes advantage of the vision of death to find out what can be seen through it. Her mistake is only initial. The rebirth is accompanied by an exorcism, which she sees and feels but which, so great is the force of the world, she does not at once recognize for what it is. She has become single; it seems to be by renunciation; actually it is by an access of devotion—for she is not a woman gifted with renunciation, and her first practice of it shows as irritation and inability, as something to overcome and something to perfect. Had Vronsky not come, had he not rushed in, and stroked her cropped hair, calling her a pretty boy, she might never have found out in actuality what her new singleness was. Instead of positive desperation she would have ended in self-contemptuous despair. There would have been nothing to break down, only the collapse of a dry shell. As it is, she begins at once, against the world-and-his-wife and contemptuous of both, the long course of building her own desperation, the positive desperation of her own cause, to the point where her own strength but not that of her cause should be exhausted.

That is the nature of her tragedy, that her own strength cannot be equal to her cause. The independence of the individual is never equal to the cause of independence. And the flaw is as it should be, both in her and in the nature of things, and not at all less guilty for that (or if you like, less innocent): a flaw in any case, a human need, which as it finds its mode of action and creates its motive becomes less and less the kind of flaw that asks for the forgiveness of understanding and is more and more revealed as a single, eminent aspect of the general nature of things which brings the mind to compassion.

How otherwise—how if it is not this train that has been set going—can we look at the irony of the pure, lawful, and successful love affair of Levin and Kitty as anything but cheap and puerile "moralism"?—that is, not irony at all. Levin in new life, Levin on wings, has also singled his life, has made an act of devotion, to which he will necessarily turn out inadequate, not so much because of inadequate strength but because the cause itself (in the form of his original impulse) will desert him. The very brutal force of the world and his wife which will bring ruin to Anna and Vronsky because they contest it, is the force Levin leans on—his cause—and it is a force hardly less reliable taken as a cause than as the enemy. No institution and no individual may ever be more than a partial incarnation of the underlying or superior force; nor can any set of individuals and institutions taken together. It is only Stiva or the peasant with the pretty daughter-in-law whom Levin had seen pitching hay who can use or abuse this force indifferently: with the kind of faith that makes no enquiries and would not know a vision if it saw one. For Stiva, there is always a way out, not death. For the peasant girl—she is herself a way out, and death is a matter not yet experienced. These are the creatures not subject to individual rebirth, they are the nearest thing to permanence: momentum, or recurrence.

But the shoe of Anna's rebirth pinches sharpest, under the impact of symbolic death, on Karenin and Vronsky: the one with his head in the hollow of Anna's elbow, the other with his face in his hands: the one suffering total and permanent spiritual change, the other suffering total humiliation followed by recovery through violence: the one inwardly transcending his society, the other rejecting his society and both to be ever afterwards victimized by it—though one, Karenin, is put in contempt by society, and the other, Vronsky, is made a hero so to speak outside society. Karenin can never get back into society and is in a misunderstood position above it. Vronsky can never leave society behind him: it goes with him: he is a kind of pet public outcast. They have passed, by humiliation and self-contempt, through their relations to Anna's symbolic death, to the roles most nearly opposite to those in which we first saw them.

That is, to each of them comes a deep reversal of role through a direct, but miscomprehended, experience of the force of life in the phase of sex under the image of an incomplete death. We shall see the deaths completed diversely. Meanwhile we see Anna, Vronsky, Karenin, and Levin tied in the hard knot of individual goodness, and each, in that goodness, in a different relation to the manners and momentum of society. I mean, by goodness, that each has been reborn into a man or woman for once, and at last, proper to his or her own nature. Each has *virtu*, and to the point of excess, but—such is the power of Tolstoi's imagination—without loss of humanity. Each, seen beside the self, is more the self than ever. Levin, seen in society, is no more representative of it than the other three; who are seen against it.

It is for this goodness that they pay the cost. The good, said Aristotle, is that which all things aim at, and when an aim has been taken everything flies that way—whether the target was indeed the good or not. We see Levin in doubt and delight about everything, desiring not to desire, as we see Vronsky equally in doubt, but so full of *ennui* that he desires desire. We see that Anna's problem is to maintain the state of crisis in love, to be always a young girl in love, and that Vronsky's problem is to find substitutes, caprices of action, to prevent *ennui* from absorbing crisis. In Vronksy's house all were guests, in Levin's all were part of the household; and so on. Tolstoi gives us hundreds of comparisons and analogies of the two honeymoons. But perhaps the most instructive is the comparison of Veslovsky at Levin's and at Vronsky's. This young man with unseemly eyes, fat thighs, and hand-kissing habits was very much a gentleman of the bedchamber: altogether in place at Vronsky's, very much a part of the general pretense at occupation. Vronsky ignores in him what had genuinely put Levin in a rage, and Anna was amused at him where Kitty was ashamed. Kitty and Levin made a fight for life within the fold, Anna and Vronsky fight in abuse of the fold; and a little in the background Dolly surrenders to life within a broken fold.

Each of them is inadequate to him or herself as a solitary actor; and perhaps this is nowhere shown so clearly as in the image of Dolly making her solitary visit to Anna sitting in the coach, afraid to look in her glass, daydreaming herself a perfect paramour. Again we see it in Dolly in her darned gown listening with aversion and distrust to Anna talk of birth-control. She knows suddenly that in the very numbers of her children is her safety: not in perspective, future or past, but in numbers, in everyday life. Dolly is the monitor of all that is living: she has paid the cost of goodness without ever having had it, and in so very deep a way that no fresh start—neither rebellion nor new effort along old lines—could ever get it for her. She is neither good nor evil; neither hopeless nor desperate. She believes in high principles, and that they must not be forgotten, but in every act of her being she knows the necessity, if she is to survive, of the alternate assertion and abuse of these principles. The compassionate gesture of her visit to Anna is symbolic of all this; and it is the kind of peak of meaningfulness she can reach at any time, with no need for crisis. So we begin to see what she is doing in this novel: she is to be recognized, not understood. But we should never have believed her, or in her, had we seen her in such a moment at the beginning; nor would she have believed in herself. She would have been a bad Varenka, a hypocrite unendurable. It was right that she had to be brought round by Anna, just as it is right now that her presence should remind Anna of all the life she was smothering. But best of all is to think of Dolly with the road dust in the creases about her eyes, imagining at the end of her daydream of illicit love, what the expression on Stiva's face would be, when, like Anna to Karenin, she flaunted her infidelity in his face.

This image of Dolly may have come to Tolstoi as an afterthought, as a debt to his novel he had not known he was incurring and which he had therefore all the more obligation to pay. He had thought of Rachel, but not of Leah. But with the other image in this part of the book—the death of Nikolay—it is the other way round. This is the death that lived in Tolstoi all his life, for which he made three great images of which this is the first and greatest—the others are "Ivan Ilyitch" and *The Living Corpse*. Death is the inevitable thing from which there is no freedom by recognition but only by enactment. Where Anna (as Dolly saw) has learned a new gesture, to half close her eyes on what is threatening her and cannot be dealt with, Tolstoi himself has to force a steady gaze on death physical, spiritual, and dramatic (poetic, dialectic, rhetorical). He has to mime death. He has to show in fact that death, as well as good, is what all things aim at; that death is the moving *and* the fixed background of life. He knows and must show that it is a commonplace truth and illusion that men die well. The whole commonplace is there in the physical—the terribly physical—death of Nikolay: and in the longing for death that surrounds it.

This death—the most innocent and most mature in all fiction—though it has nothing to do directly with the plot is yet a center of attractive force presiding over its whole course. Everything else is drawn to it, across a gap. It is this attractive force that begins to complete the actions of each of our persons, those actions which were focussed in the partial deaths endured by Anna and Levin in the middle portion of the book, and which were initiated by the death of Frou Frou at the first crisis in the action: it is the solitary and menacing incarnation of all these. And it should be well noted that in this death everything is as near the physical as possible without affront to the spiritual and the dramatic. The turbulence is all of something watched by Kitty or felt by Levin. It is death as raw force, a concrete, focal, particular epiphany of the raw force of death. It is the after part of every forethought.

Surely that is what is somehow in Levin's mind when, in making his one call, on Anna in her Coventry, he sees her face as stone and more beautiful than ever, the very Medusa-face of life (Henry James's phrase) to which for a moment he succumbs. Altogether these nine or ten pages of Levin's vision of Anna are a high example of what may be meant in the novel by full drama. As in the modern stage drama, a great deal depends on what has gone before, now summarized and brought to a fresh and conclusive action against a background which may and will come forward when the action is done: when the violent inner light of conflagration in Anna is changed to the lightning that momentarily obscures the stars for Levin. That is what the dramatic action is for, to pull the whole background forward. It is the background in which they are all implicated, and in which the action is a series of parallels and a series of analogies which show all our principal persons in deeply but narrowly different responses to the same force: each lawful, each valid, complementing each other like ice and water, or night and day, converging like slush or twilight, like midnight and noon. Each is brought to a clarity, of which the meaning is seen, not alone in relation to the other persons, but also with respect to the sweep of things: the sweep which moves with the strange intimate noise which Shakespeare calls the endless jar of right and wrong in which justice resides. It is against this that Anna's face was stone and more beautiful than ever.

There is a nakedness in this sort of experience for Anna which ends in death, and an unarmored defencelessness for Levin which begins in birth. It leaves both of them without the protection or clothes of the intellect. And there is a harshness in the compassion required of total response to each— the compassion of peace with a sword—which is possible only to a saint or a great artist. Such response touches what is under our behavior, and what comes into our behavior, which whether we shun it or salute it, remakes, while the contact lasts, our sense of relation with ordinary life. We cannot live at crisis, at the turning point, but must make out of it either a birth or a death in the face of ordinary life. This is what happens to morality in art. It is an image of passing one way or the other; which may explain what Eliot had in mind when he observed that as morals are only a preliminary concern to the saint so they are only a secondary concern to the artist. That is the condition, between the preliminary and the secondary, of harsh compassion that made Tolstoi reject his novels, including this one, along with Shakespeare. He rejected the uncopeable truth, because he wanted to remake the world piecemeal in terms of morality as a central authority. In the novels he wanted only the mimesis of morality as a central experience, both in the world and in the crisis of individuals who were somehow, because of the crisis, removed from it.

The novels wanted to show the tacit, potential crisis which gave the ordinary world meaning, and which in turn put individuals to the test. It is in contest and concert with the ordinary world that crisis is reached and given worth; and it is into the ordinary world that things break through and are bodied forth, visibly in crisis, actually all along. The last two parts of *Anna Karenina* put into parallel and analogy such recognitions as these. Under pressure of the action even the parallels seem to become analogies, to be in proportional relation to each other: as in the stream of consciousness— the articulate hysteria—in which Anna's last hours are recorded, which is both parallel and analogous to Levin's final conversion in company with the beetle under the dusty shade of the poplars at noon.

For a major parallel which is also analogy, let us look at the whole structure in the next to last part of the book. We begin with Kitty's delayed confinement and from it see Levin moved through Moscow's "society," intellect, and club life, to reach that other form of delayed or arrested vitality which is Anna, and in which he is for a moment absorbed. Then through quarrel and jealousy we are moved sharply to the scream of birth for Kitty and the plunge to death for Anna: the birth which for Anna meant death not herself, which to Kitty meant new life not herself, and which to Levin were one and the same. Between the two sets of movements there is a chapter in which an independent evil spirit grew up in Anna because there was a delay in her affairs, just as there was an independent new life in Kitty in the delay of *her* affairs. The one ends in senseless rage, the other in senseless joy. In either case it is the uncopeable power not themselves which moves them, and to each it shows with the terrible ambiguity of an immediate experience.

Surely it is not providential that before returning to Anna and her death, Tolstoi carries us to Petersburg, the city of government and decorum and manners, and gives us, so we may make our own irony, images of what happens when people insist on coping with their own troubles in terms of the unilluminated ordinary world. We see all this in Stiva pursuing his double errand, to get himself a better job and to get Anna her divorce. To get the job he has to descend into humiliation. To prevent himself from giving the divorce, Karenin, with Lidia aiding, has to descend to a false appeal to a false force pretending to govern a false society: he descends to the clairvoyance of a charlatan, to an "induced" change of heart. By betrayal of his own traditions, Stiva gets his job; so does Karenin refuse the divorce. Anna is not a matter of genuine consideration. In this analogy, Tolstoi presents all that is left, in these people, of the true force: he sees that Stiva and Karenin have become all manners and no men.

Nor is it providential, it is the very essence of the prepared drama, that we return from Stiva in Petersburg to find Anna in Moscow, herself clutching at manners—in the form of quarrels, jealousies, formal emotions—in the one place where manners cannot act but can only cover up ugly action—the place where people are outside society, but where, since so little else is left except the raw emotion of the self, appearances must be kept up. It is their manners, failing, that keep Anna and Vronsky from joining their emotions. They neither do their part nor keep pace. It is when her manners wholly fail that Anna brims over, sees herself clear, and comes on that unintermediated force which makes her suffer, and it is in desperate pursuit of some manners into which she can deliver that suffering that she finds her death: precisely as she thought she had done so long ago in her false death. Her tragedy is that she has destroyed too much of the medium, too many of the possibilities, of actual life, to leave life tolerable, and she has done this partly by dissociating manners from the actual world and partly by losing her sense of the sweep of things. Thus her last turning point, her last effort at incarnation, was death.

With no less of the force in him that drove Anna, Levin turned the other way. He too had been at the point of death and for months at a time, but through the death of his brother and the delivery of his wife found himself alive instead. It could have been the other way; Levin and Anna were aimed equally at life or at death. Human life cannot stand the intensity of Anna, but works toward it; human life requires the diminution of intensity into faith and of faith into momentum which is Levin. The one is very near the other. Only Anna's face was stone and more beautiful than ever. Yet it is in the likeness not the difference that the genuineness and the dialectic of Tolstoi's incarnation lies.

ISAIAH BERLIN

Tolstoy and Enlightenment

'Two things are always said about Tolstoy,' wrote the celebrated Russian critic Mikhailovsky, in a largely forgotten essay published in the 'eighties, 'that he is an outstandingly good writer of fiction and a bad thinker. This has become an axiom needing no demonstration'. This almost universal verdict has reigned, virtually unchallenged, for something like a hundred years; and Mikhailovsky's attempt to question it remained relatively isolated. Tolstoy dismissed his left-wing ally as a routine radical hack, and expressed surprise that anyone should take interest in him. This was characteristic but unjust. The essay, which its author called 'The Right Hand and the Left Hand of Leo Tolstoy', is a brilliant and convincing defence of Tolstoy on both intellectual and moral grounds, directed mainly against those who saw in the novelist's ethical doctrines, and in particular in his glorification of the peasants and of natural instinct and his constant disparagement of scientific culture, merely a perverse and sophisticated obscurantism which discredited the liberal cause, and played into the hands of priests and reactionaries. Mikhailovsky rejected this view, and in the course of his long and careful attempt to sift the enlightened grain from the reactionary chaff in Tolstoy's opinions, reached the conclusion that there was an unresolved and unavowed conflict in the great novelist's conceptions both of human nature and of the problems facing Russian and Western civilization. Mikhailovsky maintained

From *Mightier Than the Sword* by Charles Morgan, J.B. Priestley, et al. © 1964 by The English Centre.

that, so far from being a 'bad thinker', Tolstoy was no less acute, clear-eyed and convincing in his analysis of ideas than of motive, character and action. In his zeal for his paradoxical thesis—paradoxical certainly at the time at which he wrote it—Mikhailovsky sometimes goes too far. My own remarks are no more than an extended gloss on his thesis; for in substance it seems to me to be correct, or at any rate more right than wrong. Tolstoy's opinions are always subjective and can be (as for example in his writings on Shakespeare or Dante or Wagner) wildly perverse. But the questions which in his more didactic essays he tries to answer nearly always turn on cardinal questions of principle, and his analysis is always first hand, and cuts far deeper, in the deliberately simplified and naked form in which he usually presents it, than those of more balanced, concrete and 'objective' thinkers. Direct vision often tends to be disturbing: Tolstoy used this gift to the full to destroy both his own peace and that of his readers. It was this habit of asking exaggeratedly simple but fundamental questions, to which he did not himself—at any rate in the 'sixties and 'seventies—claim to possess the answers, that gave Tolstoy the reputation of being a 'nihilist'. Yet he certainly had no wish to destroy for the sake of destruction. He only wanted, more than anything else in the world, to know the truth. How annihilating this passion can be, is shown by others who have chosen to probe below the limits set by the wisdom of their generation: the author of the *Book of Job*, Machiavelli, Pascal, Rousseau. Like them, Tolstoy cannot be fitted into any of the public movements of his own, or indeed any other, age. The only company to which he belongs is the subversive one of questioners to whom no answer has been, or seems likely to be, given—at least no answer which they or those who understand them will begin to accept.

As for Tolstoy's positive ideas—and they varied less during his long life than has sometimes been represented—they are his own but not unique: they have something in common with the French enlightenment of the eighteenth century; something with those of the twentieth; little with those of his own times. He belonged to neither of the great ideological streams which divided educated Russian opinion during his youth. He was not a radical intellectual with his eyes turned to the West, nor a Slavophil, that is to say, a believer in a Christian and nationalist monarchy. His views cut across these categories.

Like the radicals, he had always condemned political repression, arbitrary violence, economic exploitation and all that create and perpetuates inequality among men. But the rest of the 'westernizing' outlook—the overwhelming sense of civic responsibility, the belief in natural science as the door to all truth, in social and political reform, in democracy, material progress, secularism—this celebrated amalgam, the heart of the ideology of the intelligentsia—Tolstoy rejected early in life. He believed in individual liberty and indeed in progress too, but in a queer sense of his own.[1] He looked with contempt on liberals and socialists, and with even greater hatred on the right-wing parties of his time. His closest affinity, as has often been remarked, is with Rousseau; he liked and admired Rousseau's views more than those of any other modern writer. Like Rousseau, he rejected the doctrine of original sin, and believed that man was born innocent and had been ruined by his own bad institutions; especially by what passed for education among civilized men. Like Rousseau again, he put the blame for this process of decadence largely on the intellectuals and the institutions which they support—in particular the self-appointed *élites* of experts, sophisticated *côteries*, remote from common humanity, self-estranged from natural life. These men are damned because they have all but lost the most precious of all human possessions, the capacity with which all men are born—to see the truth, the immutable, eternal truth, which only charlatans and sophists represent as varying in different circumstances and times and places—the truth which is visible fully only to the innocent eye of those whose hearts have not been corrupted—children, peasants, those not blinded by vanity and pride, the simple, the good. Education, as the West understands it ruins innocence. That is why children resist it bitterly and instinctively: that is why it has to be rammed down their throats, and, like all coercion and violence, maims the victim and at times destroys him beyond redress. Men crave for truth by nature; therefore true education must be of such a kind that children and unsophisticated, ignorant people will absorb it readily and eagerly. But to understand this, and to discover how to apply this knowledge, the educated must put away their intellectual arrogance and make a new beginning. They must purge their minds of theories, of false, quasi-scientific analogies between the world of men and the world of animals, or of men and inanimate things. Only then will they be able to re-establish a personal relationship with the uneducated—a relationship which only humanity and love can achieve. In modern times only Rousseau, and perhaps Dickens, seem to him to have seen this. Certainly the people's condition will never be improved until not only the Czarist bureaucracy, but the 'progressists', as Tolstoy called them, the vain and doctrinaire intelligentsia, are 'prised off the people's necks'—the common people's, and the children's too. So long as fanatical theorists bedevil education, little is to be hoped for. Even the old-fashioned village priest—so Tolstoy maintains in one of his early tracts—was less harmful: he knew little and was clumsy, idle and stupid; but he treated his pupils as God's creatures, not as scientists treat specimens in a laboratory; he did what he could; he was often corrupt, ill tempered, ignorant, unjust, but these were human—'natural'—vices, and therefore their effects, unlike those of machine-made modern instruction, inflicted no permanent injury.

With these opinions it is not surprising to find that Tolstoy was personally happier among the Slavophil reactionaries. He rejected their ideas, but at least they seemed to him to have some contact with reality—the land, the peasants, traditional ways of life. At least they believed in the primacy of spiritual values, and in the futility of trying to change men by changing the superficial sides of their life by means of political or constitutional reforms. But the Slavophils also believed in the Orthodox Church, in the unique historical destiny of the Russian people, in the sanctity of history as a divinely ordained process and therefore as the justification of many anomalies because they were native and ancient, and thus instruments in the divine tactic; they lived by a Christian faith in the mystical body—at once community and church—of the generations of the faithful, past, present and yet unborn. Intellectually, Tolstoy utterly repudiated all this; temperamentally he responded to it all too strongly. As a writer he truly understood only the nobility and the peasants: and the former better than the latter. He shared many of the instinctive beliefs of his country neighbours: like them he had a natural aversion from all forms of middle-class liberalism: the *bourgeoisie* scarcely appears in his novels: his attitude to parliamentary democracy, the rights of women, universal suffrage, was not very different from that of Cobbett or Carlyle or Proudhon or D. H. Lawrence. He shared deeply the Slavophil suspicion of all scientific and theoretical generalizations as such, and this created a bridge which made personal relations with the Moscow Slavophils congenial to him. But his intellect was not at one with his instinctive convictions. As a thinker he had profound affinities with the eighteenth-century *philosophes*. Like them, he looked upon the patriarchal Russian State and Church, idealized by the Slavophils (and the implication that common ideals united the educated ruling minority and the uneducated masses) as organized, hypocritical conspiracies. Like the moralists of the Enlightenment, he looked for true values not in history, nor the sacred missions of nations or cultures or churches, but in the individual's own personal experience. Like them, too, he believed in eternal (and not in historically evolving) ends of life, and rejected with both hands the romantic notion of race or nation or culture as creative agencies, still more the Hegelian conception of history as the self-realization of self-perfecting reason incarnated in men, or movements, or institutions (ideas which had deeply influenced the Slavophils); all his life he looked on this as cloudy metaphysical nonsense.

Tolstoy's cold, clear, uncompromising realism is quite explicit in the notes, diaries and letters of his early life. The reminiscences of those who knew him as a boy or as a student in the University of Kazan, reinforce this impression. His character was deeply conservative, with a streak of caprice and irrationality; but his mind remained calm, logical and unswerving; he followed the argument easily and fearlessly to whatever extreme it led and then embraced it—a typically Russian, and sometimes fatal, combination of qualities. What did not satisfy his critical sense, he rejected, he left the University of Kazan because he decided that the professors were incompetent and dealt with trivial issues. Like Helvétius and his friends in the mid-eighteenth century, Tolstoy denounced theology, history, the teaching of dead languages and literatures—the entire classical curriculum—as an accumulation of data and rules that no reasonable man could wish to know. History particularly irritated him as a systematic attempt to answer trivial or non-existent questions, with all the real issues carefully left out. 'History is like a deaf man answering questions which nobody has put to him,' he announced to a startled fellow student while they were both locked in the University detention room for some minor act of insubordination. The first extended statement of his full 'ideological' position belongs to the 'sixties. The occasion for it was his decision to compose a treatise on education. All his intellectual strength and all his prejudice went into this attempt.

II

In 1860 Tolstoy, then thirty-two years old, found himself in one of his periodic moral crises. He had acquired some fame as a writer: *Sebastopol*, *Childhood*, *Adolescence and Youth* and two or three shorter tales had been praised by the critics. He was on terms of friendship with some of the most gifted of an exceptionally talented generation of writers in his country— Turgenev, Nekrassov, Goncharov, Panaev, Pisemsky, Fet. His writing struck everyone by its freshness, sharpness, marvellous descriptive power and the precision and originality of its images. His style was at times criticized as awkward and even barbarous; but he was the most promising of the younger prose writers; he had a future; and yet his literary friends felt reservations about him. He paid visits to the literary salons, both right and left-wing, but he seemed at case in none of them. He was bold, imaginative and independent; but he was not a man of letters, not fundamentally concerned with problems of literature and writing, still less of writers; he had wandered in from another, less intellectual, more aristocratic and more primitive world. He was a well-born dilettante; but that was nothing new: the poetry of Pushkin and his contemporaries—unequalled in the history of Russian literature—had been created by amateurs of genius. It was not his origin but his unconcealed indifference to the literary life as such—to the habits and problems of professional writers, editors, publicists—that made his friends among the men of letters feel uneasy in his presence. This worldly, clever young officer could be exceedingly agreeable; his love of writing was genuine and very deep; but he was too contemptuous, too formidable and reserved, he did not dream of opening his heart in a *milieu* dedicated to intimate, unending self-revelation. He was inscrutable, disdainful, disconcerting, a little frightening. It was true that he no longer lived the life of an aristocratic officer. The wild nights on which the young radicals looked with hatred or contempt as characteristic of the dissipated lives of the reactionary *jeunesse dorée* no longer amused him. He had married, he had settled down, he was in love with his wife, he became for a time a model (if at times exasperating) husband. But he did not trouble to conceal the fact that he had infinitely more respect for all forms of real life—whether of the free Cossacks in the Caucasus, or of the rich young Guards officers in Moscow with their racehorses and balls and gypsies—than for the world of books, reviews, critics, professors, political discussions and talk about ideals, or philosophy and literary values. Moreover, he was opinionated, quarrelsome, and at times unexpectedly savage; with the result that his literary friends treated him with nervous respect, and, in the end, drew away from him; or perhaps he abandoned them. Apart from the poet Fet, who was an eccentric and deeply conservative country squire himself, Tolstoy had scarcely any intimates among the writers of his own generation. His breach with Turgenev is well known. He was even remoter from other *littérateurs*. There were times when he was fond of Vassili Botkin; he liked Nekrassov better than his poetry; but then Nekrassov was an editor of genius and had admired and encouraged him from his earliest beginnings.

The sense of the contrast between life and literature haunted Tolstoy all his life, and made him doubt his own vocation as a writer. Like other young men of birth and fortune, he was conscience stricken by the appalling condition of the peasants. Mere reflection or denunciation seemed to him a form of evasion. He must act, he must start at home. Like the eighteenth-century radicals, he was convinced that men were born equal, and were made unequal by the way in which they were brought up. He established a school for the boys of his own village; and, dissatisfied with the educational theories then in vogue in Russia, decided to go abroad to study Western methods in theory and in practice. He derived a great deal from his visits to England, France, Switzerland, Belgium, Germany—including the title of his greatest novel. But his conversations with the most advanced Western authorities on education, and his observation of their methods, had convinced him that they were at best worthless, at worst harmful, to the children upon whom they were practised. He did not stay long in England and paid little attention to its 'antiquated' schools. In France he found that learning was almost entirely mechanical—by rote; prepared questions, lists of dates, for example, were answered competently, because they had been learnt by heart. But the same children, when asked for the same facts from some unexpected angle, often produced absurd replies, which showed that their knowledge meant nothing to them. The schoolboy who replied that the murderer of Henry IV of France was Julius Caesar seemed to him typical: the boy neither understood nor took an interest in the facts he had stored up: all that was gained, at most, was a mechanical memory. But, the true home of theory was Germany. The pages which Tolstoy devotes to describing teaching and teachers in Germany rival and anticipate the celebrated pages in *War and Peace* in which he makes savage fun of admired experts in another field—the German strategists employed by the Russian Army—whom he represents as grotesque and pompous dolts.

In *Yasnaya Polyana*, the journal called after his estate, which he had had privately printed in 1859–61, Tolstoy speaks of his educational visits to various schools[2] in the West and, by way of example gives a hair-raising (and exceedingly entertaining) account of the latest methods of elementary teaching used by a specialist trained in one of the most advanced of the German teachers' seminaries. He describes the pedantic, immensely self-satisfied schoolmaster, as he enters the room and notes with approval that the children are seated at their desks, crushed and obedient, in total silence, as prescribed by German rules of behaviour. 'He casts a look round the class and is quite clear in his mind about what they ought to understand; he knows it all already, he knows what the children's souls are made of and a good many other things that the seminary has taught him.' The schoolmaster enters, armed with the latest and most progressive pedagogic volume, called *Das Fischbuch*. It contains pictures of a fish.

'What is this, dear children?' 'A fish,' replies the brightest. 'No, no. Think. Think!' And he will not rest until some child says that what they see is not a fish, but a book. That is better. 'And what do books contain?' 'Letters,' says the bravest boy. 'No, no,' says the schoolmaster sadly. 'You really *must* think of what you are saying.' By this time the children are beginning to be hopelessly demoralized: they have no notion of what they are meant to say. They have a confused and perfectly correct feeling that the schoolmaster wants them to say something unintelligible—that the fish is not a fish; they feel that whatever it is that he wants them to say is something that they will never think of. Their thoughts begin to stray. They wonder (this is very Tolstoyan) why the master is wearing spectacles, why he is looking through them instead of taking them off, and so on. The master urges them to concentrate; he harries and tortures them until he manages to make them say that what they see is not a fish, but a picture, and then, after more torture, that the picture represents a fish. If that is what he wants them to say, would it not be easier, Tolstoy asks, to make them learn this piece of profound wisdom by heart, instead of tormenting them with the idiotic Fishbook method, which so far from causing them to think 'creatively', merely stupefies them? The genuinely intelligent children know that their answers are always wrong; they cannot tell why, they only know that this is so; while the stupid, who occasionally provide the right answers, do not understand why they are praised. All that the German pedagogue is doing is to feed dead human material—or rather living human beings—into a grotesque mechanical contraption invented by fanatical fools who think that this is a way of applying scientific method to the education of men. Tolstoy assures us that his account (of which I have quoted only a short fragment) is not a parody, but a faithful reproduction of what he saw and heard in the advanced schools of Germany and in 'those schools in England which have been fortunate enough to acquire these wonderful modern methods'.

Disillusioned and indignant, Tolstoy returned to his Russian estate and began to teach the village children himself. He built schools, continued to study and reject and denounce current doctrines of education, published periodicals and pamphlets, invented new methods of learning geography, zoology, physics; composed an entire manual of arithmetic of his own, inveighed against all methods of coercion, especially those which consisted of forcing children against their will to memorize facts and dates and figures. In short, he behaved like an energetic, opinionated, somewhat eccentric eighteenth-century landowner, who had become a convert to the doctrines of Rousseau or the abbé Mably. His accounts of his theories and experiments fill two stout volumes in the pre-revolutionary editions of his collected works. They are still fascinating, if only because they contain some of the best descriptions of village life, and especially of children, both comical and lyrical, that even he had ever composed. He wrote them in the 'sixties and 'seventies, when he was at the height of his creative powers. The reader tends to lose sight of Tolstoy's overriding didactic purpose before the unrivalled insight into the twisting, criss-crossing pattern of the thoughts and feelings of individual village children, and the marvellous concreteness and imagination of the descriptions of their talk and their behaviour and of physical nature round them—of trees, meadows, sky, light and darkness and winter in a village in Central Russia. Yet side by side with this expression of a direct vision of human experience there run the clear, firm dogmas of a fanatically doctrinaire eighteenth-century rationalist—doctrines not fused with the life that he describes, but superimposed upon it, like windows with rigorously symmetrical patterns drawn upon them, unrelated to the world on which they open, and yet achieving a kind of illusory artistic and intellectual unity with it, owing to the unbounded vitality and constructive genius of the writing itself. It is one of the most extraordinary performances in the history of literature.

The enemy is always the same: experts, professionals, men who claim special authority over other men. Universities and professors are a frequent target for attack. There are intimations of this already in the section entitled *Youth* of his earlier autobiographical novel. There is something eighteenth century, reminiscent both of Voltaire and of Bentham, about Tolstoy's devastating accounts of the dull and incompetent professors and the desperately bored and obsequious students in Russia in his youth. The tone is unusual in the nineteenth century: dry, ironical, didactic, mordant, at once withering and entertaining; the whole based on the contrast between the harmonious simplicity of nature and the self-destructive complications created by the malice or stupidity of men—men from whom the author feels himself detached, whom he affects not to understand and mocks at from a distance.[3] We are at the earliest beginnings of a theme which grew obsessive in Tolstoy's later life, that the solution to all our perplexities stares us in the face—that the answer is about us everywhere, like the light of day, if only we would not close our eyes or look everywhere but at what is there, before our very eyes, the clear, simple irresistible truth.

Like Rousseau and Kant and the believers in Natural law, Tolstoy was convinced that men have certain basic material and spiritual needs in all places, at all times. If these needs are fulfilled, they lead harmonious lives, which is the goal of their nature. Moral, aesthetic and other spiritual values are objective and eternal, and man's inner harmony depends upon his correct relationship to these. Moreover, Tolstoy constantly defended the proposition that human beings are more harmonious in childhood than under the corrupting influence of education in later life;[4] and also something that he believed much more deeply and expressed in everything he wrote or said—

that simple people, peasants, Cossacks, and the like have a more 'natural' and correct attitude than civilized men towards these basic values and that they are free and independent in a sense in which civilized men are not. For (he insists on this over and over again) peasant communities are in a position to supply their own material and spiritual needs out of their own resources, provided that they are not robbed or enslaved by oppressors and exploiters; whereas civilized men need for their survival the forced labour of others—serfs, slaves, the exploited masses, ironically called 'dependents' because their masters depend on them. The masters are parasitic upon others: they are degraded not merely by the fact that to enslave and exploit others is a denial of such objective values as justice, equality, human dignity, love—values which men crave to realize because they must, because they are men—but for the further and, to him, even more important reason, that to live on robbed or borrowed goods and so fail to be self-subsistent, falsifies 'natural' feelings and perceptions, corrodes men morally, and makes them both wicked and miserable. The human ideal is a society of free and equal men, who live and think by the light of what is true and right, and so are not in conflict with each other or themselves. This is a form—a very simple one—of the classical doctrine of Natural law, whether in its theological or secular, liberal-anarchist form. To it Tolstoy adhered all his life, as much in his 'secular' period as after his 'conversion'. His early stories express this vividly. The Cossacks Lukashka or Uncle Yeroshka in *The Cossacks* are morally superior as well as happier and aesthetically more harmonious beings than Olenin. Olenin knows this; indeed that is the heart of the situation. Pierre in *War and Peace* and Levin in *Anna Karenina* sense this in simple peasants and soldiers; go does Nekhlyudov in *The Morning of a Landowner*. This conviction fills Tolstoy's mind to a greater and greater degree, until it overshadows all other issues in his later works; *Resurrection* and *The Death of Ivan Ilyich* are not intelligible without it.

Tolstoy's critical thought constantly revolves round this central conflict—nature and artifice, truth and invention. When in the 'nineties he laid down conditions of excellence in art (in the course of an introduction to a Russian translation of some of Maupassant's stories), he demanded of all writers, in the first place, the possession of sufficient talent; in the second, that the subject itself must be morally important; and finally, that they must truly love and hate what they describe—'commit' themselves—retain the direct moral vision of childhood, and not maim their natures by practising self-imposed, self-lacerating and always illusory objectivity and detachment. Talent is not given equally to all men; but everyone can, if he tries, discover what is good and what is bad, what is important and what is trivial. Only false—'made up'—theories blind men and writers to this, and so distort their lives and creative activity. He applies his criteria quite literally. Thus Nekrassov, according to Tolstoy, treated subjects of profound importance, and possessed superb skill as a writer; but he failed because his attitude towards his suffering peasants and crushed idealists remained chilly and unreal. Dostoevsky's subjects, Tolstoy concedes, lack nothing in seriousness, and his concern is profound and genuine; but the first condition is not fulfilled: he is diffuse and repetitive, he does not know how to tell the truth clearly, and then to stop—one can, after the first hundred pages or so, predict all the rest. Turgenev writes well and stands in a real, morally adequate, relationship to his subjects; but he fails fearfully on the second count: the level is too superficial—the issues are too trivial—and for this no degree of integrity or skill can compensate. For, Tolstoy insists again and again, content determines form, never form content; and if the topic is too small, nothing will save the work of the artist. To hold the opposite of this—to believe in the primacy of form—is to sacrifice truth: to end by producing works that are contrived. There is no harsher word in Tolstoy's entire critical vocabulary than 'made up'—indicating that the writer did not truly experience or imagine, but merely 'composed', 'contrived', 'made up' that which he is purporting to describe. So, too, Tolstoy maintained that Maupassant, whose gifts he admired greatly (and perhaps overestimated), betrayed his genius precisely owing to false and vulgar theories of this kind; yet he was judged, none the less, to be a good writer to the degree to which, like Balaam, although he might have meant to curse the good, he could not help discerning it: and this perception inevitably attracted his love to it and forced him against his own will towards the truth. Talent is vision, vision reveals the truth, truth is eternal and objective. To see the truth about nature or about conduct, to see it directly and vividly as only a man of genius (or a simple human being or a child) can see it, and then, in cold blood, to deny or tamper with the vision, no matter with what motive, is always monstrous, unnatural, a symptom of a deeply, perhaps fatally, diseased condition.

III

Truth, for Tolstoy, is always discoverable, to follow it is to be good, inwardly sound, harmonious. Yet it is clear that our society is not harmonious or composed of internally harmonious individuals. The interests of the educated minority—what he calls 'the professors, the barons and the bankers'—are opposed to those of the majority—the peasants, the poor.

Each side is indifferent to, or mocks, the values of the other. Even those who, like Olenin, Pierre, Nekhlyudov, Levin, realize the spuriousness of the values of the professors, barons and bankers, and the moral decay in which their false education has involved them, even those who are truly contrite, cannot, despite Slavophil pretensions, go native and 'merge' with the mass of the common people. Are they too corrupt ever to recover their innocence? Is their case hopeless? Can it be that civilized men have acquired (or discovered) certain true values of their own, which barbarians and children may know nothing of, but which they—the civilized—cannot lose or forget, even if, by some impossible means, they could transform themselves into peasants or the free and happy Cossacks of the Don and the Terek? This is one of the central and most tormenting problems in Tolstoy's life, to which he goes back again and again, and to which he returns conflicting answers.

Tolstoy knows that he himself clearly belongs to the minority of barons, bankers, professors. He knows the symptoms of his condition only too well. He cannot, for example, deny his passionate love for the music of Mozart or Chopin or the poetry of Pushkin or Tyutchev—the ripest fruits of civilization. He needs—he cannot do without—the printed word and all the elaborate paraphernalia of the culture in which such lives are lived and such works of art are created. But what is the use of Pushkin to village boys, when his words are not intelligible to them? What real benefits has the invention of printing brought the peasants? We are told, Tolstoy observes, that books educate societies ('that is, make them more corrupt'), that it was the written word that has promoted the emancipation of, the serfs in Russia. Tolstoy denies this: the government would have done the same without books or pamphlets. Pushkin's *Boris Godunov* pleases him, Tolstoy, deeply, but to the peasants means nothing. The triumphs of civilization? The telegraph informs him about his sister's health, or about the political prospects of King Otto I of Greece; but what benefit do the masses gain from it? Yet it is they who pay and have always paid for it all, and they know this well. When peasants in the 'cholera riots' kill doctors because they regard them as poisoners, what they do is no doubt wrong, yet these murders are no accident: the instinct which tells the peasants who their oppressors are is sound, and the doctors belong to that class. When Wanda Landowska played to the villagers of Yasnaya Polyana, the great majority of them remained unresponsive. Yet can it be doubted that it is these simple people who lead the least broken lives, immeasurably superior to the warped and tormented lives of the rich and educated? The common people, Tolstoy asserts in his early educational tracts, are self-subsistent not only materially but spiritually—folksong, ballads, the *Iliad*, the Bible, spring from the people itself, and are therefore intelligible to all men everywhere, as Tyutchev's magnificent poem *Silentium*, or *Don Giovanni*, or the Ninth Symphony are not. If there is an ideal of human life, it lies not in the future but in the past. Once upon a time there was the Garden of Eden, and in it dwelt the uncorrupted human soul—as the Bible and Rousseau conceived it—and then came the Fall, corruption, suffering, falsehood. It is mere blindness (Tolstoy says over and over again) to believe, as liberals or socialists—'the progressives'—believe, that the golden age is still to come, that history is the story of improvement, that advances in natural science or material skills coincide with real moral progress. The truth is the reverse of this.

The child is closer to the ideal harmony than the man, and the simple peasant than the torn, 'alienated', morally and spiritually unanchored, self-destructive parasites who form the civilized *élite*. From this doctrine springs Tolstoy's notable anti-individualism; and in particular his diagnosis of the individual's will as the source of misdirection and perversion of 'natural' human tendencies, and hence the conviction (derived largely from Schopenhauer's doctrine of the will as the source of frustration) that to plan, organize, rely on science, try to create ordered patterns of life in accordance with rational theories, is to swim against the stream of nature, to close one's eyes to the saving truth within us, to torture facts to fit artificial schemes, and torture human beings to fit social and economic systems against which their natures cry out. From the same source, too, comes the obverse of this moral: Tolstoy's faith in the intuitively grasped direction of things as being not merely inevitable but objectively—providentially—good; and therefore belief in the need to submit to it: his quietism.

This is one aspect of his teaching, the most familiar, the central idea of the Tolstoyan movement. It runs through all his mature works, imaginative, critical, didactic, from *The Cossacks* and *Family Happiness*, to his last religious tracts; this is the doctrine which both liberals and Marxists duly condemned. It is in this mood that Tolstoy (like Marx whom he neither respected nor understood) maintains that to imagine that heroic personalities determine events is a piece of colossal megalomania and self-deception. His narrative is designed to show the insignificance of Napoleon or Alexander, or of aristocratic and bureaucratic society in *Anna Karenina*, or of the judges and official persons in *Resurrection*; or again, the emptiness and intellectual impotence of historians and philosophers who try to explain events by employing concepts like 'power' attributed to great men, or 'influence' ascribed to writers, orators, preachers—words, abstractions, which, in his view, explain nothing, being themselves more obscure than the facts for which they purport to account. He maintains that we do not begin to understand, and therefore cannot explain or analyse, what it is to wield authority or strength, to influence, to dominate. Explanations that do not explain, are, for Tolstoy, a symptom of the destructive and self-inflated intellect, the faculty that kills innocence and leads to false notions and the ruin of human life.

That is one strain, inspired by Rousseau and present in that early romanticism which inspired primitivism in art and in life, not in Russia alone. Tolstoy imagines that this state can be achieved by observing the lives of simple people and by the study of the Gospels.

His other strain (interwoven with the first) is the direct opposite of this. Mikhailovsky in his essay on Tolstoy says, justly enough, that Olenin cannot, charmed as he is by the Caucasus and the Cossack idyll, transform himself into a Lukashka, return to the childlike harmony, which in his case has long been broken. Levin knows that if he tried to become a peasant this could only be a grotesque farce, which the peasants would be the first to perceive and deride; he and Pierre and Nicolai Rostov know obscurely that in some sense they have something to give that the peasants have not. In the famous essay entitled *What is Art?* Tolstoy unexpectedly tells the educated reader that the peasant 'needs what your life of ten generations uncrushed by hard labour has given you. You had the leisure to search, to think, to suffer—then give him that for whose sake you suffered; he is in need of it ... do not bury in the earth the talent given you by history ...' Leisure, then, need not be merely destructive. Progress can occur; we can learn from what happened in the past, as those who lived in that past could not. It is true that we live in an unjust order. But this itself creates direct moral obligations. Those who are members of the civilized *élite*, cut off as they tragically are from the mass of the people, have the duty to attempt to rebuild broken humanity, to stop exploiting other men, to give them what they most need—education, knowledge, material help, a capacity for living better lives. Levin in *Anna Karenina*, as Mikhailovsky remarks, takes up where Nicolai Rostov in *War and Peace* leaves off; they are not quietists, yet what they do is right. The emancipation of the peasants, in Tolstoy's view, although it did not go far enough, was nevertheless a powerful act of will—good will—on the part of the government, and now it is necessary to teach peasants to read and write and grasp the rules of arithmetic, which the peasants cannot do for themselves; to equip them for the use of freedom. I may be unable to merge myself with the mass of peasants; but I can at least use the fruit of the unjustly obtained leisure of myself and my ancestors—my education, knowledge, skills—for the benefit of those whose labour made it possible. This is the talent which I may not bury. I must work to promote a just society in accordance with those objective standards which all men, except the hopelessly corrupt, see and accept, whether they live by them or not. The simple see them more clearly, the sophisticated more dimly, but all men can see them if they try; indeed, to be able to see them is part of what it is to be a man. When injustice is perpetrated, I have an obligation to speak out and act against it; nor may artists, any more than other men, sit with folded hands. What makes good writers good is first and foremost, ability to see truth—social and individual, material and spiritual—and so present it that it cannot be escaped. Tolstoy holds that Maupassant, for example, is doing exactly this, despite all his aesthetic fallacies. Maupassant may, because he is a corrupt human being, take the side of the bad against the good, write about a worthless Paris seducer with greater sympathy than he feels for his victims. But provided that he tells the truth at a level that is sufficiently profound (and men of talent cannot avoid doing this) he will face the reader with fundamental moral questions—even though this may not be his intention— questions which the reader can neither escape nor answer without severe and painful self-examination. This, for Tolstoy, opens the path to regeneration, and is the proper function of art. Vocation, talent, artistic conscience—all these are obedience to an inescapable inner need: to satisfy it is the artist's purpose and duty. Nothing therefore, is more false than the view of the artist as a purveyor or a craftsman whose sole function is to create a beautiful thing, as the aesthetes—Flaubert, or Renan or Maupassant[5] (or Mr. Evelyn Waugh) maintain. There is only one true human goal, and it is equally binding on all men—landowners, doctors, barons, professors, bankers, peasants: to tell the truth and act according to it, that is, to do good and persuade others to do so. That God exists, or that the *Iliad* is beautiful, or that men have a right to be free and to be equal, are all eternal and absolute truths. Therefore, we must persuade men to read the *Iliad* and not pornographic French novels, and to work for an equal society, not a theocratic or political hierarchy. Coercion is evil; this is self-evident and men have always known it to be true; therefore they must work for a society in which there will be no wars, no prisons, no executions, in any circumstances, for any reason—for a society in which there is the highest attainable degree of individual freedom. By his own route Tolstoy arrived at a programme of Christian anarchism which had much in common with that of the 'realist' school of painters and composers—Mussorgsky, Repin, Stassov—and with that of their political allies, the Russian Populists, although he rejected their belief in natural science and their doctrinaire socialism and faith in the methods of terrorism. For what he now appeared to be advocating was a programme of action, not of quietism; this programme underlay the educational reforms that Tolstoy attempted to carry out. *L'éducation peut tout*, said Helvétius a hundred years before, and Tolstoy in effect agreed. Ignorance is responsible for misery, inequality, wars. He writes with indignation about the prevalent 'inequality of education', and in particular 'the disproportion of the educated and uneducated, or more exactly the savage and the literate'.

If it were not for ignorance, human beings could not be exploited or coerced. 'One man cannot compel others—only a dominant majority can do that, united in its lack of education. It only looks as if Napoleon III concluded the peace of Villafranca, suppresses newspapers or wants to conquer Savoy, actually all this is done by the Félixes and Victors who cannot read newspapers' (*ibid.*, p. 329). This is the seed of the doctrine that henceforth determines all his thoughts—that the real agents of history are the masses—the collection of obscure individuals, the Félixes and Victors, although responsibility for them is mistakenly attributed to leaders and great men. If the Félixes and Victors refused to march, there would be no wars; if they were educated and could read newspapers—and if these newspapers contained truth instead of falsehood—they would not march. This is eighteenth-century rationalist doctrine in its clearest form. For Tolstoy, at this stage, all social movements can be analysed into the specific behaviour of specific individuals. Peoples, governments, nations, armies, are only collective nouns, not genuine entities—to attribute to them the characteristics of human beings, to speak of them as literally active or powerful, as authors of this achievement or that feature—is not misleading only if it is remembered that they can (and not in principle only) be analysed into their constituent elements. This positivist conviction Tolstoy holds in a stronger form than Marx or Comte—as strongly as the most extreme empiricists of our own time: like them, he denounces as myth, as metaphysical obfuscation, anything that implies that collective behaviour is not analysable into the behaviour of the individuals who compose the collective; and to this he adds the corollary that the real activity of a man is the 'inner' activity of his spirit, and not the 'outer' activity as expressed in social or political life. And he quotes the activist and revolutionary Herzen towards whom his attitude was at all times highly ambivalent in support of this position.[6] It is hardly necessary to add that the whole of *War and Peace* and much of *Anna Karenina* and *Resurrection* is an incarnation of this central idea. All the results of advancing civilization—the telegraph, steamers, theatres, academies, literature, etc.—are useless so long as only one per cent of the people are receiving education. 'All this (i.e. universities, etc.) is useful, but useful as a dinner in the English Club might be useful if all of it were eaten by the manager and the cook. These things are created by all the seventy million Russians, but are of use only to thousands.' Who shall determine what is the right kind of education? When in doubt Tolstoy returns to Rousseau. 'The will of the people is the sole factor by which our (educational) activity should be guided.'

'If we offer the people certain kinds of knowledge ... and find that they have a bad influence on it, I conclude not that the people is bad because it doesn't absorb this knowledge, nor that the people, unlike ourselves, is not adult enough to do so ... but that this kind of knowledge is bad, abnormal, and that with the help of the people we must work out new sorts of knowledge more suitable for us all—that is both for the educated and for the common people ...' 'Someone might ask: Why should we assume that the arts and sciences of our own educated class are false? Why should you infer their falsity from the mere fact that the people does not take to it? This question is answered very easily: because there are thousands of us, but millions of them.'

This democratic programme is Tolstoy's answer to the hated 'liberals' and 'progressives' and the specialists and civilized *élites* to whom they look for salvation. Faithful to Rousseau (and if he had but known it), to Kant, he strove to discover, collect, expound eternal truths; awaken the spontaneous interest, the imagination, love, curiosity, of children or simple folk; above all liberate their 'natural' moral, emotional and intellectual powers, which he did not doubt, as Rousseau did not doubt, would achieve harmony within men and between them, provided that we took care to eliminate whatever might cramp, maim, and kill them.[7]

IV

This programme—that of making possible the free self-development of all human faculties—rests on one vast assumption that there exists at least one path of development which ensures that these faculties will neither conflict with each other, nor develop disproportionately—a sure path to the complete harmony in which everything fits and is at peace; with the corollary that we can find it—that knowledge of man's nature gained from observation or introspection or moral intuition, or from the study of the lives and writings of the best and wisest men of all ages or of the simple hearts of the 'millions' and not of the 'thousands', will show it to us. This is not the place for considering how far this doctrine is compatible with ancient religious teachings or modern psychology. The point I wish to stress is that it is, above all, a programme of action, a call for universal education and re-education, a declaration of war against current social values, against the tyranny of states, societies, churches, against brutality, injustice, ignorance, stupidity, hypocrisy, weakness, above all, against vanity and moral blindness. A man who has fought a good fight in this war will thereby expiate the sin of having been a hedonist and an exploiter, and the son and beneficiary of robbers and oppressors.

This is what Tolstoy believed, preached and practised. His 'conversion' altered his view of what was good and what was evil. It did not weaken his faith in the need for action. His belief in the principles themselves henceforth never wavered. The enemy entered by another door: Tolstoy's sense of reality was too inexorable to keep out a terrible doubt about how these principles—no matter how true themselves—should be applied. Even though *I* believe some things to be beautiful or good, and others to be ugly and evil, what right have *I* to bring up others in the light of my convictions, when I know that, do what I might, I cannot help liking Chopin and Maupassant, while these far better beings—peasants or children—do not? Have I, who stand at the end of a long period of decadence—of generations of civilized, unnatural living—have *I* the right to touch *their* souls?

To seek to influence someone, however mysterious the process, is to engage in a dark, morally suspect enterprise. This is obvious in the case of the crude manipulation of one man by another. But in principle it holds equally of education. All educators seek to shape the minds and lives of human beings in the direction of a given goal, or in the light of a specific ideal model. But if we—the sophisticated members of a deeply corrupt society—are ourselves unhappy, inharmonious, gone astray, what can we be doing but trying to change children who are born healthy into our own sick semblance, to make of them cripples like ourselves? We are what we have become; we cannot help our love of Pushkin's verses, of Chopin's music; we discover that children and peasants find them unintelligible or tedious. What do we do? We persist, we 'educate' them, until they too, appear to enjoy these works, or, at least, grasp why we enjoy them. What have we done? We find the works of Mozart and Chopin beautiful only because Mozart and Chopin were themselves children of our degenerate culture, and therefore their words speak to our diseased minds; but what right have we to infect others, to make them as corrupt as ourselves? ('The works of Pushkin, Gogol, Turgenev, Derzhavin ... are not needed by the people and will bring it no benefit.') We see the blemishes of other systems. We see all too clearly how the human personality is destroyed by Protestant insistence on blind obedience, by Catholic belief in social emulation, by the appeal to material self-interest and the value of social rank and position on which Russian education, according to Tolstoy, is based. Is it not, then, either monstrous arrogance or a perverse inconsistency to behave as if our own system of education—something recommended by Pestalozzi, or by the inventors of the Lancaster method, or by some other expert, systems that reflect their inventors' civilized and consequently perverted, personalities—as if such ideas were necessarily superior, or even less destructive than what we condemn so readily and justly in the superficial French or the stupid and pompous Germans?

How is this to be avoided? Tolstoy repeats the lessons of Rousseau's *Emile*. Nature, only nature will save us. We must seek to find what is 'natural', spontaneous, uncorrupt, sound, in harmony with itself and other objects in the world, and then to clear paths for development on these lines; not seek to alter, to force into a mould. We must listen to the dictates of our stifled original nature—not look on it as mere raw material on which to impose our unique individual personalities and powerful wills. To defy, to be Promethean, to create goals and build worlds in rivalry with what our moral sense knows to be eternal truths, given once and for all to all men, truths, knowledge of which alone renders them men and not beasts—that is the monstrous sin of pride, committed by all reformers, all revolutionaries, all men judged by the world to be great and effective. It is committed in just as large a measure by those in authority—by legislators, bureaucrats, judges, country squires who, out of liberal convictions or simply caprice or boredom, dictate, bully and interfere with the lives of peasants.[8] Do not teach: learn; that is the central notion of Tolstoy's essay, written nearly a hundred years ago, '*Should we teach the peasants' children how to write, or should they teach us?*' and it goes through all the notes on education, published in the 'sixties and 'seventies and written with his customary freshness, attention to detail and unapproachable power of direct perception. In one of these he gives examples of stories written by the children in his village, and speaks of the awe which he felt, face to face with the act of pure creation in which, he assures us, he played no part himself, these stories would only be spoilt by his 'corrections'; they seem to him far deeper than anything by Goethe. He speaks of how deeply ashamed they made him feel of his own superficiality, vanity, stupidity, narrowness, lack of moral and aesthetic sense. If, he tells us, one can help children and peasants at all, it is only by making it easier for them to advance freely along their own instinctive path; to direct is to spoil; men are good and only need freedom to realize their goodness.

'We speak,' writes Tolstoy in the 'seventies, 'of bringing a man up to be a scoundrel, a hypocrite, a good man: of the Spartans as bringing up brave men, of French education as producing one-sided and self-satisfied persons, and so on.' But this is speaking of, and using, human beings as so much raw material for us to model, this is what 'to bring up' to be like this or like that, means. We are evidently ready to alter the direction spontaneously followed by the souls and wills of others, to deny them independence—in favour of what? Of our own corrupt, false, or, at best, uncertain values? 'Education', Tolstoy says elsewhere, 'is the action of one person on another with a view to causing the other to acquire certain moral habits'; but this always involves some degree of moral tyranny. And in a wild moment of panic, he adds 'Is not the ultimate motive of the educator envy—envy of the purity of the child; desire to make the child more like himself, that is to say, more corrupt?' he goes on to add, 'What has the entire history of education been?' he answers: 'All philosophers of education, from Plato to Kant, professed to want one thing: to free education from the chains of the evil past—from its ignorance and its errors—to find out what men truly need, and adjust the new schools to that.' They struck off one yoke only to put another in its place. Certain scholastic philosophers insisted on Greek, because that was the language of Aristotle who knew the truth. Luther, Tolstoy continues, denied the authority of the Fathers and insisted on inculcating the original Hebrew, because he *knew* that that was the language in which God had revealed eternal truths to men. Bacon looked to empirical knowledge of nature, and his theories contradicted those of Aristotle. Rousseau proclaimed his faith in life—life as he conceived it—and not in theories. But about one thing they were all agreed: that one must liberate the young from the blind despotism of the old; and each immediately substituted his own fanatical, enslaving dogma in its place. If I am sure that I know the truth and that all else is error, does that alone entitle me to superintend the education of another? Is such certainty enough? Whether or not it disagrees with the certainties of others? Have I the right to put a wall round the pupil, exclude all external influences, and try to mould him as I please, in my own, or somebody else's, image? The answer to this question, Tolstoy passionately says to the 'progressives', 'must be "yes" or "no" ..., if it is "yes", then the church schools and the Jews' schools have as much right to exist as our universities'. He declares that he sees no moral difference, at least in principle, between the compulsory Latin of the traditional establishments and the compulsory materialism with which the radical professors indoctrinate their captive audiences. There might indeed, be something to be said for the things that the liberals delight in denouncing: education at home, for example; for it is surely natural that parents should wish their children to resemble them. Again there is a case for a religious upbringing, since it is natural that believers should want to save all other human beings from what they are certain must be eternal damnation. Similarly the Government is entitled to train men, for society cannot survive without some sort of government, and governments cannot exist without some qualified specialists to serve them. But what is the moral basis of 'liberal education' in schools and universities, staffed by men who do not even claim to be sure that what they teach is true? Empiricism? The lessons of history? The only lesson that history teaches us is that all previous educational systems have proved to be despotisms founded on falsehoods, and later roundly condemned. Why should the twenty-first century not look back on us in the nineteenth with the same scorn and amusement as that with which we now look on mediaeval schools and universities? If the history of education is the history merely of tyranny and error, why should we, and what right have we, to carry on this abominable farce? And if we are told that it has always been so, that it is nothing new, that we cannot help it and must do our best—is this not like saying that murders have always taken place, so that we might as well go on murdering even though we have now discovered what it is that makes men murder? In these circumstances, we should be villains if we did not say at least this much: that since, unlike the Pope or Luther or modern positivists, we do not ourselves claim to base our education (or other forms of interference with human beings) on knowledge of absolute truth, we must at least stop torturing others in the name of something that we do not know. All we can know for certain is what men actually want. Let us at least have the courage of our admitted ignorance, of our doubts and uncertainties. At least, we can try to discover what others— children or adults—require, by taking off the spectacles of tradition, prejudice, dogma, and making it possible for ourselves to know men as they truly are, by listening to them carefully and sympathetically, and understanding them and their lives and their needs, one by one, individually. Let us at least try to provide them with what they ask for, and leave them as free as possible. Give them *Bildung* (for which Tolstoy produces an equivalent Russian word—pointing out with pride that it has none in French or English), that is to say, seek to influence them by precept and by the example of your own lives; but not apply 'education' to them, which is essentially a method of coercion and destroys what is most natural and sacred in man—the capacity for knowing and acting for oneself in accordance with what one thinks to be true and good—the power and the right of self-direction.

But he cannot let the matter rest there, as many a liberal has tried to do. For the question immediately arises; how are we to contrive to leave the schoolboy and the student free? By being morally neutral? By imparting only factual knowledge, not ethical, or aesthetic, or social or religious doctrine?

By placing the 'facts' before the pupil, and letting him form his own conclusions, without seeking to influence him in any direction, for fear that we might infect him with our own diseased outlooks? But is it really possible for such neutral communications to occur between men? Is not every human communication a conscious or unconscious impression of one temperament, attitude to life, scale of values, upon another? Are men ever so thoroughly insulated from each other that the careful avoidance of more than the minimum degree of social intercourse will leave them unsullied, absolutely free to see truth and falsehood, good and evil, beauty and ugliness, with their own, and only their own eyes? But this is an absurd conception of individuals as creatures who can be kept pure from all social influence, and seemed absurd in the world even of Tolstoy's middle years, even, that is, without the new knowledge of human beings that we have acquired today as the result of the labours of psychologists, sociologists, philosophers. We live in a degenerate society; only the pure, Tolstoy says, can rescue us. But who, he reasonably asks, will educate the educators? Who is so pure as to know how, let alone be able, to heal our world or anyone in it?

Between these poles—on one side the facts, nature, what there is; on the other duty, justice, what there should be; on one side innocence, on the other education; between the claims of spontaneity and those of obligation, of the injustice of coercing others, and of the injustice of leaving them to their own ways, Tolstoy wavered and struggled all his life. And not only he, but all those populists and socialists, the doctors, engineers, agricultural experts, painters and composers and idealistic students in Russia who 'went to the people' and could not decide whether they had gone to teach or to learn, whether the 'good of the people' for which they were ready to sacrifice their lives, was what 'the people' in fact desired, or something that the reformers and they alone knew to be good for it—something which the 'people' should desire—would desire if only they were as educated and wise as their champions—but, in fact, in their benighted state, often spurned and violently resisted. These contradictions, and his unswerving recognition of his failure to reconcile or modify them, are, in a sense, what gives its special meaning both to Tolstoy's life and to the morally agonized, didactic pages of his art. He furiously rejected the compromises and alibis of his liberal contemporaries as mere feebleness and evasion. Yet he believed that a final solution to the problem of how to apply the principles of Jesus must exist, even though neither he nor any one else had wholly discovered it. He rejected the very possibility that some of the tendencies and goals of which he speaks might be literally both valid and incompatible. Historicism versus moral responsibility; quietism versus the duty to resist evil; teleology or a causal order against the play of chance and irrational force; on the one hand, spiritual harmony, simplicity, the mass of the people, and on the other, the irresistible attraction of the culture of minorities and their sciences, and arts, the conflict between corruption of the civilized portion of society and its direct duty to raise the masses of the people to its own level; the dynamism and falsifying influence of passionate, simple, one-sided faith, as against the clear-sighted sense of the complex facts and inevitable weakness in action which flows from enlightened scepticism—all these strains are given full play in the thought of Tolstoy. His adhesion to them appears as a series of inconsistencies in his system, because the conflicts may, after all, exist in fact and lead to collisions in real life.[9] Tolstoy is incapable of suppressing, or falsifying, or explaining away or 'transcending' by reference to dialectical or other 'deeper' levels of thought, any truth when it presents itself to him, no matter what this entails, where it leads, how much it destroys of what he most passionately longs to believe. Everyone knows that Tolstoy placed truth highest of all the virtues. Others have made such declarations and have celebrated her no less memorably. But Tolstoy is among the few who have truly earned that rare right: for he sacrificed all he had upon her altar— happiness, friendship, love, peace, moral and intellectual certainty, and, in the end, his life. And all she gave him in return was doubt, insecurity, self-contempt, insoluble contradictions. In this sense (although he would have repudiated this most violently) he is a martyr and a hero in the central tradition of the European enlightenment. This seems a paradox: but then his entire life is in this sense a great paradox, inasmuch as it bears constant witness to a proposition to the denial of which his last years were dedicated— that the truth is seldom wholly simple or clear, or as obvious as it may sometimes seem to the eye of the ordinary, sensible man.

NOTES

1. Education is for him 'a human activity based on a desire for equality, and a constant tendency to advance in knowledge'. Equality, that is, between the teacher and the taught. This desire for equality on the part of both is itself for him the spring of progress—progress in the 'advance of knowledge' of what men are and what they should do.

2. These were the very years of Matthew Arnold's tours of inspection of the French and German educational systems. A comparison of their impressions might prove illuminating; they admired each other's writings and outlooks, but did not, so far as is known, know one another.

3. This is one of the best examples of what the excellent Soviet critic Victor Shklovsky has called the descriptive method of ostraneniye— 'rendering strange'—not to be confounded with either Hegelian or Brechtian 'alienation'—founded on a pretended inability to discover any rational explanation for behaviour which the author seeks to deride.

4. 'Man', he wrote in 1862, 'is born perfect—that is the great word spoken by Rousseau, and it will, like a rock, remain strong and true.'

5. Tolstoy is moved to indignation by Maupassant's celebrated dictum (which he quotes) that the business of the artist is not to entertain, delight, move, astonish, cause his reader to dream, reflect, smile, weep or shudder, but 'faire quelque chose de beau dans la forme qui vous conviendra le mieux d'après votre tempérament'.

6. *Literaturnoye Nasledstvo*, No. 41 42, 1941, p. 517.

7. These quotations come from Tolstoy's writings in 1862, most of which are to be found in vol. 8 of the Jubilee Edition of his works. Informative remarks on this topic may be found in an article by E. N. Kupreyanova in *Yasnopolyanski Sbornik* (Tulai, July, 1955).

8. Mikhailovsky maintains that in *Polikushka*, one of Tolstoy's best stories, composed during the months in which he wrote his educational tracts, he represents the tragic death of the hero as being ultimately caused by the wilful interference with the lives of her peasants by the well meaning, but vain and stupid, landowner. His argument seems to me exceedingly convincing.

9. Some Marxist critics, for instance Lukács, represent these contradictions as the expression in art of the crisis of the semi-feudal social structure in Russia, and in particular of the condition of the peasants whose predicament Tolstoy's writing is held to reflect. This seems to me too optimistic: the destruction of Tolstoy's social world should have rendered his dilemmas obsolete. The reader can judge for himself whether this is so.

JOHN BAYLEY

Anna Karenina
and What is Art?

"The sense of shame is lost, the sense of aesthetic shame. I
wonder if you know the feeling? I feel it most strongly when I
read something that is artistically false, and I can call it nothing
else but shame."

TOLSTOY to GOLDENWEISER, 1901

The meeting of Vronsky and Anna in Italy with the Russian painter
Mikhaylov is particularly interesting for the light it throws on Tolstoy's views
on art at the time, and on the relation between the artist and society.
Mikhaylov, a self-educated painter of considerable talent, is probably
modelled on the painter Kramskoy, who did a portrait of Tolstoy and with
whom he became very friendly. The introduction of the theme of art at this
moment in the lovers' relation has a special significance, because their lives
are no longer given but chosen; no longer taken up with involuntary emotion
and event. They have, in a sense, stopped living, and so have leisure for art.

The timing of the incident reveals what Tolstoy was afterwards to state
theoretically in *What is Art?*—his distrust for art which is not an involuntary
and necessary part of the life of the individual and society. Italy is an aesthetic
enclave; it symbolises the status of art as a fashionable upper-class amusement.

From *Tolstoy and the Novel* by John Bayley. © 1966 by Chatto & Windus Ltd.

"Being a Russian and an intelligent man," Vronsky cannot feel for sightseeing "that inexplicable importance the English manage to attach to it"; even though the Palazzo they have rented contains a fine Tintoretto—"one of his later period." The information comes from Golenishchev, the eternal parasite on art, who "never missed an opportunity of instilling into Mikhaylov a true understanding of it." He thinks Vronsky has talent, "his conviction being supported by the fact that he required Vronsky's praise for his articles and ideas, and felt that praise and encouragement should be mutual. Tolstoy's analysis of Golenishchev is deadly but not unfair. No doubt he is a man of genuine sensibility who can distinguish the good from the bad, but his power of doing so has been fatally compromised by his own social and personal needs, the chief of which is the need to avoid recognising his own sterility. Vronsky, on the other hand, "left off painting without any explanations or excuses" when he became aware he had no talent for it, and this is of a piece with his experience as a lover—he feels he has no real talent for that either, and finds it impossible eventually to disguise the fact. Anna's refusal to face this fact torments and embitters her until she cannot leave love alone any more than Golenishchev can leave art alone.

Tolstoy's central conviction that bad art is an affair of the will is expressed more powerfully in the narration of *Anna* than in his theoretical statements. Such artistic activity—whether as producer or spectator—means that one's life is not proceeding along natural, simple and inevitable lines. To amuse oneself with art is like amusing oneself with food, or with sex, and making a diversion out of something that should be an essential. Vronsky discovers "the eternal error men make in supposing that happiness consists in the gratification of their wishes": art, like happiness, is not a question of gratifications but of necessities. And it is through the essential that art and life coincide; soldiers sing songs and tell stories as a part of their way of life; a Vogul audience groan, weep and shout with joy at a dramatic representation of a hunting scene. Pozdnyshev, in *The Kreutzer Sonata*, makes Tolstoy's general point specifically about music.

> When a march is played the soldiers march to the music and the music has achieved its object. A dance is played; I dance, and the music has achieved its object.... Music ... otherwise is only agitation, and what ought to be done in that agitation is lacking.

Passivity,[1] instead of participation, leads to the abuse of art and to its decadence. Karataev, Natasha and 'Uncle' sing like birds: in "an unendurable scene," as Tolstoy calls it, Wagner imitates birdsong.

There is a remarkable analogy, whether or not Tolstoy intended it, between his conception of what is bad in art and his presentation of what happens to Anna and Vronsky's love. Anna's passion was spontaneous, but the things that woman's love needs to perpetuate itself as necessary and good—family, home, husband—are lacking. Anna has no time for the English novel she tries to read in the train to Petersburg, because her excitement over Vronsky makes her want to live; but later we see her living with Vronsky very much the kind of life which that novel described as fashionable and offered as a distraction. Mikhaylov is silent about Vronsky's pictures because as a true artist he is bewildered and repelled by the atmosphere with which art is surrounded by those who want to use it as a distraction. For him, Vronsky is like a man who in the presence of a lover caresses a big waxen doll. The striking and sinister metaphor cannot but infect our idea of Vronsky as a lover as well as an artist. When Dolly goes to stay with Anna and Vronsky she is somewhat in the position of Mikhaylov—she is repelled by what she instinctively feels to be an imitation of family life and affections. Love is mocked as art can be mocked; as the life of the intellect is mocked for Levin by the intellectual dilettante Sviyazhsky, and as the love of country is mocked by the Pan-Slav enthusiasts.

But because *Anna* puts Tolstoy's view of art into a deeper and closer relation with the rest of life than does *What is Art?* it also reveals the inherent objections to that view. The novel does not deny that the love of Anna and Vronsky is still alive at the end, still capable and potential, and this fact dissolves dogma. What seems bogus and dead can still come alive—as his picture did for Mikhaylov—and display "the inexpressible complexity of everything that lives." Because this is so, it is not meaningless for Anna to interest herself in the groom's little girl and to plan a book for children, or for Vronsky to build a hospital and take part in the local elections. Because she no longer has the inevitabilities of a woman's life (Tolstoy brilliantly and convincingly suggests their loss in the fact that she cannot love her daughter by Vronsky as she loved her son by Karenin) it does not mean that affection and interest cannot revive in Anna, as art renews itself in new ways in new societies. Being itself a work of art the novel admits this in a way that *What is Art?* does not. In the later treatise Tolstoy merely asserts the comparison that "real art, like the wife of an affectionate husband, needs no ornaments ... counterfeit art, like a prostitute, must always be decked out".

Tolstoy frequently compares counterfeit art to eating for gratification, but Stiva's mere presence contradicts this in the memorable scene where he and Levin have lunch together. He lends a scene which might have been—on Tolstoy's theory must have been—pretentious, gluttonous and mechanical, his own individual zest and spontaneity. He is a living proof that art can be a relaxation, a lightness that infects us with gaiety and spontaneous pleasure. It is the same with Sviyazhsky, who according to Levin/Tolstoy represents counterfeit intellectual activity, the wish for knowledge as an amusement and distraction. But the novel admits, and admits with authority, that Sviyazhsky is not 'placed' by Levin, who cannot "get beyond the reception rooms of his mind"; that he has "other bases of life which Levin could not discern"; that he has the mysteriousness of human individuality which, like the individuality of art, cannot be categorised and dismissed just because it is not understood. It continually happens in novels and plays that a character is not created enough to make the author's point of view about him convincing[2]; Tolstoy is the rare example of the opposite taking place. The reality of his characters breaks the dogmatic pattern into which they were made to fit, and suspends the judgments prepared against them.

Anna Karenina does not only contain its own qualification and contradiction of Tolstoy's attitude to art—it also gives unexpected support to the examples of good and bad art that Tolstoy chooses. When we read *What is Art?* we may assent to many of his general propositions, but we are staggered by the apparent perversity of his taste. *Hamlet* and *Lear* are notorious instances, but even more disheartening is the offer of Hugo, *Uncle Tom's Cabin*, his own stories *God Sees the Truth but Waits* and *The Prisoner of the Caucasus* (his only works of good art according to Tolstoy) and of the crudest kind of *genre* painting. He singles out for special praise a sketch by Kramskoy (the Mikhaylov of *Anna*)

> showing a drawing-room with a balcony past which troops are marching in triumph on their return from the war. On the balcony stands a nurse holding a baby, and a boy. They are admiring the procession of the troops, but the mother, covering her face with a handkerchief, has fallen back on the sofa sobbing.

In spite of the different moral, this sounds horribly like the modern Russian *genre* painting *The Letter from the Front*, said to be Kruschev's favourite. But when with Anna and Vronsky we suddenly catch sight in a corner of Mikhaylov's studio of his picture of two boys angling, we are, like them, completely won over by it. Tolstoy makes a picture seem good which cited as an example in *What is Art?* would seem awful, and the reason is that he can make the picture alive for us in the novel by the element of *participation*. We are vividly aware of the attitudes of the three spectators, of their ennui with Mikhaylov's big religious work and their need to say something intelligent about it; of their attempt to express appreciation by means of the word 'talent', "which they understood to mean an innate ... capacity, independent of mind and heart, and which was their term for everything an artist lives through"; and of how their bogus appreciative vocabulary is extinguished by spontaneous delight at the sight of the angling picture, which Mikhaylov has forgotten all about, as he has forgotten "the sufferings and raptures" he went through while painting it. The point is not that the painting is 'good art'— the novel does not pronounce on this—but that it gives these people whom we know real pleasure instead of merely engaging with their aesthetic expectations; that it leads us, therefore, into a true and penetrating study of the relation of artist, art and spectator. Tolstoy has made it come alive "with the inexpressible complexity of everything that lives."

It is precisely the absence of this life which condemns the examples thrust down our throats in *What is Art?*. Tolstoy had little experience of pictorial art and less education in it. He saw it in terms of the bad painting of his own time, but given this large limitation (of which he admittedly seems unaware) his taste is singularly just. He preferred the bad picture with feeling to the bad picture with none. Though he might not have cared for Piero della Francesca, and still less for Cézanne, he none the less urges upon us the considerations in art which makes those artists great; the dependence of skill upon 'mind and heart'; the true invitation to the whole of human experience. He detests art that stops short at beauty, or indeed that stops short anywhere.

All treatises on art are unsatisfactory—the issue is at once too simple and too complex for any theorist to do justice to—and Tolstoy's is no exception. What he says is profoundly true, but it is not the sort of truth which can be set out in the way he chooses to do so. As polemic, the effectiveness of *What is Art?* lies not so much in its positive assertions as in its rejection of much that was taken for granted in the aesthetic theories of the time, particularly as these relate to the story and the novel. Tolstoy explicitly rejects the Kantian isolation of art as the realm of decoration and play, and all the nineteenth-century doctrines of art for art's sake which stem from it. He points out that the word for beauty in Russian, *Krasotá*, applies only to what is seen, so that it makes no sense to speak of beauty in an action or a novel, or even in poetry or music. The interchangeability of words meaning *good* and *beautiful* in Western languages has, he implies, resulted in the notion of some sort of beauty, verbal or aesthetic, as the goal of art.

The admired literature of the nineties could hardly defend itself against a charge like Tolstoy's. Even Wagner and Ibsen—to say nothing of Maupassant, Huysmans, Mallarmé, Rilke, Bryusov and the symbolists—they *are* inferior to great writers and for the reason Tolstoy gives, a lack of that wide and involuntary humanity which unites the writer's consciousness with the human experience that "knew the thing before but had been unable to express it". We are reminded of the eighteenth-century pre-Kantian view of art here—"what oft was thought but ne'er so well expressed"—and we remember the reaction of Vronsky to Anna's portrait by Mikhaylov (where the general point is characteristically sharpened by Vronsky's unconscious assumption of his superior background and culture.)

> "One needed to know and love her as I do to find that ... expression of hers," thought Vronsky, though he himself had only learnt to know it through the portrait. But the expression was so true that it seemed both to him and to others that they had always known it.

Tolstoy perceives with great clarity the connection between 'art for art's sake' and the new morality associated with Nietzsche and his followers. "It is said that art has become refined. On the contrary, thanks to the pursuit of effects, it has become very coarse." Art for art's sake aims at the pure 'effect,' but because art cannot but mirror the religious feeling of the age, the new aestheticism has become the prophet and religion of a new barbarity; and this applies not only to trivial works like the *Contes Cruels*, *Salome*, Andreyev's *The Red Laugh*, and so forth, but to such otherwise dissimilar writers as Flaubert, Kipling and Gerhard Hauptmann. Tolstoy detests the notion of the *Zeitgeist*, and with some justification sees the new aestheticism as pandering to it and dependent upon it.

Even when the moral is supposedly good, the craze for what Tolstoy calls "physiological effect" vitiates it—the writer is concerned not to infect the audience but to play upon their nerves, as at the climax of Hauptmann's play, *Hanneles Himmelfahrt*. It is instructive to compare Tolstoy's caustic comments on this piece, in which the part of the ill-used girl might have been expected to arouse his sympathy, with the enthusiastic preface he wrote for a German novel—Von Polenz's *Der Büttnerbauer*—with its similar part of a meek and injured wife. In the play there is "no infection between man and man" but only a deliberate attempt to excite the audience. The novelist on the other hand "loves his protagonists", and in an equally pathetic and terrible scene compels the reader not only to pity but also to love them.

Irrespective of the merits of the actual play and novel, Tolstoy's criteria are cogent. He considers the play form more subject than the novel to the crudity of the author's intention and desire for effect, and it is notorious that he considers Shakespeare as guilty in this respect as Hauptmann. As in the case of pictorial art, it is his lack of knowledge that is at fault here rather than his critical sense. He supposes that Shakespeare, like other playwrights, is chiefly concerned to secure an effect, and he denounces such an intention untiringly. "You see his intention," he observes of a new composer, "but no feeling whatever, except weariness, is transmitted to you." And again—when attacking Kipling and Zola—"from the first lines one sees the intention with which the book is written, the details all become superfluous, and one feels dull." When praising Chekhov's story *The Darling* he asserts that Chekhov intended to make fun of 'the darling', "but by directing the close attention of a poet upon her he has exalted her." The best books, the most full of infectious feeling, are those in which the author's intention is lost sight of, or even contradicted by, the close attention or 'love' which he devotes to his characters. Tolstoy is here implying a criticism of himself and revealing why we feel as we do about Stiva or about Anna.

Only once does he come near to perceiving that Shakespeare might have the same gift of 'close attention', and that is when he observes that Falstaff is his only non-theatrical character, the only one who does not behave like an actor, "He alone speaks in a way proper to himself." It is an illuminating comment. Again we feel that the novel, and in particular the naturalism of the Russian novel, is being called in to condemn the theatre. Falstaff is the only occasion when Shakespeare, like a novelist, set out to do one thing, and by becoming involved with his hero, did another. Such is Tolstoy's view, and he implies that Falstaff moves us for this reason, and that Lear and Cordelia do not move us because they are not seen in this way and not, as people, involuntarily loved. For this to happen they must be seen (like Falstaff) as if in real life and surrounded by the complex detail of real life.[3] Tolstoy is of course committing here the common critical fault of attacking a work because it has not the form that he prefers and refusing to understand the form in which it is actually written. And even on his own ground he is wrong, for the most obvious thing about almost all Shakespeare's characters is how continuously—and often, in terms of dramatic requirement, how unnecessarily—like 'real people' they are! Had Tolstoy known it, Shakespeare was really on his side.

Moreover, his criticism of *Lear* indicates not, as Tolstoy holds, what is wrong with the play, but what is remarkable and unique about it. It is true that Lear and Cordelia are actors whose parts are almost impossible to present and sustain, and that when Tolstoy speaks of "Lear's terrible ravings which make one feel as ashamed as one does when listening to unsuccessful jokes" he describes with uncomfortable accuracy the kind of embarrassment we feel at pretentious acting and an insensitive production. But we never know where we are with the play, as Tolstoy wished always to know where he was. Edging bathos and weird farce, it confounds our instinctive desire (which in Tolstoy had become an obsession) to see life steadily and whole. There is no clarity or security in which close attention might be paid to the individual—indeed the most unnerving thing about the play is the irrelevance of the character indications that do none the less appear, to be burnt up in the human reduction. Edmund's flashy comprehensibility gets us nowhere, nor does the puffing humanity of old Gloucester so brilliantly hit off in the opening scene—a scene that might well prelude a different kind of work altogether. Strangely enough, the openings of *Lear* and of *Anna* are by no means so different: we feel we know Gloucester as we know Stiva, but it would be unthinkable for Stiva to surrender his personality in some extraordinary metaphorical climax, to be blinded and driven to despair for his misdemeanours with governesses and ballet girls. For Tolstoy this would indeed be a flagrant case of a character being made to "do what was not in his nature," or to suffer what was not. But it is at once Tolstoy's strength and limitation that he will not relinquish his grasp on the individual nature—he cannot tolerate the thought of a total human reduction. On the retreat from Moscow Pierre still remains Pierre, and hence there is 'nothing terrible': Father Sergius cannot renounce his pride and desire to excel; and in spite of his moment of impersonal greatness Karenin cannot shake off his old persisting self.

This is certainly true of human beings in society as we usually know it. But in *Lear* Shakespeare presents us with another truth, no more profound but equally convincing. He could have understood and rendered Auschwitz in art: Tolstoy could not have done. When men are indistinguishable in animal evil and animal suffering, love and goodness seem no longer qualities connected with the whole complex of a personality but as graces entering as if from outside. Tolstoy's final charge against Shakespeare—curiously echoing Dr Johnson's less censorious comment—is that his reader "loses the capacity to distinguish between good and evil". His plays, and plays generally (Tolstoy specifically includes his own) have "no religious basis", and because they depend on effect and sensation "even lack any human sense". One sees what he means, but 'human sense' is not everything, and religion—in Tolstoy's use of the term—most certainly is not. In his passion for common sense and common virtue he turns his back on the extreme situation which deprives us of personal differentiation, of the habit of being ourselves. For Tolstoy "the capacity to distinguish between good and evil" must come out of close attention to the individual self. In Shakespeare it can also come from prolonged exposure to his poetic art, and from the range of apprehension—in the widest sense religious—with which he can infect us as Tolstoy cannot.

There is much to be learnt from Tolstoy's dislike of Wagner and Shakespeare, though in both cases what really counts is his refusal to educate himself into their created medium. When Tolstoy says that from the first reading "I was at once convinced that it is obvious Shakespeare lacks the main, if not the only, means of portraying character, which is individuality of language"—one can only suggest that he should have read more Shakespeare and learnt more English. If all art were simple, transparent, and international it would not even be necessary to attack Shakespeare and Wagner—they would hardly have been heard of. Tolstoy's method of attacking them is the same: he describes the action of *Lear* and of *The Ring* in his Masonic "making it strange" language, a kind of seemingly guileless esperanto, so that the whole complex appeal and participation through music and language is lost. When he tells us that though *Lear* may sound absurd in his version it is even more absurd in the original, he speaks truer than he knows: but the real absurdity of *Lear* is that of life, not that of basic English. None the less, Tolstoy did show up the chorus of nineteenth-century European pedants who proclaimed Shakespeare's beauties and profundities without any regard for the living complex of linguistic and national sensibility in which they have their being: just as he showed up the *Ring* worshippers who went into mass hypnosis at Bayreuth without any understanding of what Wagner was trying to accomplish in the tradition of Germanic self-awareness and Germanic dream. By being deliberately insensitive himself, Tolstoy revealed the insensitivity of those who profess to adore the great, but this is not the same as revealing that the great are not great at all.

"Great works of art are only great because they are accessible and comprehensible to everyone." By insisting on this principle Tolstoy asserts that a Vogul hunting-mime is far superior as art to *Hamlet*. The mime may indeed be true art, but its level of operation is sufficiently summed up by Henry James's comment on the puppet show: "What an economy of means—and what an economy of ends!" Moreover, 'everyone' is not—though Tolstoy would no doubt like to have him so—in a fixed state of being but in a state of becoming. His level of participation rises with education, becomes more complex and more demanding. "Groaning, weeping, and holding their breaths with suspense", the primitive audience of the mime were clearly participating much more than the average audience of *Hamlet*; but one can be sure that they would respond to *Hamlet*, in so far as they understood it, with just as much interest and enthusiasm, and more so as they got to know more about it. The trouble with drama is not the art but the audience, and the uneasy and pretentious relation between drama and audience—the desire to shock and be shocked—which Tolstoy saw as characteristic of nineteenth-century drama, and which he would recognise in drama today. That is why he returns, perversely, to the most primitive audience/drama relation. He ignores the fact that the Vogul audience would have delighted in the climax of *Hanneles Himmelfahrt,* and by their delight would have purged it of those elements of invited embarrassment and planned sensationalism which he rightly detected in the relation between Hauptmann and his audience. The gruesome thing about modern Shakespeare productions is precisely the mutual wish to shock and be shocked, to give and take gimmicks, but that is not Shakespeare's fault, though Tolstoy said it was. His real target, to a greater extent perhaps than he realised, is not counterfeit art that has been mistaken for great art, but the bad taste that has become accepted and standardised between producer and consumer. This is why much of what he has to say about art is so relevant today.

Unexpectedly, *What is Art?* is an assertion of the solitude of good art in the modern age. It leads us back, deviously but unmistakably, to Tolstoyan solipsism. Tolstoy's shame before the speeches of Lear, or before a performance of Beethoven's Ninth Symphony, reveals an overwhelming fastidiousness, a refusal to find the communal art of his own day anything but false, coarse and embarrassing. His solution—a return to primitive mime and to communal story—telling like that of Karataev in *War and Peace*—is of course a hopeless one, and there is no reason to suppose Tolstoy did not realise it. He disliked public art as much as public government, and the television age would not have given him cause to change his mind about either the one or the other. Tacitly he accepts the novel—the most private form—as the form in which good art still appeared in the modern age, and again and again in his criticism he makes things easy for the novel, allowing it a degree of sophistication which other forms—poetry, music, drama—are not allowed to share. Chekhov's *The Darling* and Von Polenz's novel are cases in point: can Tolstoy really have thought that his hypothetical 'everyone' would grasp the issues that he draws attention to in them, the grounds of appreciation which he indicates? The great irony is that he did not perceive how, with the decay of public art, Shakespeare's works—by one of those transformations of form in time of which supreme art is capable—had come to exhibit themselves, and to be treated, as the most comprehensive of novels—or non-novels perhaps, like *War and Peace* itself. The great unadmitted and perhaps unconscious assumption and conclusion of *What is Art?*—all the more evident from his rejection in it of his own best work—is that art is the novel, Tolstoy's novel.

NOTES

1. Tolstoy's argument is strengthened today by the denaturing which art undergoes when packaged for passive consumption by a television audience.

2. E.g. we do not believe enough in Kipling's soldiers to accept their creator's conception of military life. The same is true of Pinter's play *The Homecoming*, where the contrast between ways of life depends on a true realisation of the individuals which is not achieved. This criticism does not of course apply to either Shaw's or Tolstoy's own plays, where the characters are not intended to be fully realised and, as it were, topographically true.

3. Essays by Professors Wilson Knight ('Shakespeare and Tolstoy') and L. C. Knights ('*King Lear* as Metaphor') are illuminating on the question of Tolstoy's presuppositions about character and naturalism in Shakespeare. L. C. Knights also compares the 'realistic' method of Turgenev's *nouvelle*, *King Lear of the Steppe*, with the 'metaphorical' method of Shakespeare's play.

ANNA A. TAVIS

Authority and its Discontents
in Tolstoy and Joyce

The authority of the author is the authority of the chorus.
—Mikhail Bakhtin[1]

This study continues the tradition of critical approaches to literary texts as sources of potential subversion; it engages the early works of Leo Tolstoy and James Joyce in a dialogue on *authority*. Authority, needless to say, is a less enticing subject than the body, the carnivalesque, and the grotesque— prominent themes in recent re-readings of Tolstoy and Joyce.[2] For these authors, however, authority is as obsessively present as more popular themes. The polemical thrust with which both Tolstoy and Joyce simultaneously address and evade, expose and disguise, posit and dissect authority gives their argument a provocative dialogical edge and makes authority in their texts ubiquitously present. To take on responsibility with respect to any form of authority functioning as a form of exterior discourse in the novel, the author must not dismiss it, but enter into a dialogue with it, argues Mikhail Bakhtin, a Russian thinker who examined discourses of authority in literary works.[3] With Bakhtin in mind, we need to see how Tolstoy and Joyce enter into a dialogue with authority in their novels; how they 'test, assimilate, and reaccentuate' authoritative discourses and transform the disquisitions on authority into a dialogic drama of their narratives, particularly because

From *Irish Slavonic Studies* 12. © 1991 by *Irish Slavonic Studies*.

Tolstoy's and Joyce's ideologies of authority have been represented as diametrical opposites.[4] For all practical and political purposes of current criticism, Tolstoy's practice of *telling* is usually censured as being overbearingly authoritarian, while Joyce's way of *showing* is endorsed as rebelliously libertarian.[5] To define what narrative authority represents and what purposes it serves in Tolstoy's and Joyce's prose, we need to see where the existing political and ideological polarising of the two authors' positions originates, how it gains currency and circulation.

Tolstoy's and Joyce's biographies have remained prominent in critical discussions of their work, although our age has become particularly sceptical about the uses of biography in text interpretation, and although we argue that literary lives are themselves no more than discursive constructs. Nonetheless, some literary theorists continue to mobilise writers' biographies to support their interpretative positions. In so doing, they themselves participate in creating the author's narrative authority. Even a perceptive reader like Bakhtin departs from his critical principle in Tolstoy's case, despite the fact that he reads other authors as 'points of view' and insists that the 'spirit of the time' resides in the novelist's word and not in his life. In his study of *The Problems of Dostoyevsky's Poetics*, for example, Bakhtin refuses to see the creative roles that discourses of authority play in Tolstoy's work and banishes the writer to the monologists' camp not for his literary practice but for his personal ideology. As for Joyce, Richard Ellmann's classic biography has dominated the Joycean canon for the last three decades and has competed for authority with Joyce's own word about himself and with the word of his narratives. The biographical point of view often interferes with the literary interpretative one. To reopen the question of narrative authority in Tolstoy's and Joyce's novels we must first subject the old stereotypes to serious questioning, and consider how Tolstoy's and Joyce's personal rebellion against the authority of the State, the Church and their institutions had undergone transformation before it surfaced in the narrative politics of their works.

We begin with Tolstoy. A common joke abroad at the time of Tolstoy's excommunication from the Orthodox Church in 1901 had it that there were two tsars in Russia: Nicholas II and Leo Tolstoy. In the Russian popular imagination, Tolstoy's moral authority was metaphorically linked with the authority of the autocrat. It made little difference in the struggle waged between the two centres of authority that Tolstoy had neither a positive programme nor an agenda to offer. His sympathies were neither with the liberals who clamoured for legislative reforms not with the anarchic revolutionaries who resorted to violence. Tolstoy's authority was equal to that of the tsar only in the intensity of his defiance; his was the most thorough-going and radical reform of anarchism: that is to say, total rejection of the principle of authority and force. It was precisely because he was so 'insistently not of any party', commented his biographer A. N. Wilson, that he could gain the anti-authority that he did. It was precisely because

> his howls of rage against the authorities [were] so irrational, and because he [produced] no serious programme of alternative action. He [was] no good at saying what should be done, but very good at saying what [was] wrong.[6]

By excommunicating Tolstoy the Orthodox Church exercised its powers where even the tsar's government feared to tread. The Synod's edict was framed in non-canonical language which summoned the authority of the whole Christian world to condemn the writer as an iconoclast and 'false teacher'. The language of Tolstoy's response to church hierarchs at once represented his anarchic rebellion against imposed dogmas, religious and political, and delivered a counter-statement of faith. The world, Tolstoy knew, was polyphonous with the voices of Confucius, Buddha, Solomon, Socrates, and to this roster of the world's sages he added the name of Jesus Christ. 'I believe,' Tolstoy wrote, 'that the will of God is most clearly and intelligibly expressed in the teaching of the man Jesus, whom to consider as God and pray to, I esteem the greatest blasphemy.'[7] Tolstoy himself wanted to be known not as a propagator of ideologies but as a teacher of life. The image of Tolstoy, the browbeating didact, is a simplistic proposition which significantly weakens effective readings of his texts. He was, rather, a utopian insurgent in search of an anti-authoritarian centre, and his delusion was only in the mistaken conviction that 'there could be an absolute likeness between means and ends'[8] and that search for Truth (istina) had to be carried out under monologic conditions.[9] In his Confession, Tolstoy explained the nature of his belief when he wrote:

> Whether or not these beliefs of mine offend, grieve, or prove a stumbling block to anyone, or hinder anything, or give displeasure to anybody, I can as little change them as I can change my body.... But I can no more return to that from which with such suffering I have escaped, than a flying bird can re-enter the eggshell from which it has emerged.[10]

But it was precisely Tolstoy, as Nikolai Berdiaev aptly observed, who demanded foolishness in life, precisely he 'who would not admit any sort of compromise between God and the world; he who proposed to venture everything.'[11] Tolstoy was a rebel in his own right, no less than Joyce.

Joyce's anarchism was of another kind. He built a bond of exile with Ireland and became compulsively dependent on his own dissent. His strategy was that of combat, and he thrived, in Ellmann's words, on 'the incursions he could make upon conventions and upon the resistance he could stimulate'.[12] Joyce made a striking statement of his intellectual doctrine when he left Ireland. 'My mind rejects the whole present social order and Christianity—home, the recognized virtues classes of life, and religious doctrines.' 'I cannot enter the social order except as a vagabond,' he wrote in a letter to Nora.[13] Yet after annihilating and rebuilding experience out of his own life in the name of artistic freedom, he developed a dependency on his own denial from which there was no escape. Ellmann recorded in his biography of Joyce:

> [...] whenever his relationship with his native land was in danger of improving, he was to find a new incident to solidify his intransigence and to reaffirm the rightness of his voluntary absence. In later life he even showed some grand resentment at the possibility of Irish independence on the grounds that it would change the relationship he had so carefully established between himself and his country. 'Tell me.' he said to a friend, 'why you think I ought to change conditions that gave Ireland and me a shape and destiny.'[14]

The Bakuninesque urge for violence and destruction was foreign to Joyce as he 'piously forged'[15] and re-forged the Irish national consciousness in a decidedly heretical manner of his works. Joyce's articulation of goals in his confessional letters reminds one of Tolstoy:

> Yet I have certain ideas I would like to give form to: not as a doctrine but as the continuation of the expression of myself. [...] These ideas or instincts or intuitions or impulses may be purely personal. I have no wish to codify myself as anarchist or socialist or reactionary.[16]

When subjected to questioning, the two biographies and the writers' own statements about themselves do not support the suggested opposition between Tolstoy the didact and Joyce the rebel. The two authors were great anarchists in life; and chose different ways to negotiate their narrative authority. The image of the upper-class landowner Tolstoy who shed his aristocratic garb for peasant clothes in order to stay in touch with his native land and traditions fascinated the entire early modernist generation. The simplicity of Tolstoy's demand for basic justice and universal tolerance appealed to Joyce's sense of how art should work: 'in spite of a little propaganda in it'.[17] Joyce learned from Tolstoy's essays on child education, for example, that the pattern of authority and submission is fundamental to human existence 'however much we may talk [...] about equality and the brotherhood of man'.[18] The attitudes of Stephen Dedalus and Leopold Bloom dovetailed with those of Tolstoy, for whom 'governments need armies particularly to protect them against their oppressed and enslaved subjects'.[19] Joyce's own message was a simple one. His mind moved circuitously, however, and his art proceeded in the same manner as Tolstoy's. 'I want the reader to understand always through suggestion rather than direct statement,' he declared.[20]

How does narrative authority function in the writings of Tolstoy and Joyce if it is not a guaranteed image of strength and not a solidly delivered monologue? In most general terms, authority functions, for Tolstoy and Joyce as an interpretative process, as a conversation and a struggle of discrepant voices (words) speaking from different positions and invested with different degrees and kinds of authority. Tolstoy and Joyce put authority on trial by making it a matter of the self's fine-tuning of the world.

The scene in *War and Peace* in which Petya Rostov blindly follows the crowd welcoming the Emperor at the Kremlin offers an illustration of Tolstoy's frequent and deliberate unmaskings of the mind befuddled by authority's illusory power. Tolstoy first sets up a situation of mass intoxication from the aura of autocratic authority:

> Quite beside himself, Petya, clenching his teeth and rolling his eyes ferociously, pushed forward, elbowing his way and shouting 'hurrah!' as if he were prepared that instant to kill himself and everyone else, but on both sides of him other people with similarly ferocious faces pushed forward and everybody shouted 'hurrah!' [p. 747][21]

Petya's desire to love and worship is so obsessive that in the mindless absurdity of the situation the object of his worship becomes irrelevant:

> Which is he? Which? asked Petya in a tearful voice, of those around him, but no one answered him, everybody was too excited; and Petya, fixing on one of those four men, whom he

could not clearly see for the tears of joy that filled his eyes,
concentrated all his enthusiasm on him—though it happened not
to be the Emperor frantically shouted 'Hurrah!' and resolved that
tomorrow, come what might, he would join the army. [p. 749]

Tolstoy shows the irrelevance of Petya's patriotic zeal in contrast with the
Tsar's grotesque gesture of throwing biscuits into the stampede:

> [The] Emperor had a plateful of biscuits brought him and began
> throwing them down from the balcony. Petya's eyes grew
> bloodshot, and still more excited by the danger of being crushed,
> he rushed to the biscuits. He did not know why, but he had to
> have a biscuit from the Tsar's hand and he felt that he must not
> give way. He sprang forward and upset an old woman who was
> catching at a biscuit. [...] Petya pushed her hand away with his
> knee, seized a biscuit, and as if fearing to be too late, again
> shouted 'Hurrah!'. [p. 750]

Much like Petya, most of Tolstoy's principal characters with some trace
of psychological complexity experience tests of authority: they learn to
recognise and resist its false aura. Examples are Andrei Bolkonsky's worship
of Napoleon and his disenchantment, Pierre Besukhov's membership of the
Masons, and Natasha Rostova's failed elopement with Anatol Kuragin.
Tolstoy shows authority not as an already given but as an organic process,
giving examples of its making, its interrogation and its ultimate rejection by
his principal characters. This narrative strategy distracted critics like Bakhtin
into thinking that Tolstoy's intention was monologic and authoritarian rather
than polyphonically inclusive of different positions and viewpoints.

Stephen Dedalus, Joyce's *alter ego*, is a doubter from the very start.
Unlike Petya Rostov, Stephen of *A Portrait of the Artist as a Young Man* is an
outsider who 'keeps on the fringe of his line, out of sight of his prefect, out
of reach of the rude feet, feigning to run now and then' (p. 246).[22] The story
of the artist which Joyce unfolds is a story of a discovery and achievement of
identity through rebellion against spiritual and secular authorities. Joyce's
hero starts where Tolstoy's characters have gone half-way. Stephen learns
early that one form of authority sustains and perpetuates the other. He lost
respect for patriarchal authority by having experienced shame for his
disreputable father at an early age, and he subsequently carries within himself
suspicion and doubt about all authorities. In the Whitsuntide play scene, the
'plump freshfaced jesuit' reminds him of his father. Stephen 'thought he saw

a likeness between his father's mind and that of this smiling welldressed priest,' writes Joyce, 'and he was aware of some desecration of the priest's office or of the vestry itself, whose silence was now routed by loud talk. [...]' (p. 334). Police and the clergy are similarly discredited by association when in *Stephen Hero*, for example, Stephen tells a joke about the old peasant down the country who says

> I will put the priest on Tom an'all, put the polisman on Mickey' ... he balances the priest against the polisman and a very nice balance it is for they are both of good girth. A nice compensative system![23]

The more Stephen feels that he is put 'under ban' the more reluctant he is to 'give pledges'. He is determined to launch single-handedly an attack on all authorities, even his own. 'I will not serve that in which I no longer believe whether it calls itself my home, my fatherland or my church,' he tells Father Cranly towards the end of the novel (p. 519). Tolstoy's principle of dissection becomes vivisection for Joyce ('Vivisection itself is the most modern process one can conceive,' Joyce commented, 'which examines its territory by the light of the day').[24]

For Tolstoy and Joyce, discourse is the principal site where all authority (narrative, personal, social, political) is created, where it is interpreted and where it exercises its power. As verbal artists, Tolstoy and Joyce find themselves in an ambivalent position towards authority, for it is not accidental that the words *author* and *authority* share a common origin.[25] Rebellious of control in their own families, religious communities and societies, they are free to exercise authority over their characters tantamount to that of the Creator himself. The author's authority begins at the juncture of *monological* and *dialogical* world-views which correspond to two types of words in any discursive space: *authoritative* (avtoritarnoe slovo) and *internally persuasive* (vnutrenne ubeditel'noe slovo).[26] *Authoritative* discourse, as Bakhtin explains it, corresponds to the monologic worldview and allows for no contradiction, excludes diversity and tolerates no questioning; *internally persuasive* word, by contrast, invites a plurality of views and celebrates a polyphony of opinions. Tolstoy's and Joyce's literary practices, when investigated in their own terms, display to an equal extent the plurality of voices and monologic slippages, the diversity of opinions and continuity of intention. To trace and compare the politics of their discourse is to match and contrast the dynamic patterns present in their work.

To begin with Tolstoy, Leo Nikolaevich started his literary career with a unique performance, a journal *The History of Yesterday*, which traced 'the intimate side of life through an entire day'. Tolstoy registered his conscious and subconscious thoughts and feelings minutely in response to particular situations of the day. This exuberance of unexpected and confused associations anticipated Joyce and Proust and resurfaced with diminishing frequency in Tolstoy's subsequent works. His master novels, *War and Peace* and *Anna Karenina*, did not allow his language to become non-dialogic, and he succeeded, as Gary Saul Morson remarks, 'in changing the nature of the dialogue' to suit his individual intention. Even when he turned to straightforward prophesy in his last novel, *Resurrection*, 'what dialogized Tolstoy's absolutes was not the surrounding language of the particular novel and not the immediate word or a single utterance' (which by themselves may, indeed, appear didactic) but 'the genre of the novel as a whole'.[27]

Joyce began to confront authority where Tolstoy stopped. In his first draft of *Portrait of the Artist* he envisaged for an artist a utopian future of socialistic enlightenment with a single purpose: to 'reunite "the children of the spirit" against "fraud and principality"' he abandoned.[28] The artist should not rely on outspokenness, Joyce concluded; indirectness and 'obliquity'[29] became his literary agenda. But if the project of *Ulysses* investigated the workings of the mind much as Tolstoy's earlier *History of Yesterday*, in *Finnegans Wake* the thoughts already 'hop, step, jump, and glide without the self-consciousness of a journal'.[30] Joyce's liberation of thought from intentionality of discourse and his ultimate denial of centre led him to the edge of incomprehensibility.

Both Tolstoy and Joyce skirted the boundaries of the absolute: Tolstoy nostalgically searched for the moral centre, while Joyce experimented with anarchic 'dis-centring'. What saved their projects from the collapse into the black hole of totalitarianism and chaos was their unsurpassed mastery of the concrete world and their interest in the organic passage of the man from childhood to old age. Human birth and growth, the body's passage through stages of physical and sexual maturity, the precariousness of the relationship between the sexes, and bodily decay and death—altogether these were ineluctable organic processes which for Tolstoy and Joyce naturally disrupted every solidity which made authority transient. The two writers' narratives were punctuated with the portrayals of periodic crises of authority as their protagonists underwent physical change. George Lukács misunderstood Joyce when he assumed that if 'Joyce had set Napoleon on the toilet of the petit bourgeois Bloom, he would merely have emphasised what was common to both Napoleon and Bloom'.[31] Napoleon, whom Tolstoy showed in the midst of his daily routine, would not have escaped Joyce's ironic treatment either. Similarly to Tolstoy's iconoclasm, Joyce offered a perspective which prevents us from assuming that one man is all grandeur and the other is all triviality: 'men [are always] in the process of becoming', and authority which claims permanence is always inherently suspect.[32] Tolstoy's early novel *Childhood* and Joyce's *Portrait of the Artist* depended on this organic undermining of authority.

Tolstoy's *Childhood* opens when the ten-year-old Nikolenka Irten'ev awakes to his tutor's noisy hunt for flies over his head. This amusing scene introduces Nikolenka's thoughts about his relationships with the members of his household: with his brothers and sisters, parents, tutors and servants. Karl Ivanych, his German tutor, dares to wake him up in such a disrespectful manner, Nikolenka thinks, because he is the youngest member of the household. For Nikolenka, his tutor is an ambiguous figure to comprehend. As a living-in, salaried domestic, he is of service to the children, and at the same time he is an adult and a teacher ('In the schoolroom Karl Ivanych was an entirely different person: there he was the tutor' [p. 15]).[33] The scene of Karl Ivanych's dismissal by his father, for example, is full of ambiguity for Nikolenka. Karl Ivanych humbly pleads to be allowed to look after the children without salary and at the same time demands payment on a bill for petty expenses which he incurred for children's presents. 'That Karl Ivanych was speaking in all sincerity [...] I can affirm but how he reconciled the bill with his words remains a mystery to me' (p. 42). Half a year later, the dilemma of Karl Ivanych is resolved: to Nikolenka, who is now a sophisticated young gentleman living in Moscow, Karl Ivanych is a domestic whom 'grandmamma called the "school-usher" and who—heaven knows why—had suddenly [exchanged] his venerable long-familiar baldness for a red wig'. He 'looked so strange and ridiculous' to Nikolenka that he is 'surprised he had never struck [him] so before' (p. 120). The passage of time helps Nikolenka sort out his complex attitudes to the authorities which surround him.

A medley of voices which crowd in on Stephen's mind introduces Stephen Dedalus in Joyce's *Portrait of the Artist*. 'The wide playgrounds were swarming with boys. All were shouting and the prefects urged them on with strong cries' (p. 246). Towards the middle of the novel, the multi-voiced background builds up in a crescendo, in which all voices, except for Stephen's, drown one another. Stephen's thoughts, as Joyce describes them after Stephen's arrogant classmates have beaten and humiliated him, offer a good illustration of how Joyce's polyphonic method functions in the novel:

While his mind had been pursuing its intangible phantoms and turning in irresolution from such pursuit he had heard about him the constant voice of his father and of his masters, urging him to be a gentleman above all things and urging him to be a good catholic above all things. These voices had now come to be hollowsounding in his ears. When the gymnasium had been opened he had heard another voice urging him to be strong and manly and healthy and when the movement towards national revival had begun to be heard in the college yet another voice had bidden him to be true to his country and help to raise up his father's fallen state by his labours and, meanwhile, the voice of his school comrades urged him to be a decent fellow, to shield others from blame or to beg them off and to do his best to get free days for the school. And it was the din of all these hollowsounding voices that made him halt irresolutely in the pursuit of phantoms. He gave them ear only for a time but he was happy only when he was far away from them, beyond their call, alone or in the company of phantasmal comrades. [pp. 332–3]

Through the inner speech of his protagonist, Joyce moves his aesthetic visualisation to the new depths and the new strata of the unconscious. For Stephen, competing for authority means winning back control over discursive space. For Tolstoy, 'consciousness remains to be much more terrifying than any unconsciousness would be' and Nikolenka comes to terms with authority only when he is able to gain distance from it and evaluate it rationally.

The most significant difference between the two writers' approach is their understanding of freedom from authority and the connection they make between the breaking and making of authority. There could never be a complete vacuum of authority for Tolstoy; everything has its limits. Tolstoy's is a vision of freedom as rational self-direction which he often identifies with self-improvement and self-mastery by bringing the 'lower' subconscious part of the psyche in line with the 'higher' rational and spiritual self. The danger of this line of argument led him to the premise that in the present imperfect world it may be the duty of the more enlightened to preach to the less fortunate how to be free. He called to learn from the 'less fortunate', from the 'natural men', from the peasants. For example, in *War and Peace* Pierre Bezukhov sets out to assassinate Napoleon, to eliminate evil power by force; he ends up in captivity where he learns from a simple Russian peasant Platon Karataev, a fellow captive, a new philosophy of freedom. 'He had learned,'

Tolstoy writes of Pierre, 'that as there is no condition in which man can be happy and entirely free, so there is no condition in which he need be unhappy and lack freedom. He learned that suffering and freedom have their limits and that those limits are very near together' (p. 1176). Yet, paradoxically, Tolstoy's interpretation of 'more enlightened' was a post-modern one in erasing the difference between freedom and its opposite, captivity.

Joyce's drama was modernist. He always had to struggle but never quite triumph in his revolt against prevalent style and his unyielding rage against the official order, and then, after a time, had to 'struggle in order not to triumph'.[34] Joyce's protagonists become adept at speaking the language of discontent, but rarely do they attempt to disengage themselves from their bonds of rejection. 'Welcome, Oh life!' says Stephen Dedalus in celebration of his departure from Ireland at the end of *A Portrait of the Artist*, but in the final entry of his diary he interrupts his jubilant mood by bringing back the rejected image of his father which continues to haunt him: 'Old father, old artificer, stand me now and ever in good stead.' Ironically, even rejected authority continues to dictate the terms of Stephen's contract with Ireland.

The foregoing comparison between different ways in which Tolstoy's and Joyce's protagonists construct, dismantle and reconstitute authority suggests a paradigm of contingency rather than dichotomy. Tolstoy and Joyce complement rather than cancel each other's positions on authority. Tolstoy's heroes overcome the illusions of authority with the passage of time and exemplify Tolstoy's temporal, organic approach to social phenomena. All Tolstoy's locations—his nurseries and bedrooms, studies, drawing rooms, and battlefields—are marked as stages in human development, as spaces in which different types of authority are exercised. For Joyce's protagonists, authority is given all at once, and all at once it loses its legitimacy. Joyce's school grounds, city streets and theatrical backstages are sites of simultaneity in moments of crises.[35] Temporally or spatially, the two writers dismantled authority as it was given and elevated a new form of authority which had no current legitimacy: Tolstoy believed in the Russian peasant, while Joyce trusted in the artist.

To conclude, authority in the work of Tolstoy and Joyce is a fluid process of interpreting power rather than a solid image of strength and domination. Like a two-faced Janus, the Roman god of doors, authority is an act of imagination as much as it is an act of coercion. To negotiate authority Tolstoy devises the strategy of recognition while Joyce enacts the drama of rejection, but for neither of the two does authority ever disappear: it periodically renews itself like the Phoenix, rejected and reconstituted from the ashes. Both Tolstoy's and Joyce's works show a way of disorienting authority's controls and dispersing its powers by introducing alternative discourses. For Tolstoy these discourses are temporal and organic, while for Joyce they are multiple and coexistent. As novelists, Tolstoy and Joyce know that authority is a proposition rather than an axiom, and their frank unmaskings of how authority makes itself, breaks into multiple meanings and reconstitutes its solidity again, allows us to question our own relationship with authority. When we erroneously contrast Tolstoy and Joyce as examples of authoritarian–anti-authoritarian centre we internalise our own modern fear of authority as a seductive agency which usurps our individual freedoms. When we indict Tolstoy for his authoritarian lapses, we reveal our own fear of personal dependence; when we praise Joyce for his defiant autonomy, we desire our own liberation. In the heat of the current polemic about authority, we forget that we need at least two consciousnesses and two presences to make authority work. Authority may seek permanence in churches, government buildings, Berlin Walls and propaganda posters; but, as Tolstoy and Joyce have shown, it can never be immune to the beholder's investigatory eye.

NOTES

1. M. M. Bakhtin, 'Avtor i geroi', in *Estetika slovesnogo tvorchestva* (Iskusstvo, Moscow, 1986), p. 158.

2. See among others Sidney Monas's essay 'Verbal Carnival: Bakhtin, Rabelais, "Finnegans Wake" and the Growthesk', *Irish Slavonic Studies*, 6, 1985, pp. 35–45, and R. B. Kershner's study, *Joyce, Bakhtin, and Popular Literature: Chronicles of Disorder* (The University of North Carolina Press, Chapel Hill, NC, and London, 1989).

3. Mikhail Bakhtin, 'The Problem of Speech Genres', in *Speech Genres and Other Essays*, edited by Caryl Emerson and Michael Holquist (Austin, TX: University of Texas Press, 1986), p. 89. For an examination of Bakhtin's views on authoritative discourse see also Gary Saul Morson and Caryl Emerson, *Mikhail Bakhtin: Creation of a Prosaics* (Stanford University Press, Stanford, CA, 1990), pp. 218–23.

4. Dominic Manganiello, *Joyce's Politics* (Routledge & Kegan Paul, London and Boston, MA, 1980). This very thorough study tends to polarise Tolstoy and Joyce.

5. Wayne Booth concludes in his 'Introduction to *Problems of Dostoyevsky's "Poetics"*', that Bakhtin favoured 'telling' over 'showing'. This

preference shows that despite this outspoken rejection of Tolstoy's practices Bakhtin's bonds with the Russian novelist were closer than he wanted us to believe.

6. A. N. Wilson, *Tolstoy* (Norton, New York, 1968). p. 460.

7. Quoted in Ernest Simmons, *Leo Tolstoy* (Little, Brown, Boston, MA, 1949), p. 599.

8. Nicolas Berdiaev, *The Russian Idea* (Beacon Press, Boston, MA, 1962), p. 150.

9. Caryl Emerson, 'The Tolstoy Connection in Bakhtin', in Caryl Emerson and Gary Saul Morson, eds, *Rethinking Bakhtin* (Northwestern University Press, Evanston, IL, 1989), p. 166.

10. Quoted in Simmons, *Leo Tolstoy*, p. 600.

11. Berdiaev, *The Russian Idea*, p. 150.

12. Richard Ellmann, *James Joyce* (Oxford University Press, New York, 1959), p. 114.

13. Stuart Gilbert and Richard Ellmann, eds, *Letters of James Joyce* (Viking, New York, 1959), Vol. II, p. 48.

14. Ellmann, *James Joyce*, pp. 113–14.

15. James Joyce, *Finnegans Wake* (Viking, New York, 1961), p. 182.

16. *Letters of James Joyce*, Vol. II, p. 217.

17. Ibid., p. 183.

18. Quoted in Thomas E. Connoly, *The Personal Library of James Joyce* (University of Buffalo, Buffalo, NY, 1955), p. 40.

19. Quoted in Paul Eltzbacher, *Anarchism*, translated by Steven T. Byington (New York, 1908).

20. Frank Budgen, *James Joyce and the Making of Ulysses and Other Writings* (Oxford University Press, London, 1972), p. 21.

21. All quotations from Leo Tolstoy, *War and Peace*, edited by George Gibian (Norton Critical Editions, New York, 1966),

22. All quotations from *The Portable James Joyce* (Penguin, Harmondsworth, 1978).

23. James Joyce, *Stephen Hero*, edited by John J. Slocum and Herbert Cahoon (Cape, London, 1969), p. 69.

24. Ibid., pp. 190–1.

25. As we see it from the language-oriented twentieth century, the question of authority is contingent on authority's relation to discourse: see, *inter alia*, M. Bakhtin, *The Problems of Dostoyevsky's Poetics* (University of Minnesota Press, Minneapolis, MN, 1984) and 'Discourse in the Novel', in *Dialogic Imagination*, edited by Michael Holquist and Caryl Emerson

(University of Texas Press, Austin, TX, 1981); also Michel Foucault, *Discipline and Punish* (Vintage Books, New York, 1979).

26. Bakhtin, 'Discourse in the Novel', *loc. cit.*, p. 345.

27. Gary Saul Morson, *Hidden in Plain View* (Stanford University Press, Stanford, CA, 1989), p. 20.

28. Robert Scholes and Richard M. Kain (eds), *The Workshop of Daedalus* (Northwestern University Press, Evanston, IL, 1965), pp. 56–74.

29. Richard Ellmann, *The Consciousness of James Joyce* (Oxford University Press, New York, 1977), p. 77.

30. Ellmann, *James Joyce*, p. 369.

31. George Lukács, *Writer and Critic* (Grosset & Dunlop, New York, 1971), p. 180.

32. For the discussion of 'men in the process of becoming' see Bakhtin, 'The *Bildungsroman* and its Significance', in Caryl Emerson and Michael Holquist (eds), *Speech Genres and Other Late Essays* (University of Texas Press, Austin, TX, 1986), p. 19.

33. All quotations from Leo Tolstoy, *Childhood, Boyhood, Youth*, translated by Rosemary Edmonds (Penguin, Harmondsworth, 1985).

34. Irving Howe's words about modernism are quoted in Richard Sennett, *Authority* (Vintage Books, New York, 1980), p. 49.

35. Bakhtin, 'Towards the Reworking of Dostoyevsky Book' in Caryl Emerson (ed.), *Problems of Dostoyevsky's Poetics* (University of Minnesota Press, Minneapolis, MN, 1984), p. 288.

AMY MANDELKER

A Painted Lady:
The Poetics of Ekphrasis

THE POETICS OF *EKPHRASIS*

In *What Is Art?* Tolstoy discusses a play in which "the author wishes to transmit to the spectators pity for a persecuted girl. To evoke this feeling in the audience by means of art, the author should either make one of the characters express this pity in such a way as to infect everyone, or he should describe the girl's feelings correctly."[1] Instead, Tolstoy complains, most authors fail because they do not utilize these techniques but rely on verisimilitudinous or extreme effects. In *Anna Karenina* there is a spectator in the text who reflects the audience's act of viewing and judging the heroine we are meant to pity. The scene where Lyovin and Anna meet is preceded by Lyovin's viewing of Mikhailov's portrait of Anna. Lyovin's response to the artwork and to the actual woman infects the reader and simultaneously directs our gaze to Anna as a represented character, and to art—the portrait, the novel—as the means for infecting us with pity and compassion. Thus, the description of Lyovin's act of gazing and the verbal description of the visual work of art constitute an *ekphrasis* (the term is used here in the sense developed by classicists, that is, the verbal description of a visual work of art).[2] This moment allows Tolstoy the opportunity for meta-aesthetic commentary.

From *Framing Anna Karenina: Tolstoy, the Woman Question, and the Victorian Novel.* © 1993 by Ohio State University Press.

79

Roland Barthes describes *ekphrasis* as "a brilliant detachable morsel [of description], sufficient unto itself," and introduced solely for the "pleasure of verbal portraiture."[3] His surprisingly limited definition disregards the potential for *ekphrasis* to function not just as a description of art but as art criticism and meta-aesthetic discourse. For example, it is possible to read Homer's description of the shield forged by Hephaestus for Achilles as a pretext for describing the customs of the day; however, no one could read Virgil's description of Aeneas's shield in this fashion. Because of its intertextual relationship to Homer's description, the passage expresses a reflexivity and awareness of the value of art and description that Virgil employs to valorize Rome; as Lessing comments: "Homer makes Vulcan devise decorations because he is to make a shield worthy of a divine workman. Virgil seems to make him fashion the shield for the sake of the decorations."[4]

Similarly, since John Keats's extended *ekphrasis* in his "Ode on a Grecian Urn" exalts the classical ethos in its visual inscription, it also necessarily comments on form and on the apparent superiority of visual over verbal or aural representation: "Heard melodies are sweet, but those unheard / Are sweeter; therefore, ye soft pipes, play on; / Not to the sensual ear, but, more endear'd, / Pipe to the spirit ditties of no tone." On the one hand, the visual form is superior to other media because it preserves forever the ecstatic moment: "Forever panting, forever young." On the other hand, the ode comments on the representational conventions and constraints of that "Cold Pastoral." *Ekphrasis* thus establishes a tension between narrativity and stasis: in the ekphrastic moment, the stilling of the narrative flow required for ekphrastic exposition is renarrativized in the course of the temporally elaborated descriptions of the visual work of art. This paradox of modes returns us to the problem referred to in aesthetics by the term *ut pictura poesis* ("poetry is like painting"). This notion developed from a casual analogy in Horace's *Ars poetica* into a precept of aesthetics and literary theory that poetry *should* be like painting. The classical emphasis on *mimēsis* or imitation as the ultimate goal of a work of art informed the critical debate on the limitations of representation within and between the two media. The accepted notion, as stated by Longinus in his treatise *On the Sublime* and later developed by Burke in his *Philosophical Inquiry into the Origin of Our Ideas of the Sublime and Beautiful*, exalted the capacity of painting to represent things themselves. Poetry, on the other hand, could only "affect by sympathy rather than imitation; to display rather the effect of things on the mind of the speaker, or of others, rather than to present a clear idea of the things themselves" (172).[5]

Ut pictura poesis thus engages the phenomenological issue of traditional aesthetics as to whether or not poetry constitutes thinking in images. This latter view implies that the contemplation or creation of images facilitates the primary cognitive processes associated with the preverbal or extraverbal states of childhood, mysticism, and ecstatic visions. The association of literary pictorialism with primal vision and epiphany privileges *ekphrasis* and, by extension, other descriptive moments in a text that organize visual perceptions in a pictorial manner. Such "framed" and "frozen" moments reflect the degree to which art is taken to inform and form our vision, and the extent to which vision is exalted as the conveyer of untranslatable and unnameable spiritual grace. The capacity of verbal texts to create vivid pictorial effects is seen as a fulfillment of *energeia*, expressed by the term *hypotyposis*, which Barthes claims may serve to place things right beneath the eyes of the listener, not in a neutral way but in a manner that releases into the representation all the force of desire ("mettre les choses sous les yeux de l'auditeur, non point d'une façon neutre, constative, mais en laissant à la représentation tout l'éclat du désir").[6] When the *hypotyposis* is self-conscious, that is, aesthetically framed (ekphrastic), literary pictorialism becomes a commentary on all visual practice. Thus, as Mary Ann Caws suggests, this technique "makes a statement of coherence against the narrative flux and against the flux of our own time, so that our reading of frames and of the framed passages ... is the model of not just reading, but of what, while reading, we live."[7]

The fact therefore that we organize our life experiences into narratives and our views of the world into pictures exposes us to the risk of being poor storytellers and mediocre artists. At worst, we are victims of the clichés and conventions that tell us how to make pictures; at best, our artistic structuring of experience lends coherence and epiphanic illumination to otherwise random and chaotic experience, and a sense of aesthetic closure weaves together the loose and unfinished, raveled threads of life. The danger is that we risk the enclosure that constricts, the form that deforms, or the representation that misrepresents.

A desire for coherence in the presentation of self or the quest for psychic unity and meaning in existence, the urge to contextualize life experiences, increases our desire for the end of the story or the frame of the picture. Thus, ominously, the desire for a finished self-portrait or a comprehensive icon is subtended by the death instinct, as critics like Mikhail Bakhtin and Peter Brooks have noted. As Jean-Paul Sartre commented about the process of writing his autobiography, "I became my own obituary."[8] Both the main protagonists of *Anna Karenina*, Anna and Lyovin, pursue meaning through visions, both rely on frames to secure understanding, and both find themselves drawn toward death. Their desire to frame and compose their views of self and their interpretations of life according to artistic models suggests that we may read them as artist figures.[9] Anna willfully completes her self-portrait by committing suicide while, in the essential contrast of the novel, Lyovin leaves his narrative unfinished and open ended and "goes on living." This contrast is overdetermined by the exigencies of plot and gender: many novelistic heroines, whose only two choices are oppression in marriage or liberation through death, "choose to die in order to shape their lives as whole."[10] Lyovin's vision of Anna, occurring at a critical moment in the novel when the intersecting trajectories of the two protagonists' lives emphasize their essential kinship and differences, is doubly marked as the viewing of a woman and the viewing of a representation of a woman. It is a great work of art, Mikhailov's portrait of Anna, that occupies central view.[11]

LYOVIN'S *LAOCOÖN*

The power of the ekphrastic moments in *Anna Karenina* motivated John Bayley to draw the conclusion that Tolstoy's views on art "are expressed more powerfully in the narration of *Anna* than in his theoretical statements on art."[12] Certainly, the passages in *Anna Karenina* dealing with the artist Mikhailov and the other moments where art is discussed by the novel's characters allow Tolstoy to delineate the creative process and to comment on aesthetic theory. Thus, Lyovin's observations while attending a concert of modern music become a disquisition on aesthetics in general. In this episode, Lyovin attends a concert of Balakirev's *King Lear in the Steppe*,[13] a piece "in the modern style" of the Wagnerian *Gesamtkunstwerk*. During the entr'acte, Lyovin enters into a debate with his friend:

> Lyovin maintained that the mistake of Wagner and all his followers lay in their trying to take music into the sphere of another art, just as poetry goes wrong when it tries to paint a face, which is what should be left to painting, and as an instance of this mistake he cited the sculptor who carved in marble certain shadows of poetical images flitting around the figure of the poet on the pedestal. "These shadows were so far from being shadows that they were positively clinging to the ladder," said Lyovin. The comparison pleased him, but he could not remember whether or not he had used the same phrase before. (714)

Lyovin is right to question the originality of his statement. In fact, his habit of unconscious quotation overtakes him in this section of the novel, where the pressures of urban social life seduce him into a constant theft of bons mots in pursuit of the appearance of wit. For example, earlier in this chapter, Lyovin quips that punishing a revolutionary by exiling him to Europe is like casting a pike back into the water. Lyovin later realizes that he had "borrowed" the bon mot from an acquaintance who had read it in a newspaper article that in turn quoted from Krylov's fables. Lyovin's indictment of the sculptural (material) representation of poetic (intangible) ideas is similarly not original but derivative: it strongly echoes, at several points, Lessing's *Laocoön* (1766), the classic polemic on the Horatian precept of *ut pictura poesis*.

Lyovin wants to argue against the doctrine of *ut pictura poesis*; yet his sculptural example as he describes it does not serve as an apt illustration to support the separation of painting (specifically, portraiture) from poetry. The sculptural example is only effective when read against the intertext of *Laocoön*. Lessing's discussion focuses on the critical controversy over whether Virgil's description of the agony of Laocoön antecedes or is derivative of the classical sculpture of Laocoön being devoured by serpents, and it concludes with his famous theses on the need to modify the subject to accommodate different modes of representation. Imitating Lessing, Lyovin employs a sculptural work for his example, but he replaces the figure of the high priest Laocoön with the figure of a poet.[14] Lyovin describes the sculptural work as hampered by clinging shadows that were meant to represent "poetic ideas." We may see the shadows in terms of the Laocoön sculpture as a recasting of the serpents that encircle Laocoön and whose different positions in the two works (poem and sculpture) form the basis for much of Lessing's argumentation. In *The Aeneid* (2. ll. 305–307), the serpents mount Laocoön's body and engulf him totally: "Twice round his waist their winding volumes rolled, / And twice about his gasping throat they fold. / The priest thus doubly choked,—their crests divide, / And towering o'er his head in triumph ride" [Dryden]. As Lessing points out, a literal rendering of this description would have obliterated any visual expression of Laocoön's agony; therefore, the sculptor winds the serpents about Laocoön's wrists and ankles, "parts which might be concealed and compressed without injury to the expression ... [and which] also convey the idea of arrested flight."[15]

Lyovin's clinging shadows illustrate the problem of the embodiment of the spiritual in the material: the indefinite, cerebral creative ideas of the poet are invisible mental constructs that manifest themselves only in the artist's own work and appear ridiculous when represented as concrete objects attendant upon it. Lyovin's image evokes Lessing's indictment[16] of the artistic conventions employed for representing the cloud of invisibility cast over the hero by the deus ex machina in classical canvases: the solution, a "cloud" painted to one side of the "invisible" figure, Lessing argues, is beyond "the limits of painting. His cloud is a hieroglyphic, a purely symbolic sign, which does not make the rescued hero invisible, but simply says to the observers, 'You are to suppose this man to be invisible.' It is no better than the rolls of paper with sentences upon them which issued from the mouths of personages in the old Gothic pictures."[17] The echo of *Laocoön* in Lyovin's brief treatise on aesthetics is enhanced by the subject of Lyovin's statue: a poet, surrounded by his poetic ideas; the creator about to create and seeking an appropriate embodiment for his artistic vision. The choice of flitting shadows to represent creative inspiration suggests a demonic rather than a divine source and raises the question of good and evil in creation.

Thus through Lyovin's illustration Tolstoy subtly debates the question of how or whether art may achieve its theurgic potential. This is an issue of central importance in the most sustained *ekphrasis* in *Anna Karenina*, the description of Mikhailov's painting *Pilate's Admonition*. Mikhailov's problem, as Anna, Vronksy, and Golenishchev perceive it, is how to represent a human, real Christ, or whether such a representation is possible or even desirable; whether a spiritual entity can be materially embodied or represented; whether divine or demonic inspiration is required for such a manifestation; whether the material representation deforms or profanes the spiritual.[18] Tolstoy's indebtedness to Lessing is again discernible in the Platonic distinction he draws between Vronsky's dilettantism and Mikhailov's genius. In *Laocoön* Lessing differentiates between artworks that imitate nature directly and those that imitate other artworks (imitations of imitations); the latter category, Lessing argues, utterly degrades the artist; primacy of *mimēsis* is thus the criterion by which genius is distinguished from talent. Therefore, Vronsky is automatically indicted as an epigone who cannot discriminate between truth and illusion (recall the memorable analogy of a man caressing a doll as if it were a real woman) and who therefore paints after the style of other artistic schools: "He appreciated all kinds [of art], and could have felt inspired by any of them; but he had no conception of the possibility of knowing nothing at all of any school of painting, and of *being inspired directly by what is within the soul*, without caring whether what is painted will belong to any recognized school" (489) (emphasis added). In contrast, Mikhailov paints directly from the heart: "I cannot paint a Christ who is not in my heart" (499), drawing inspiration from "inner vision" (painting is "removing the coverings" from the true insight) while "[Vronsky] drew his inspiration, not directly from life, but indirectly from life embodied in art" (489). Thus it is that Vronsky's portrait of Anna ("in Italian costume in the French style") fails and remains unfinished while Mikhailov succeeds in creating a portrait that "impressed everyone, especially Vronsky, not only by its likeness, but by its characteristic beauty," and by its revelation of "the very sweetest expression of [Anna's] soul" (501).

THE PORTRAIT

In his study of *ekphrasis* in the European novel, Mack Smith determines that Mikhailov's portrait is successful because it lives and "stands out from its frame."[19] This organicist valuation of the creative process, which invests the created object with a life of its own, is exemplified in Mikhailov's experience with his sketch of a "man in a violent rage" onto which a drop of wax falls. The new shape lent to the figure by the drop of wax inspires Mikhailov. As he works, "(t)he figure, from a lifeless imagined thing, had become alive and could not be changed. The figure lived, and was clearly and unmistakably defined" (463). Mikhailov's view of the creative process, "removing the coverings from already existing figures," is counterposed to Vronsky's belief in "technique." Victor Terras has glossed this passage as "a classical statement of the Neoplatonic organic concept of the creative process."[20] In his study of *War and Peace*, Gary Saul Morson terms this process "creation by potential," a notion opposed equally to the classical, programmatic/algorithmic principle of composition and to the romantic conception of poetic madness or the frenzy of inspiration caused by divine or demonic possession. The autonomous, organic status of the artwork suggests that the artist is not in full control of his text and that the work of art evolves autonomously and organically, developed by the artist's delicate manipulations, as Plotinus's sculptor "liberated" his vision of Beauty from the prison of the unformed block of marble.

Mikhailov's struggle to uncover the true forms within his art might be considered as exemplifying of the mode of sincerity Tolstoy would demand of the great artist in *What Is Art?* Tolstoy characterized art according to three main precepts:

1. An artist is successful if he or she succeeds in conveying through the force of his artwork his own genuine feelings (the work's "sincerity" and its capacity for "infection").

2. Art is successful only if it is universal; that is, if it is accessible to all people, regardless of their class, education, formation, culture, and any other characteristic.

3. A work of art succeeds as Christian art not necessarily because of its choice of Christian or biblical subject matter but because of its ability to inspire brotherly love and to unite humanity with divinity.

If we evaluate the three paintings by Mikhailov that we are shown in *Anna Karenina* according to Tolstoy's own aesthetic principles, we find that the painting *Pilate's Admonition* fails, despite its biblical subject matter and Mikhailov's sincerity, because, by Mikhailov's own admission, it requires education to understand it; even then Vronsky and Anna do not fully appreciate it. By contrast, the less ambitious secular painting of two boys fishing in a stream is a success, not merely because it infects the viewers with the bucolic mood of a lazy afternoon fishing expedition but because it appeals to a wide audience and, most important, stimulates the viewer's desire to share the thoughts and experiences of another: "Two boys were angling in the shade of a willow tree. The elder had just dropped in the hook and ... was entirely absorbed in what he was doing. The other ... was lying in the grass leaning on his elbows, with his tangled, flaxen head in his hands, staring at the water with his dreamy blue eyes. What was he thinking of?" (500).

By Tolstoy's own criteria, Mikhailov's portrait of Anna is the most successful artistic creation in the novel, and as such it is contrasted to the various other portraits of Anna presented in and by the text. In addition to the three painted versions and the verbal portraits sketched by other characters, there are Anna's own ekphrastically presented self-portraits; that is, Tolstoy's framings of Anna's presentations of herself as an art object. The most notable scenes in which Anna is overtly framed and aestheticized are her first and last public appearances at the ball in Moscow and at the opera in Petersburg. Anna's presentation of herself as spectacle and art object (portrait or bust) meant to be admired and desired for its beauty alone is contrasted in the novel to Lyovin's sublime visions of the world (landscapes) that become iconic emblems of his spiritual development. Thus, Tolstoy appears to perpetuate the romantic tradition of elevating the category of the sublime over that of the beautiful and preferring the landscape to the portrait.

Although described briefly in the section of the novel in which it is painted, Mikhailov's portrait of Anna receives its most sustained ekphrastic treatment in the scene where the novel's two leading protagonists meet, when Lyovin is coerced by his brother-in-law, Stiva, into visiting Anna. Tolstoy has been criticized for failing to exploit the full dramatic potential of this scene; for example, Boris Eikhenbaum characterizes the connection established at Anna's and Lyovin's meeting as a "light dotted line" having no significance for the plot.[21] In fact, their meeting inaugurates Lyovin's education or *Bildung*, which is achieved through his contemplation of an image.[22] So powerful and crucial is this scene that Joan Grossman has argued that the episode be regarded as the keystone in the arch of *Anna Karenina*,[23] although, on purely architectural grounds, the placement of the keystone in this chapter would make it asymmetrical to the novel's balanced structure, as elegantly diagrammed by Elisabeth Stenbock-Fermor.[24] If the scene is not the keystone, it is nonetheless highly demarcated and circumscribed in the text. Lyovin's viewing of the portrait is multiply framed and deeply imbedded in the narrative; the ornate setting of the portrait and its viewing similarly frame Anna's entrance, which is in turn framed by Lyovin's vision of her. The most exterior frames of this episode, the two occasions on which Lyovin and Stiva dine together, neatly bracket the novel structurally and thematically since both occasions serve as Platonic symposia where the various types of love are discussed, defined, and, on the second occasion, witnessed. Novelistically, and proleptically, the placement of the chapter in the plot serves as an additional frame. As has often been noted, Anna is contiguously and metaphorically located in a brothel, or women's quarters (*teremok*).[25] In terms of temporal sequence, Stiva and Lyovin fulfill the novelistic convention of having dinner, drinks, playing cards, and then going off to ——; a notion that is rendered explicit by Kitty in her subsequent argument with Lyovin: "You were drinking at the club, drinking and gambling, and then you went ... to her of all people!" (732). The setting of the scene is itself seductive: dark lighting, soft carpets, even the treillage reminiscent of the trellis work in the traditional Islamic *teremok*, from behind which Anna emerges. It is this context, in addition to what Lyovin knows of Anna's history, that informs his sense of guilt and embarrassment and predisposes him to a harsh judgment of Anna as a fallen woman.

In the dialogue with Stiva when they are en route to Anna, Lyovin reaffirms his attitudes toward fallen women and his negative expectations of Anna as he frames and stereotypes his projected image of her. The reader is reminded of his disquisition on fallen women in the symmetrically opposed first dinner scene with Stiva: "I have a loathing for fallen women. You're afraid of spiders, and I of these vermin ... those who know only the nonplatonic love have no need to talk of tragedy. In such love there can be no tragedy" (46).

As in their first dinner discussion, on this occasion Stiva tries again to solicit Lyovin's tolerance for human imperfection. As Stiva and Lyovin ride in the carriage to Anna's, Stiva attempts, in three short narratives, to win Lyovin over with his descriptions of Anna. Stiva's sketches are dialogized by Lyovin's resistance and by Stiva's own sense of verbal incompetence, as well as by their lack of fitness to frame the subject. Not only does Stiva fail to draw a portrait of Anna to his own satisfaction (he concludes each sketch by falling back on, "but you'll see for yourself...."); the pictures of Anna he presents are unrecognizable even to the reader since they introduce events and actions that are new in the narrative. The resulting sense of estrangement (*ostranenie*) has the effect of distancing and renewal, so that we, like Lyovin, seem to be hearing about a stranger and anticipate seeing Anna as if for the first time. Stiva begins by describing Anna as "calm and dignified," when the reader last saw her in a state of psychic disintegration, rebelliously flouting social convention at the opera. Stiva then seeks to arouse Lyovin's sympathies by describing Anna's writing of children's books, but then he immediately negates this portrayal: "But are you imagining she's an authoress? Not at all." Finally, he attempts to present Anna as a "woman with a heart" who has adopted a protégée and her family, a description he proceeds to deconstruct: "It's not philanthropy.... She saw them, helped them.... But not by way of patronage.... But you'll see for yourself" (724). But prior to seeing for himself, Lyovin is aided by another, more accurate interpretation of Anna's character: Mikhailov's portrait.

Upon entering Anna's house, Lyovin's first action is to examine his face in the mirror. His face is red, but he denies to himself that he is drunk.[26] Lyovin's second action is to contemplate Mikhailov's portrait of Anna. The juxtaposition of the two portraits—one real in a mirror, the other so real it seems to step from its frame—reinforces our sense of Anna and Lyovin as alter egos, a view buttressed by the novel's structure, which continually juxtaposes parallel events from these two characters' lives. In psychoanalytic terms,[27] the act of viewing the "other" necessarily involves the projection of self, the conflation of portrait with reflection is emphasized linguistically by the description of a reflector lamp (*lampa-refraktor*) that overhangs Anna's portrait and suggests the double function of illumination and reflection. Lyovin's presence as the observer in the text mirrors the reader's role as voyeur and introduces the implicit comparison of Mikhailov's painted portrait with Tolstoy's verbal one. The ultimate effect of the framing of the heroine is to focus our attention, and to estrange us from our familiar interiorized relationship to Anna in order to see her through others' eyes.

This makes Lyovin's mental and spiritual transformation before the painting all the more effective.

Lyovin's *Bildung* consists in his acceptance of human, specifically feminine imperfection, as expressed in his attitude toward "those vermin," fallen women, whom he has traditionally and conventionally stereotyped as vulgar, lower-class, uneducated, and lacking in the capacity for suffering or consciousness. His Victorian ("Dickensian," in Stiva's term) prejudice is well described by Anna, who thus defines Stiva's similar views on women to Dolly: "I know how men like Stiva look at it.... Their own home and wife are sacred to them. Somehow or other these [fallen] women are looked on with contempt by them.... They draw a sort of line that can't be crossed between them and their families" (76). Lyovin's encounter with Anna, an educated woman of high society with a complex, sensitive character, necessarily breaks the frame of his own expectations and provokes in him not the feeling of disgust he had anticipated but "a tenderness and pity which surprised him" (729). What brings about the birth of compassion and tolerance for human frailty and imperfection, a capacity for forgiveness that is the beginning of true faith on Lyovin's part? It is not simply a case of physical attraction, although Lyovin is by no means immune to Anna's attempt to "arouse in [him] a feeling of love" (733); yet even in this response we must ask if the resulting feeling is that of *erōs* or *agapē*. Lyovin's first examination of the portrait of a fallen woman of high society, coming immediately on the heels of his glimpse of his own guilty face "caught in the act," undermines his self-righteousness and harsh judgment of others and produces the requisite sense of humility. And then the portrait itself immediately enchants Lyovin:

> He could not tear himself away from it. He positively forgot where he was and not even hearing what was said, he could not take his eyes off the marvellous portrait. It was not a picture, but a living, charming woman, with black curling hair, with bare arms and shoulders, with a pensive smile on lips covered with soft down; triumphantly and softly she looked at him with eyes that baffled him. (725)

Lyovin is captivated not only by the exceptionally lifelike quality of the portrait, or by its beauty, but by the mysterious expression of Anna's eyes, a mystery that perhaps implies the inner life of the subject, which can only be represented enigmatically.[28] In its act of framing, the portrait paradoxically shows what cannot be framed. The viewer's response to beauty framed is to sense the sublimity of spirit that escapes those borders. Thus, Lyovin's vision of Anna is expanded rather than contained by the portrait, although when Anna first appears to Lyovin, she appears as "the very woman of the portrait ... with the same perfection of beauty which the artist had caught" (725). But it is when Lyovin recognizes the disjunction between the Anna before him and the character of the ideal Anna in the portrait that he begins to appreciate and to commiserate her agony:

> [H]er face, suddenly taking on a hard expression, looked as if it were turned to stone. With that expression on her face she was more beautiful than ever; but the expression was new; it was utterly unlike that expression, radiant with happiness and creating happiness, which had been caught by the painter in her portrait. *Lyovin looked once more at the portrait and at her figure ...* and he felt for her a tenderness and pity which surprised him. (729) (emphasis added)

By the end of the evening during which he "all the while was thinking of her inner life, trying to divine her feelings ... though he had judged her so severely hitherto, now *by some strange chain of reasoning* he was justifying her and also sorry for her" (730) (emphasis added).

It is the portrait that leads Lyovin to wonder at the mysteries of Anna's spiritual or inner life and thus to recognize the conflict and agony she endures. Lyovin achieves this understanding by "some strange chain of reasoning," because it is not by reason at all but by intuition and empathy, stimulated by contemplation of a true work of art that gives him insight. In a similar way, Vronsky had earlier marveled that Mikhailov, without knowing Anna, had managed to portray her soul: "'One has to know and love her as I have loved her to discover the very sweetest expression of her soul,' Vronsky thought, though *it was only from the portrait that he had himself learned* the sweetest expression of her soul" (501) (emphasis added).

Lyovin's revelation before Anna's portrait initiates the spiritual conversion he will achieve by the close of the novel: his acceptance of an intuitive faith that is not based on reason; his recognition of and tolerance for the imperfection of human life and his resulting compassion. Lyovin thus plays the role of Christ asked to judge the fallen woman. In response to the Pharisee's demand for judgment, Christ bent down in silence and began to write in the dirt, as if revising Mosaic law. While seeming to perpetuate the tradition of scribal elitism, Christ tempered its dicta by maintaining oral silence, thus drawing a distinction between the abstract realm of the logos and the real plane of human response. Forgiveness transforms even Kitty, who, although she condemns Lyovin for his compassion for Anna, will herself instantly forgive her when she sees her. Thus, Mikhailov's portrait fulfills Tolstoy's requisite for true Christian art as stated in *What Is Art?*: that it unite people in compassionate love.

Lyovin's viewing of Mikhailov's portrait of Anna is contrasted to an earlier scene where a portrait of Anna is also contemplated by a man sitting in judgment of her. In the chapter that follows the one in which Anna reveals to Karenin her liaison with Vronsky, Karenin attempts to pursue his usual evening's diversions after having written his wife a letter requiring her to continue their married life as before. He attempts to read a French work on the Eugubine Tables but finds himself unable to concentrate and instead contemplates his wife's portrait:

> Over the armchair there hung in a gold frame an oval portrait of Anna, a fine painting by a celebrated artist. Aleksey Aleksandrovich glanced at it. The *unfathomable eyes* gazed ironically and insolently at him. Insufferably insolent and challenging was the effect, in Aleksey Aleksandrovich's eyes, of the black lace about the head, admirably done by the painter, the black hair and handsome white hand with one finger lifted, covered with rings. After looking at the portrait for a minute, Aleksey Aleksandrovich shuddered, so that his lips quivered, and uttered the sound "brrr." (301) (emphasis added)

Karenin proceeds to solve not the mystery of his wife's "unfathomable gaze," which he now interprets as insolence, nor the (for him) unsolvable mystery of the Eugubine Tables, but "a complication that had arisen in his official life" (301). Anna, like the Eugubine Tables, remains a cipher.[29] The effect of the black lace about the head and the "insolent" expression both recall Anna's earlier appearance at the ball and predict her later fatal appearance at the opera. In both public appearances, Anna is depicted as an aesthetic object, framed by her attire.

At the ball:

> Anna was not in lilac, as Kitty had so urgently wished, but in a black, low-cut, velvet gown, showing her full shoulders and bosom that looked as though *carved of old ivory*, and her rounded arms, with tiny, slender wrists. The whole gown was trimmed with Venetian lace. In her black hair, all her own, was a little wreath of pansies, and there were more of the same in the black

ribbon winding through the white lace encircling her waist. Her coiffure was not striking. All that was noticeable were the little wilful tendrils of her curly hair that would always break free about her neck and temples. Around her finely *chiseled*, strong neck was a thread of pearls.... Now [Kitty] understood that Anna could not have been in lilac, and that her charm was just that *she always stood out from her attire*, that her dress could never be conspicuous on her. And her black dress, with its sumptuous lace, was not conspicuous on her; *it was only the frame and all that was seen was she*. (85) (emphasis added)

In contrast to Anna, who is presented both as a chiseled ivory statue and as a work of art within a frame, Kitty appeals in such a way that her attire is part and parcel of her character, "as if she had been born in that tulle and lace, with her hair done up high on her head and a rose and two leaves on the top of it" (83). Despite the apparent "natural" quality of Anna's coiffure and toilette, the reader recognizes, with some irony at Kitty's expense, what the more experienced Dolly will later understand as she examines Anna's gown: "Anna had put on a very simple batiste dress. Dolly scrutinized that simple dress attentively. She knew what it meant, and the price at which such simplicity was obtained" (645). It is a supreme artistry that creates the impression of being natural whereas only genuine innocence could render the frills and furbelows of Kitty's attire natural.

Anna's conscious presentation of herself as an aesthetic object is even more pronounced in the later scene where she attends the opera. As in the ballroom scene and in the portrait contemplated by Karenin, lace is again the framing feature. In fact, this scene becomes an enactment of the features Karenin sees in the portrait, while Vronsky's role and reactions throughout this chapter parallel those of Karenin in the earlier scenes between Anna and her husband. Vronsky now assumes Karenin's role as Anna becomes a "closed book" (or cipher) to him:

He looked at her with searching eyes, but she responded with that defiant, half-mirthful, half-desperate look, *the meaning of which he could not comprehend*.... Anna was already dressed in a low-necked gown of light silk and velvet that she had had made in Paris, with costly white lace on her head *that framed her face* and was particularly becoming, *setting off her dazzling beauty*. (569) (emphasis added)

In the following exchange, Vronsky, "appealing to her exactly as her husband once had done" (570), feels an increasing hostility toward Anna as his respect for her diminishes, "although his sense of her beauty [is] intensified" (570). After pursuing her to the opera, Vronsky watches as Anna, framed by the proscenium of her opera box, upstages the diva:

> Vronsky ... caught sight of Anna's head, proud, strikingly beautiful, *and smiling in the frame of lace. The setting of her head* ... reminded him of her just as he had seen her at the ball in Moscow. But he felt utterly different toward her beauty now. In his feeling for her now there was no element of mystery, and so her beauty, though it attracted him even more intensely than before, now offended him too. (573) (emphasis added)

Vronsky feels no sense of mystery, although he has never understood Anna less than at this moment, when he is ignorant of her tragic meeting with her son and cannot comprehend her behavior. What Vronsky sees in Anna's self-portrait is the presentation of beauty without barriers to the sexual knowledge he has of her; as a result, his aesthetic experience of Anna is empty and superficial, virtually pornographic, and therefore offensive.

Such a reading is defensible when we recall Tolstoy's later dictum in *What Is Art?* that true art requires no ornament or technique while false art relies on convention and decorations. In his famous analogy, Tolstoy argues:

> However strange it may be to say this, the art of our time and circle has undergone that same thing that happens to a woman, whose feminine charms, destined for motherhood, are sold for the satisfaction of those who lust after such satiations.
>
> The art of our time and circle has become a fallen woman....
> It is just as made-up, just as commercialized, just as deceptive and ruinous....
>
> True art does not require any adornment, like a wife beloved of her husband. False art, like a prostitute, must always be adorned.[30]

Anna as a fallen woman, is contrasted in the novel to Dolly, who is concerned about her appearance only as the mother of her children: "Now she did not dress for her own sake, not for the sake of her own beauty, but simply so that, as the mother of those exquisite creatures [her children], she might not spoil the general effect" (278). Despite her lack of feminine vanity, however, Dolly is no stranger to the impulse to be aestheticized in a picture, although in her case it is as the mother of "exquisite creatures" that she desires to be framed. Thus, meeting Lyovin as she is bathing with her children, "she was especially glad he should see her in all her glory. No one was able to appreciate her grandeur better than Lyovin. Seeing her, he found himself face to face with one of the *pictures of family life his imagination painted*" (282) (emphasis added). When Dolly exclaims, "How glad I am to see you!" the reader easily discerns that her pleasure is not in seeing but in being seen by Lyovin in a flattering picture.

In contrast to Dolly and Anna's narcissistic self-portraits, Mikhailov's portrait of Anna is transcendent. The revelatory effect of Anna's portrait on Lyovin is reminiscent of his response to a vision of Kitty earlier in the novel: a vision that, like the portrait of Anna, constitutes an *ekphrasis* and radically revises his world view. Following a night spent with the peasants after the harvest, during which Lyovin experiences a false epiphany and considers marrying a peasant woman, he catches a glimpse of Kitty traveling to her estate, framed by the window of her carriage: "At the window, evidently only just awake, sat a young girl holding in both hands the ribbons of a white cap. With a face full of light and thought, *full of a subtle, complex inner life* that was remote from Lyovin, she was gazing beyond him at the glow of the sunrise" (293) (emphasis added). Lyovin, struck by this portrait of Kitty, realizes the full falsity of his previous night's epiphany and acknowledges that the solution to the mystery of his life rests with her.

Whenever Lyovin attempts to find solutions to his philosophical dilemmas, he creates pictures by framing the vision of the real world before him and using it as an emblem or icon of his thoughts and experience. Thus, in his rodomontade in the passage preceding his vision of Kitty, Lyovin observes a "strange mother-of-pearl shell of fleecy white cloudlets" (293) in the sky that he "takes as a symbol of [his] ideas and feelings" (294) concerning the formation of his new views of life: "Just now I looked at the sky and there was nothing in it—only two white streaks. Yes, and so imperceptibly too my views of life changed!" Similarly, on the morning of his betrothal to Kitty, "what Lyovin saw then he never saw again" (424): a fortuitous, synchronic composition of birds, freshly baked loaves and children at play, drawn into a visual composition that crystallizes his spiritual state of ecstasy.

In the earlier passage, after Kitty's carriage disappears over the horizon, Lyovin glances at the sky to find that the shell has gone: "There in the remote heights above, a mysterious change had been accomplished. There was no trace of a shell, and there was stretched over fully half of the sky an even cover of tiny and ever tinier cloudlets" (294). Both images, the shell and the cover, suggest containment, physical exteriors that embody spiritual essences, and thus incorporate the theme of representation. Lyovin makes his vision stand as an emblem of the natural law of flux, of constant change and variation, of the impossibility of fixing the world and himself in an eternal state of perfection. This recognition makes possible his later acceptance of life as spiritual struggle in an ongoing process, and of himself as an imperfect creature with the intent of perfecting himself and the knowledge that this intent is as sufficient as the achievement of perfection. At the close of the novel, he accepts not only these facts but also his own flawed nature that resists process and seeks finalization by attempting to stop time and to preserve moments in a "frozen," "framed" state.

Thus, at the novel's conclusion, Lyovin acknowledges both the dangers of framing and, paradoxically, the salvific potential of such visions. Once he recognizes the limitations of earthbound vision, he can allow his tendency to organize the world into symbolic landscapes to enhance his nonrational, intuitive approach to faith without falling prey to the dangers of trusting his insight too much. Lyovin's sense of limits and acceptance of the bounded field of bodily experience that cannot contain transcendence constitutes Tolstoy's restatement of the Kantian definition of the sublime, as discussed in chapter 3. Lyovin's final epiphanic picture of the sky is bordered and framed by his awareness of his narrow scope of sight and his appreciation of the value of the sensation of limits:

> Lying on his back, he gazed up now into the high cloudless sky. "Do I not know that that is infinite space, and that it is not a rounded vault? But, however I screw up my eyes and strain my sight, I cannot see it but as round and finite, and in spite of my knowing about infinite space, I am incontestably right when I see a firm blue vault, far more right than when I strain my eyes to see beyond it." (833)

Tolstoy closes Lyovin's narrative on an exaltation of the experience of the sublime realized through the traditionally romantic vehicle of the awe-inspiring landscape. Yet this is an experience of the sublime that carries Lyovin away from human relations, which now irritate him as distractions from his spiritual growth. Indeed, he finds the mood of ecstasy difficult, if not impossible, to reconcile with the daily events and human interactions of prosaic existence, which "momentarily overshadow" his state of grace. By contrast, his viewing of Anna's portrait brought him into harmony with humanity and made it possible for him to empathize even with someone completely different from himself. Anna's portrait thus belongs in the category of the iconic and is superior to the mode of the sublime; it is a transcendent portrait that implies the continual process of perfectivization through living experience.

Lyovin's final vision is contrasted to the series of streetscapes Anna views through the frame of her carriage window en route to her suicide: she interprets these pictures as profane projections of the vanity fair and cartoonish illustrations of unmitigated human greed and self-delusion. The hyperrealist, almost naturalist, depictions of dirty ice cream and grotesque visages are neither sublime nor iconic. Instead, Anna is seduced by an implacable realism and a photographic objectivity into making these scenes stand as accurate portrayals or "physiological sketches" of the human condition. Unaware of her own hermeneutic action of framing and reading, she accepts her frame of mind as the objective truth and the candlelight by which she reads her "book filled with troubles, falsehoods, sorrow, and evil" (799) as the ultimate and final illumination.

NOTES

1. Leo Tolstoy, *What Is Art?* Trans. Aylmer Maude. New York: Macmillan, 1960, p. 105. Brief versions of this chapter were delivered as lectures at the Tolstoy Society Symposium, the annual meeting of the American Association of Teachers of Slavic and East European Languages, December 1987, and at the Slavic Seminar, Columbia University, March 1988.

2. For a standard summation of the topos, see Murray Krieger, "Ekphrasis and the Still Movement of Poetry, or Laokoön Revisited." In Frederick McDowell, ed., *The Poet as Critic.* Evanston, Ill.: Northwestern University Press, 1967, pp. 3–26.

3. Roland Barthes, "L'effect du réel." *Communications* 11 (1968):88.

4. Gotthold Ephraim Lessing, *Lacoön: An Essay upon the Limits of Painting and Poetry.* Trans. Ellen Frothingham. Boston: Little, Brown, 1910, p. 117.

5. Recent studies and bibliographies on the topic of *ut pictura poesis* may be found in Arno Dolders, "*Ut Pictura Poesis*: A Selective Annotated Bibliography," *Yearbook of Comparative and General Literature* 32 (1983):105–124; Judith Dundas, "Style and the Mind's Eye," *The Journal of Aesthetics and Art Criticism* 37 (1979):325–335; Alexander Gelley, "The

Represented World: Toward a Phenomenological Theory of Description in the Novel," *The Journal of Aesthetics and Art Criticism* 37 (1979):415–422; John Graham, "*Ut Pictura Poesis*: A Bibliography," *Bulletin of Bibliography* 29 (1972):13–15; Henry Markewicz, "*Ut Pictura Poesis* ... A History of the Topos and the Problem," *New Literary History* 18 (1987):535–558; Roy Park, "*Ut Pictura Poesis*: The 19th Century Aftermath," *The Journal of Aesthetics and Art Criticism* 28 (1969):155–164.

6. Barthes, 87.

7. Mary Ann Caws, *Reading Frames in Modern Fiction*. Princeton: Princeton University Press, 1985, p. 30.

8. Jean-Paul Sartre, *Les Mots*. Paris: Gallimard, 1968, p. 171.

9. Both Anna and Lyovin are also authors, whose books remain unfinished.

10. Margaret R. Higonnet, "Speaking Silences," in *The Female Body in Western Culture: Contemporary Perspectives*. Susan Rubin Suleiman, ed. Cambridge: Harvard University Press, 1985, 1986, p. 69.

11. The problem of the description of the personality and the failures of portraiture preoccupied Tolstoy in his earliest writings, as evidenced in a diary entry from 1851: "It seems to me that actually to *describe* a man is impossible ... words give no understanding of a man but make a pretense of delineating him while more often than not only misleading [the reader]" (*PSS* 46:67). Tolstoy then proceeds to describe a man in a manner that is reminiscent of the salon game "portrait moral": first he relates what he has heard of the man's reputation from others, then he describes his appearance, and finally he describes the impression the actual man made upon him. Tolstoy employs the same procedure in relating Lyovin's visit to Anna: first he hears Stiva's account of her, then he views her portrait, and finally he is affected by her actual presence.

12. John Bayley, *Tolstoy and the Novel*. New York: Viking, 1966, p. 235.

13. An example of a Tolstoy misquotation. M. A. Balakirev's piece is known simply as *King Lear* (1860). *King Lear of the Steppes* is a novella by Turgenev (*Stepnoi Lir*). Tolstoy's own title, *King Lear in the Steppe* (*Korol' Lir v stepi*), differs from both.

14. Tolstoy was probably referring to the projected sculpture of Pushkin submitted in competition for the centennial by M. M. Antokol'skii (1843–1902). A sketch of the planned sculpture was exhibited in 1875.

15. Lessing, 39.

16. Lessing casts the issue of invisibility in neoplatonic terms as the separation of upper and lower spheres: "with the loss of all distinction to the eye between the visible and the invisible beings, all the characteristic traits

must likewise disappear, which serve to elevate the higher order of beings above the lower." See Lessing, 77.

17. Lessing, 80–81.

18. For a more thorough discussion of these issues in relation to *What Is Art?*, see Bayley, chap. 6.

19. Mack Smith, Jr., *Figures in the Carpet: The Ekphrastic Tradition in the Realistic Novel.* Unpublished doctoral dissertation, Rice University, 1981, p. 725.

20. Victor Terras, *Belinskij and Russian Literary Criticism: The Heritage of Organic Aesthetics.* Madison: University of Wisconsin Press, 1974, p. 282.

21. Boris Eikhenbaum, *Tolstoy in the Seventies.* Trans. Albert Kaspin. Ann Arbor: Ardis Press, 1972, p. 127.

22. It is interesting to note that in Russian the word for education (*obrazovanie*), like the German word *Bildung*, is based on a root meaning "to shape, form, build." However, in Russian the root *obraz* is also used to refer to icons. Thus, in popular etymology, to acquire learning implied becoming like the images (icons)," that is, becoming like the saints. For Russians, therefore, the concept of education has a marked spiritual component as well as a visual realization.

23. In response to a letter criticizing Tolstoy for lack of structure in *Anna Karenina*, Tolstoy replied: "I pride myself on the architecture—the arches are so joined that it is impossible even to notice the keystone." Letter to S. A. Rachinsky, 27 January 1878, *PSS* 62:377. Criticism on *Anna Karenina* has taken up the metaphor; the most successful work along these lines is that of Elisabeth Stenbock-Fermor, *The Architecture of Anna Karenina: A History of Its Structure, Writing, and Message.* Lisse, Belgium: Peter de Bidder Press, 1975. Stenbock-Fermor argues quite convincingly that the keystone scene is the Oblonskys' dinner party, which contains the central, symposiac debate on the woman question. In "Tolstoy's Portrait of Anna: Keystone in the Arch," *Criticism* 18 (1976):1–14, Joan Grossman argues that Lyovin's viewing of Anna's portrait is the keystone scene.

24. Stenbock-Fermor notes a symmetrical, architectural structure in the novel, built around the opening and closing scenes at railroad stations and the symposial debates on love. According to her diagram, the keystone scene is the Oblonskys' dinner party at which Dolly pleads with Karenin to forgive Anna, Lyovin and Kitty become betrothed, and the company discuss the woman question.

25. After this manuscript was completed, Ronald LeBlanc's article, "Levin Visits Anna: The Iconography of Harlotry," appeared in *Tolstoy Studies Journal* 3 (1990):1–21. LeBlanc makes several of the same points I

make here but draws a different conclusion, that "the visit to Anna's—metaphorized as a trip to a brothel—can be seen as the culmination of a process at work throughout the novel whereby the hero gradually loses his innocence and compromises his values as he becomes less a 'savage' and more a 'civilized' nobleman" (15). LeBlanc thus adheres to the critical view of Tolstoy as holding negative opinions on women and sexuality.

26. We are reminded of David Copperfield, who, on the occasion of his first debauchery, studies his face in the mirror and concludes that only his hair looks drunk. I am indebted to Elizabeth Beaujour for drawing my attention to another intertext for this passage, Dostoevsky's *Notes from the Underground*, where the Underground Man pauses prior to consummating his purchase at the brothel and glances in the mirror. It is in keeping with his perverse, reverse logic that the recognition of his drunken, disheveled state gives way to an overcompensating narcissism: "I caught sight of myself in a mirror. My agitated face seemed to me repulsive in the extreme: pale, vicious, mean, with tangled hair. 'All right, I'm glad of it,' I thought; 'I'm glad to seem repulsive to her; I like that.'"

Looking into a mirror suggests self-examination and the awakening of the conscience, as well as psychic dissociation or projection, the emergence of the uncanny twin, or double. Other characters in the novel also look into mirrors or refuse to do so, as is the case with Dolly when she visits Anna at Vronsky's estate. In a critical scene before her suicide, Anna looks into the mirror and does not recognize herself.

27. Freud's theories on the scopic drives, voyeurism, and exhibitionism, as developed in his 1915 essay "Instincts and Their Vicissitudes" (see Sigmund Freud, *Complete Psychological Works of Sigmund Freud*, 24 vols. Revised and ed. James Strachey. London: Hogarth Press, 1953–1974) were later reworked by Jacques Lacan in his concepts of the "mirror phase" and the "Gaze." The Lacanian theory of the unconscious discourse of the "Gaze" is based on a system of shifts or alternations between voyeurism and exhibitionism. The voyeur refuses to be seen as an object and attempts to assume power through visual dominance while the exhibitionist refuses to be shown or to see and is similarly dogmatic in determining the rejection of the visual field. Lyovin's role as a voyeur and Anna's exhibitionism in the public arena and with Vronsky are echoed in Lyovin's "screwing up his eyes" while trying to see more clearly and Anna's habit of "screwing up her eyes" while refusing to see.

28. Feminist critics of the representation of women in art argue that "women cannot be represented as themselves, since we cannot know their identities. They are simply present as a consciousness of being perceived and

represented as objects. Hence the duplicitous mystery of women in portraits whose gaze outward is really turned inward on themselves." Margaret R. Higonnet's introduction in Carolyn Heilbrun and Margaret R. Higonnet, eds., *The Representation of Women in Fiction*. Baltimore: Johns Hopkins University Press, 1983, p. xx.

29. The Eugubine Tables were written in an undeciphered Northumbrian dialect and were discovered in 1444 in Eugubium, Italy. It is interesting to note that the treatise on the tables that Karenin is reading is in French. Like Vronsky's portrait in French style of Anna in Italian costume, Karenin's portrait of Anna is coded in Italian and framed by the French language.

30. *What Is Art?*, 227.

CARYL EMERSON

Tolstoy and Dostoevsky:
Seductions of the Old Criticism

George Steiner wrote his major contribution to Russian literary studies, *Tolstoy or Dostoevsky: An Essay in the Old Criticism*, in the late 1950s.[1] At the time, academic critics in the West felt much closer to nineteenth-century Russian culture than to any literary product of that forbidding and well-sealed monolith, the Soviet state—even though, paradoxically, our regnant New Criticism recalled in many particulars the spirit of Russian Formalism from the Soviet 1920s. Now over thirty years old, *Tolstoy or Dostoevsky* still renders exemplary service to those two great Russian novelists. But the book casts unexpected light on our own current critical debates as well.

Steiner opens his essay with a defense of his "old" critical approach. Its primary purpose, he tells us, is to serve the text "subjectively." Thus its starting point must be a positive, almost an electrical, contact between an artwork of genius and its admiring and energized reader. In Steiner's words, "when the work of art invades our consciousness, something within us catches flame. What we do thereafter is to refine and make articulate the original leap of recognition" (45). This quasimystical mission—which, one suspects, only Steiner's astonishing erudition could bring to heel and down to earth in our secular age—is then pointedly contrasted with the spirit of the New Criticism: "Quizzical, captious, immensely aware of its philosophic ancestry and complex instruments, it often comes to bury rather than to

From *Reading George Steiner*, edited by Nathan A. Scott, Jr. and Ronald A. Sharp. © 1994 by The Johns Hopkins University Press.

praise" (4). Indeed. In retrospect Steiner is perhaps too harsh on the New Critics, whose captiousness is but a minnow to the leviathan of later, post-modernist burials of the world's great literature. Still, he sees ample evidence of a falling away from earlier, more radiant modes of reading. The unhappy vogue of "objective criticism," he claims, has made us uncertain of our great books and suspicious of tradition. "We grow wary of our inheritance," he writes. "We have become relativists" (4).

Three decades ago, then, Steiner had come out in defense of a literary canon and the reader's unmediated primary contact with it. As *Real Presences* indicates, this commitment has not changed. But what, precisely, is primary contact? It need not mean immersion in the native language of the literary text (in his dealings with Tolstoy and Dostoevsky, Steiner apologizes for his ignorance of Russian—but the deficiency hinders him much less than he fears); nor does it mandate a meticulous, insider's knowledge of the political or cultural background of every world-class text. Primary contact, for Steiner, is both more modest and more risk-laden. It requires from the reader less an intellectual than an *aesthetic* commitment, a willingness to "tune oneself" to the artwork and thus to become part of the text's glorious problem rather than its solution. In short, we have come into primary contact when, one way or another, we fall in love with a piece of art and are moved to expand on its value in ways that expose our own vulnerabilities before it. "Literary criticism should arise out of a debt of love," Steiner writes (3). From this love relation, apparently, there are no merely scientific or "secondary" ways out.

In our current age of suspicious interrogations, all this sounds very, very old. But what takes us by surprise, in rereading *Tolstoy or Dostoevsky*, is its high degree of theoretical sophistication. The number of potent critical ideas that Steiner eases directly out of primary texts (and it goes without saying that Russian scholarship has a vast "secondary" industry on each of these novelists, but Steiner is not and cannot be in thrall to it) is simply exhilarating. His resulting thesis is so expertly cobbled together from the bottom up, out of the wide-ranging and integral world views of the novels themselves, that it easily survives the language barrier and the passage of time. To reconstruct and extend that thirty-year-old thesis, with an eye to some intervening critical developments, will be the major task of this essay.

* * *

The brunt of Steiner's thesis is reducible to a topic sentence: that Tolstoy's art revives the traditions of Homeric epic, whereas Dostoevsky's reenacts, in novelistic garb, ancient tragic drama. One is immediately struck, of course, by the derivative nature of the whole dichotomy—by its apparent indifference to the manifest "novelness" of the novel, which has been justly celebrated as the most non-Aristotelian of genres. Many have argued that the novel's very messiness and indeterminacy were what appealed to these two great Russian innovators in the genre. Precisely this intractable failure of the great Russian novel to fit into a classical poetics led the twentieth century's greatest student of Dostoevsky, Mikhail Bakhtin, to posit the novel as a genre that is in principle *opposed* to both epic and drama. This dialogue between Bakhtin and Steiner, so suggestive and full of intricate complementarity, shall be pursued at the end of the essay. Let us turn first to the general lineaments of Steiner's juxtaposition of Tolstoy and Dostoevsky.

Chapter one sets the scene by marking similarities. Both novelists wrote immensely long books. But, Steiner notes, the length of these books was of a different order than the length, say, of *Clarissa* or *Ulysses*; for those latter authors, length was an invitation to elegant and precise mapping, to tying down, whereas for Dostoevsky and Tolstoy, "plenitude was an essential freedom" (14). Freedom and plenitude: out of these two ideas Steiner constructs his larger contribution to the history of the novel. Much ink has been spilt on comparisons between the "European" and "Russian" novel, Steiner remarks. But the more interesting and valid comparison is between the European novel, on the one hand, and on the other the Russian and the American novel—two generic strands fused, as it were, at the still half-savage periphery of Europe's sphere of influence. Steiner explains his typology. The European novel, he argues, arose as a private genre that was secular, rational, social. Its task was the successful portrayal of everyday life. But the genre was plagued from the start with a question of legitimacy: Could the prosaic and quotidian ever attain to the "high seriousness" expected of great art? The grand novels of the Romantic period were spared the full implications of that question, because Dickens, Hugo, Stendhal could abandon the familiar plots of classical antiquity and draw, for inspiration and grandeur, on the heroic (but still contemporary and local) events of the 1810s–40s, on the Napoleonic theme and its aftermath. The problem became more serious in the second half of the century, Steiner claims, when the mainstream European novel—tacking to and fro in search of a new word—confronted the pervasive and leveling "bourgeoisification" of everyday life. As a genre devoted to secular readings of ordinary experience, its predictable endpoint was Zola's desiccating naturalism and Flaubert's *catalogue manque*.

According to Steiner, this "dilemma of realism" was felt less acutely at the periphery of the novel's reach. "The masters of the American and the Russian manner appear to gather something of their fierce intensity from the outer darkness," he writes, "from the decayed matter of folklore, melodrama, and religious life" (30). Melville and Hawthorne are the United States' Dostoevsky: writers on an untamed frontier, creating in isolation, plagued by crises of faith in their pre-Enlightenment societies, and radically insecure in the face of Europe's complacent cultural superiority. With such a set of problems, Russian and American novelists had no trouble filling their novels with "high seriousness." Having established the special compatibility of these two quasi-civilized European outposts, Steiner then returns to the classics—and shows the Russian novel to be the salvation of that profoundly civilized legacy.

The body of the book falls into two parts, each with its own thesis and demonstration: Tolstoy as Homeric bard, and Dostoevsky as tragic dramatist. For a critic such as Steiner, utterly uninterested in such hypotheses as the death of the author or the impossibility of authorial intention, the first thesis is perhaps the easier to document. For Tolstoy himself desired to be compared with Homer. Indeed, we sense intuitively that Tolstoy's novels have some kinship with epic: in their immensity, seriousness, spaciousness, in the serene confidence of their narrative voice. But certain other parallels have been neglected, Steiner claims. The most crucial of these are Tolstoy's specific structural imitations of Homeric epic, and the concordance between Tolstoy's epic manner and his anarchic Christianity (which Steiner will later bring unnervingly close to paganism, to an anthropomorphic "theology without God" [266]). Steiner's critical method here is leisurely and learned. He constantly weaves scenes from the *Odyssey* and *Iliad* into his own paraphrases of Tolstoyan plot and doctrine. One important byproduct of these subtle penetrations is Steiner's continual reassurance that Tolstoy's novels are not unworked "slices of life," not the fluid puddings or baggy monsters that Henry James christened them—for no one would deny a great epic poem the status of real art. If the great Russian novel had little influence on its European counterpart it was not because Russian novelists had no interest in craft; it was because the craft of these Russians was unreadable in the context of the Romantic or naturalistic Continental novel (49–58).

Classicists might balk at Steiner's bold, homogenizing definition of the "epic vision." But, as Steiner gradually sculpts this vision to fit his thesis about Russian writers, Tolstoy's novels take on an integrity—both artistic and theoretical—that their bulk and their sprawl of detail usually defy. Invoking as foil and counterexample the negated, manipulative world of *Madame Bovary*, Steiner points out the deeply epic reflexes of Tolstoyan novelistic prose: the sensuous, dynamic, personal energy that physical objects continually absorb from their human context ("The sword is always seen as part of the striking arm" [51]); the frequent elevation of tiny realistic detail to a matter of passionate significance; and the utter lack of sentimentality about death and individual tragedy ("War and mortality cry havoc in the Homeric and Tolstoyan worlds, but the centre holds.... 'Keep your eyes steadfastly to the light,' says Tolstoy, 'this is how things are'" [78, 77]).

Of great and disorienting importance in the Tolstoyan vision is the effective absence of God. Steiner devotes a portion of chapter four to this seeming paradox: a deeply religious thinker who constructs his Christian theology without the Church, and his Christ without a heavenly Father.[2] A partial answer might be found, again, in the Homeric model. Tolstoy is a pagan, Steiner insists, of the most sophisticated and ethically responsible sort. Within such a world view, neither confession as a sacrament nor faith in a miracle-working savior can remedy human error; error is righted only through something akin to stoic resolve, a willingness to change one's life as a result of pained contemplation or the act of an isolated conscience. We should not be misled by the superficial frivolity of the Greek gods and their irresponsible antics on and off Mount Olympus. The continuum of Homer's world—its ultraheroism for human beings and its semidivinity for gods— suggests precisely the sort of leveling of the secular and the divine that we would expect from the author of a treatise entitled *The Kingdom of God Is within You*.

Steiner is alert, of course, to those aspects of the epic that do not match up with Tolstoyan values. He notes, for example, that the ethic of Tolstoy is profoundly antiheroic (80) and that his pacifist self would never have approved (although it always deeply understood) the epic lust of the battlefield. However, the world views of Tolstoy and the epic do share one vital and quasi-religious dimension: "The humanity of the gods signifies that reality—the controlling pivot of man's experience—is immanent in the natural world" (267).

In these ways, then, Steiner aligns Tolstoy's novel with Homeric epic. Throughout his argument, the novel appears to be the tenor of the metaphor, cast in a sort of passive holding pattern, while the epic is the more active vehicle. But in one final comparison, Steiner makes an impressive contribution precisely to understanding the novel as a genre. This is his discussion, in chapter two, of the "double and triple plot structure" of epics and of Tolstoyan narratives. Steiner does not probe the formal implications of this structure for Tolstoy's larger ethical vision—for that one must repair to Gary Saul Morson's splendid monograph on *War and Peace*[3]—but he does make numerous acute observations that assist the reader in integrating this baffling novel.

Steiner acknowledges that multiple plot structure in the epic lends it a certain narrative grandeur and disinterestedness. He sees clearly that Tolstoy employs such multiplicity for very special purposes. (On the master list of talents that Tolstoy commands as novelist, disinterestedness must rank rather low.) "Double vision" and double plots can be polemical, of course, in the overtly didactic sense: they can reinforce and generalize a particular instance (thus making it more authoritative), or they can ironize and undercut an instance, trivializing the original statement, as well as later parodic replays of it. Although Tolstoy is surely no stranger to this kind of didacticism, Steiner suggests a third possibility: that multiple vision, in the form of many blunt-edged competing plot lines, can be deployed purely to thicken the texture of the work, "to suggest realness by making the design of a work dense, jagged, and complex" (98).

So far, no surprises. But Steiner then stresses that the purpose here is not to saturate the novel with realia for its own sake, or to despise—in the name of "realism"—the need to structure some sort of coherent story. He points out, correctly, that Tolstoy's plots incorporate every bit as much artifice and coincidence as the jerry-built, crisis-driven adventure plots of Dostoevsky. However, the mesh of narrative strands in Tolstoy is so dense, and the degree of "humanization" that even the most episodic characters receive is so high and precise, that coincidence and artifice do not shock us. With that much living material it seems only natural that a great deal of it will interact.

Steiner then speculates on the connection between this thickening of texture in Tolstoy's novels and the nature of Tolstoyan closure. The mass of meticulously tended plot lines and the open, often unresolved endings of the great novels prompt Steiner to regard length, complex plotting, and multiple vision as a "stringent test" for the "aliveness" of a character: "whether or not it can grow with time and preserve its coherent individuality in an altered setting" (104). In this insight—which will not be the last such curious overlay—we see the germ of the Steiner–Bakhtin debate. At base are their deeply incompatible notions of the potential of epic. For Bakhtin, the epic hero is defined as a closed and ready-made character who fits neatly into a prescribed plot with no slack or superfluity. Bakhtin's novelistic hero, by contrast, is a character in whom "there always remains an unrealized surplus of humanness, there always remains a need for the future and a place for this future must be found."[4] What Steiner does, then, is graft on to his epic model a novelistic sensibility that undoes some of Bakhtin's most famous dichotomies—and, in the current theoretical climate that has turned so many Bakhtinian terms into mental reflexes, this is a provocative revision. Through it, Steiner proves himself as strong a reader of Tolstoy as Bakhtin was a weak one.

* * *

As a bridge to his second major theme, Dostoevsky as tragic dramatist, Steiner discusses Tolstoy and the drama—and specifically the most scandal-ridden corner of that question, Tolstoy and Shakespeare. Tolstoy's vitriolic 1904 essay "On Shakespeare and on Drama," with its mockery of *King Lear* and (implicitly) of *Hamlet*, contemptuously dismisses Shakespearean language as tedious vulgarity and the Bard himself as an immoral fraud. The piece has long been relegated to that category of eccentricity permitted great writers. Steiner, however, takes Tolstoy's essay more seriously. For one thing, it contains a lengthy passage praising Homer (for seriousness and neutral narrative voice) at Shakespeare's expense; this broadside appeals to Steiner, for he sees in Tolstoy's gravitation toward the virtues of the epic and its faith in a "totality of objects" a lodestar of Tolstoyan aesthetics. Second, and more importantly, Steiner correctly stresses that Tolstoy's writings on drama are not the ravings of a man who rejected or misunderstood the stage. Tolstoy was an excellent and effective playwright. He rejects not drama itself, but only what he perceives as Shakespeare's inability to produce on stage the right sort of illusion.

Accordingly, Steiner deals with Tolstoy's rejection of Shakespeare in terms of "two different types of illusion." The first type is straightforwardly false (the seduction of Natasha at the opera in *War and Peace*); the second type Steiner refers to, unsatisfyingly, as "some undefined notion of 'true illusion'" (122). Steiner's argument here would have been stronger had he considered a key text on aesthetics that Tolstoy wrote six years before the essay on Shakespeare. For the Tolstoyan paradox of a "true illusion" is not at all "undefined," but lies, with important modifications, at the base of Tolstoy's treatise *What Is Art?*

In his attempt to answer that title question, Tolstoy avoids the simple binary opposition "true–false." With his passion for inventories and lists, he constructs a much more interesting evaluative model of (at least) two axes. Along the first axis, an artwork can be true or counterfeit. If counterfeit, the art simply won't "take," that is, it will be deficient in aesthetic effect. If true, we enter more dangerous territory—for the artwork can be good (moral) or bad (immoral). According to Tolstoy, true art (presumably both moral and immoral) must satisfy three criteria: it must be nonderivative, lucid, and sincere. These three traits bring on the "infection" of the reader or spectator by those very emotions that the author experienced during the act of creation. The resultant communication—in essence an act of solidarity between artist (infector) and audience (infectee)—constitutes the mission and justification of art. But artists can have genuinely bad feelings, and people can be genuinely infected by bad art. Here is where the problem of Shakespeare becomes acute. For Tolstoy insists that Shakespeare's plays are *both* counterfeit art (derivative, worse than their literary prototypes, poorly motivated, and—unlike Homeric epic—the work of an insincere author who "does not believe in what he is saying") and bad and immoral art (tempting spectators with corrupt or obscene plots, trivial ideas, deceptive language). But if Shakespearean drama is both counterfeit and bad, how did "infection" occur? How did the entire European nineteenth century collapse into idolatry before this false playwright?

Tolstoy's answer to this paradox takes up a large part of *What Is Art?*, but Steiner—fastidiously and perhaps wisely—does not call him on it. For Tolstoy resolves the dilemma of false, immoral, and yet highly regarded art by an explanation as irrefutably crude and, as it were, somatic as the idea of infection itself, namely, "hypnosis," the baleful influence of fashionable critics and mere ugly vogue. Tolstoy's essay was not written to explicate Shakespeare, but to expose him. A glance at Tolstoy's letters and diaries of the time will easily document this preoccupation with the problem of "counterfeit reception." Tolstoy wrote to Vladimir Stasov in October 1903, for example, that the trouble with Shakespeare was not his aristocratism as much as "the perversion of aesthetic taste brought about by praise of unartistic works."[5] There is much that Steiner might have mined in this passion of Tolstoy's to unmask Shakespearean drama on behalf of the world's aesthetic health[6]—but here Steiner keeps his eyes perhaps too steadfastly to the light of his thesis about Tolstoy as epic bard. Three decades later, the author of *Real Presences* would have in Tolstoy a perfect candidate for his "republic of primary things," that hypothetical city from which all noncreating critics are banished. The nineteenth century's great Naysayer would keep that city from ever becoming a utopia.

* * *

If Tolstoy's understanding of the drama was hopelessly tied to a single voice with the authority of an epic narrator, then Dostoevsky represents for Steiner the opposite case: a novelist who looked to drama, and specifically to tragic drama, for both the structure and the spiritual focus of his novelistic world. Steiner begins chapter three with a most useful account of the nineteenth-century eclipse of tragic form. Music, darling of the Romantics, had accomplished less than had been hoped in the narrative arts, and the stage had been captured by popular melodrama and vaudeville. The "tragic vision" was thus picked up and perfected by Melville and Dostoevsky.

What does genuine drama require? In approaching this question, Steiner is both helped and hobbled by his reluctance to attend to specific requirements (or, for that matter, even simple definitions) of the novel as a genre. The essence of drama, for Steiner, is concentration, compression, "moments": all affects are piled into single mass confrontation, where it is imperative that "speech should move and motion speak" (163). In Steiner's view, however, this highly controlled and often stylized nature of drama does not in the least restrict its freedom of meaning, nor reduce it to cliché. This fact is of crucial importance for Steiner's next move, which is to attach to tragic drama, as a resolute genre attribute, what many (again, most famously Bakhtin) have considered the central achievement of the Dostoevskian polyphonic novel: the power to invest heroes and plots with genuinely free potential. As Steiner puts forward his thesis, "Dostoevsky, like all genuine dramatists, seemed to listen with an inward ear to the independent and unforeseeable dynamics of action.... [Thus] the characters seem admirably free from their creator's will and our own previsions" (173).

For Steiner, then, the "law of composition" in a Dostoevskian novel is dramatic in that it is "one of maximum energy, released over the smallest possible extent of space and time" (147). But this energy and compression are so volatile, so chemically unstable that the playwright cannot hope to do more than set up the scene, then stand back. Thus genuinely dramatic scenes always convey the sense that "things could be otherwise" (unlike, in Steiner's control case, the absolute determinedness of human action in the novels of Henry James). "The tightness, the high pitch of drama," Steiner writes, "are brought on by the interplay of ambiguous meanings, of partial ignorance with partial insight" (277). To be dramatic in Steiner's sense is not to be tied to specific unities, speech styles, or roles, but to be ever uncertain how the scene will end.

So much, then, for dramatic character in Dostoevsky, which is indeed saturated with polyphonic novelness. What about dramatic plot? At this point in chapter three, Steiner treats us to some European literary history (one of many such treats in the book) on a topic too often overlooked by Russianists. Steiner wishes to defend Dostoevsky's plots. These plots have taken a beating, both in their own and in our century—for their exaggerated pathos, their perversity, their apparent incompatibility with the sophisticated philosophy that Dostoevsky weaves around them in his novels. The extremism of these plots encourages critics (especially of the psychoanalytic persuasion) to seek in the personal psychology of their creator some abnormal or pathological core. But Steiner advises us to read Dostoevsky the creator against the background of his century, not our own. Our post-modern mentality now dismisses much of Dostoevskian thematics as low culture, as kitsch, or (in an alternative coping mechanism) we find it so repellent that we prefer to analyze it as a matter of "private obsession" (201). But violence against children, seduction of virgins, murder over mysterious inheritances, and related landscapes of eroticism, terror, and sadism were "the public material at hand"—that is, the set plots available to any European novelist, so familiar as to be almost invisible. This material was the indifferent, indeed the clichéd stock in trade of Gothic melodrama and the grotesque. The fact that Dostoevsky considered these conventions—which flooded the popular stage as well as the popular novel—to be acceptable material for high art provided him with a matchless opportunity. He could write best-sellers that compromised nothing in intellectual rigor; he could resurrect tragic drama on the basis of forms that were already part of the reading public's most basic literacy, namely, the Gothic romance.

Steiner argues this case with skill. What reservations one has about his thesis arise on different and prior ground, back at the point where the graft between drama and novel was originally joined. To take one example: in defense of his drama/novel analogy, Steiner notes at one point that "with each year, the list of dramatic adaptations of Dostoevskyan novels grows longer. During the winter of 1956–57 alone, nine 'Dostoevsky plays' were being performed in Moscow" (141). What Steiner does not note is that almost all the stage dramatizations of Dostoevskian novels have been spectacularly bad. This badness is not due to any lack of talent on the part of the playwrights; for example, Albert Camus's *Les Possédés*, a dramatization of Dostoevsky's massive novel-satire on revolutionary morality, *The Devils*, is clearly the work of an earnest and gifted writer.[7] It is simply that everything "Dostoevskian"—except for the melodramatic, Gothic skeleton of the plot—disappears.

In itself this is no bad thing, of course: adaptations need not imitate their parent texts, especially when cast in a new genre or medium. But the "derived" text must have its own vision and succeed on its own new terms. In this regard the adaptations and "dramatizations" of Dostoevsky—at least the ones with which I am familiar—fail more routinely and more miserably than do most such projects. This failure must at least partly be due to the temptation to extract that tragic-dramatic core that Steiner so clearly sees—to strip the novel of all that had obscured its originary scenic composition—and then to stop there. The sorry result is instructive, for the difference between the original and its stage adaptation is a measure of the crucial noncoincidence between the private, innerly realized world of the novel and the publicly performed world of drama. Dostoevsky may think through his plots as a dramatist, but he uses words as a novelist. As Bakhtin has argued this case, "drama is by its very nature alien to genuine polyphony: drama may be multi-leveled, but it cannot contain *multiple worlds*; it permits only one, and not several, systems of measurement."[8]

Near the end of chapter four, Steiner gives us one of those bold and lapidary juxtapositions that are his trademark. In what he engagingly calls a "myth of criticism, a fancy through which to re-direct our imaginings," he proposes "to read the Legend of the Grand Inquisitor as an allegory of the confrontation between Dostoevsky and Tolstoy" (328). There is much to recommend the exercise. The Inquisitor's indictment of Christ as carrier of "all that is exceptional, vague and enigmatic" is indeed Tolstoy's problem with the New Testament—and Tolstoy would like to replace its heady visions and parables with "thorough, unhesitating common sense" (337). Steiner does not take up the obvious counterargument, that the Inquisitor corrects Christ's work with the famous triad "miracle, mystery, authority" (hardly bastions of common sense), but never mind: in the tough old Cardinal there is not a drop of genuine humility or piety, and this is the point Steiner is resolved to make about that sophisticated pagan aristocrat, Leo Tolstoy. Dostoevsky, throughout his life passionately undecided about the nature of moral choice and deeply convinced that "no system of belief, however compelling, could confer immunity from guilt, doubt, or self-contempt,"[9] remained ever willing to take a chance on genuine mystery.

In the blunt contours of his Tolstoy–Dostoevsky comparison, Steiner is certainly correct. Many other students of the two novelists have elaborated this difference before and since, but one eloquent variant on the thesis can serve us as summary. In 1929, Prince D. S. Mirsky, the great Russian literary historian and critic then an émigré in England, observed that the problem of Tolstoy was indeed complicated—but, he added,

> I do not imply that he was a particularly complex character. There was no very great variety of ingredients to his personality. He cannot in this sense be compared to Rousseau, to Goethe, to Pushkin, or to Gogol. He was one of the most simply composed of great men.... His mind was essentially dialectical, in the Hegelian sense.... But, unlike Hegel's system, Tolstoy's mind did not surmount the contradiction of "thesis" and "antithesis" by any synthesis. Instead of Hegel's "triads," Tolstoy was all arranged in a small number of irreducible and intensely hostile

"dyads".... Dualism is the hall-mark of the ethical man. The
essence of ethics is a dualistic pattern, an irreducible opposition
between right and wrong or good and evil. As soon as a third
element is introduced, as soon as anything *one* is allowed to stand
above good and evil, the ethical point of view is adulterated and
ultimately lost.[10]

Perhaps here, through Mirsky's insight on Tolstoy, we can integrate the
various contradictory genre traits that Steiner sees in his two great subjects.
The Tolstoyan novel, for all its expansiveness and intricate multiplicity, is
"unitary" in the way the Manichean universe is unitary. Thus its epic
narrator, albeit often subtle in judgments of right and wrong, tends to keep
the audience distanced from the meanings of events and does not invite new
or uncontrolled synthesis. In contrast, the Dostoevskian novel—for all its
compression and ideologically precise juxtapositions—continually gives rise
to genuinely new confusions. In Steiner's terms, Dostoevsky's art is open-
ended dramatic conflict, with only the most minimal interference from
authorial stage directions.

* * *

How viable is Steiner's thesis today? And what is the "feel" of this classic
essay amid the comings and goings of current theory and criticism? What
strikes us first about *Tolstoy or Dostoevsky* is how wonderfully it is written. For
cadence and complex poetry of style, perhaps its only competition in Russian
studies is the highly personal prose of Isaiah Berlin. It is a truism—and, like
most truisms, largely true—that in this age of ideological criticism the plain
art of writing well has become terribly debased. Ground down by the ugly
and careless, however, it is easy to forget the power that a perfectly tuned
sentence can have. Some of Steiner's formulations stop you in your tracks.
"Both *The Death of Ivan Ilych* and *The Kreutzer Sonata* are masterpieces, but
masterpieces of a singular order," he writes. "Their terrible intensity arises
not out of a prevalence of imaginative vision but out of its narrowing; they
possess, like the dwarf-like figures in the paintings of Bosch, the violent
energies of compression" (283). Or on the urban landscape: "Dostoevsky
moved with purposeful familiarity amid a labyrinth of tenements, garrets,
railway yards, and tentacular suburbs.... Tolstoy was most thoroughly at
home in a city when it was being burnt down" (198).[11] Steiner has a special
way with the lower animals. "Gania's house [in *The Idiot*] is one of those
Dostoevskyan towers of Babel from whose dank rooms an army of characters
pours forth like dazzled bats" (159); and "D. H. Lawrence's dislike of the

Dostoevskyan manner is notorious; he hated the strident, rat-like confinement of it" (208).

Closely related to this exquisite literacy is a trait that Steiner shares with Vladimir Nabokov in the latter's pedagogic mode: an unembarrassed willingness to retell large amounts of plot and cite huge chunks of primary text. It is the sort of thing we always warn our undergraduates against: "Assume," we say, "that the person grading your paper will already know the plot." Now Steiner assumes that his readers will know a great deal—the depth, spread, and light touch of his allusions make that clear—but he nevertheless walks you, episode by episode, through twenty pages each on *Anna Karenina*, *The Idiot*, and *The Possessed*, for what seems to be the sheer pleasure and love of it. "Just look at how good this is," he appears to say over and over—much in the spirit of Nabokov's lecture notes on Chekhov and Tolstoy, which often do little more than note and annotate the primary author's moves over a wide stretch of text (when Nabokov really dislikes an author, as he does Dostoevsky, we get scornful and rather abstract analysis).[12]

On one level this is doubtless a common-sense acknowledgment that readers can love a novel but still benefit from some rehearsal of the plot before being asked to follow an analysis of its more subtle moves. More importantly, however, plot summary seems to be Steiner's way of leaving his readers with a fuller taste of the primary text than of its secondary critical effluvia. When the critic himself is a gifted writer, this is not an easy task. Although Steiner, to be sure, is much more the mediator and literary tour guide than Nabokov, both seem to nurse a nostalgia for that "city of primary things" from which critics have been banished.

A final general observation might be made on Steiner's evaluation of his own contribution to scholarship. At the end of chapter one, Steiner apologizes to the professionals in Russian literature: "I shall be approaching the Tolstoyan and Dostoevskyan texts by way of translation. This means that the work can be of no real use to scholars of Russian and to historians of Slavic languages and literature" (44). This is nonsense. If Steiner were analyzing poetry, or doing textological work and close reading for dialect or style, then of course; but the bulk of Dostoevsky's and Tolstoy's genius is eminently translatable. Furthermore, this body of work has been subject to at least as many constricting or superficial readings by native speakers and readers of Russian as by gifted outsiders. To assume that humanistic thought must always work with the grain of "original national languages" in order to make an authentic contribution to scholarship is to underestimate the power of ideas, the power of translation, and the value of great minds from different cultures working on one another.

Only occasionally does one remark the relative thinness of Steiner's sense of the Russian context, and the effect of these alien moments is negligible.[13] By and large, the benefits that Steiner's broadly cast net can bring to Slavists far outweigh the occasional local misprision. Through their richly nuanced European context, many of Steiner's readings oblige Russian literature professionals to confront yet again a question that never seems to go away: How much in Russia's great writers is irreducibly Russian (as the writers themselves, caught in a massive identity crisis along with their nation, would like to claim), and how much overlaps and duplicates the experience of Western Europe? We recall Steiner's thesis in chapter one: the European novel knew itself, but the American and Russian novel was always—and often unhappily—in search of itself.

Two examples from Tolstoy. What in the field is called a Tolstoyeved (a specialist on Tolstoy or, in the Soviet academic context, a scholar who has spent his or her life ingesting literally every text and commentary in the ninety-volume Jubilee Edition) will have a thick cloud of references to back up the genesis of every one of the master's ideas. All contradictions have already been classified; the novelist has long been a product, and at times even a prisoner, of his own extensive self-documentation. So has the Tolstoyeved. Steiner brings a different sort of ballast to the task—and, as it were, loosens Tolstoy's text for a moment from the paper trail of its author's life.

Consider the First Epilogue to *War and Peace*. Steiner reads these final domestic scenes in a highly peculiar—because so unredeemably negative—way. "'Brightness falls from the air'" (108), Steiner says. Natasha has become stout, stingy, untidy; Sonya is weary; the old Countess is senile. "The saddest metamorphosis is that of Pierre. With marriage to Natasha, he has suffered a sea-change into something neither rich nor strange" (109). "Tolstoy's iconoclasm is relentless," Steiner writes; "each character in turn is seen corroded" (109).

True, Steiner does see some small surviving light in the larger picture. The Epilogue can be read in two ways, he suggests: "In its corrosive account of the Rostov and Bezukhov marriages there is expressed Tolstoy's nearly pathological realism" (that is clearly the bad side); but there is also the good side, a formal loophole implicit in the very openness of the ending, which "proclaims the Tolstoyan conviction that a narrative form must endeavor to rival the infinity—literally, the unfinishedness—of actual experience" (112). Both are sound and possible readings. Then Steiner hints, albeit without enthusiasm, at a potential third reading: that Tolstoy, although he records "with the hard irony of a poet" all of Natasha's "parsimony, untidiness, and querulous jealousy," nevertheless does enunciate through her person "essential Tolstoyan doctrines" and thus probably intends us to applaud her "ferocious standards of monogamy and ... utter absorption in the details of childbearing" (110). What is missing, however, from this earnest postscript in redemptive reading is any serious attempt on Steiner's part to respect or, better, to understand from within, Tolstoy's own world view.

Why does this matter? Because anyone familiar with the long, subtle genesis of Tolstoy's views on families and on love will agree that the Epilogue provides us not with a "pathological realism" but with scenes of genuine prosaic bliss. In the late 1850s, in the final volume (*Youth*) of his childhood trilogy, Tolstoy outlined a three-part typology of love from which he henceforth never deviated. Types one and two—respectively, the "beautiful-romantic" and the "self-sacrificing" modes of loving—are mercilessly exposed as false and internally contradictory. Only type three, "active love," is genuinely worthy of the name, and its purpose is not to encourage in one's mate more of the "rich and strange," but rather to anticipate everyday necessities, to clarify, bind, and infiltrate the other life, to *serve the quotidian need*. Both Natasha and Marya accomplish that in their married states. Unmarried, Natasha was irresistible, yes, but she was also unstable, too full of self and uncertain where to invest it, a type one (so, for different reasons, was her brother); Sonya was, and remains at the end of the novel, a sterile type two. The rhythms of family—which Tolstoy deeply understands but never idealizes or presumes to be without cost—can only succeed with type-three lovers. In reading the Epilogue as negative and "corrosive," Steiner, the model pan-European, gives himself away. Courtly Renaissance moorings and conventional Tristan-and-Isolde reflexes in matters of love are precisely what Tolstoy has set out to refute with his scenes of everyday, and thus imperfect and real, human commitment.

Let us consider one more example. In his discussion (129–31) of Tolstoy as dramatist, Steiner devotes some time to his final play, that "colossal fragment" *The Light That Shines in the Darkness*. Steiner correctly reads the play—essentially a chunk of Tolstoy's own diaries cast in dramatic form—as an exercise in autobiography. Comparing Tolstoy with Molière, who is alleged to have "satirized his own infirmities in *Le Malade imaginaire*," Steiner asserts that "Tolstoy did something crueller: in his last, unfinished tragedy he held up to public ridicule and indictment his own most hallowed beliefs" (129). As Steiner interprets the play, its hero—the patriarch and pacifist Saryntsev—comes out the loser in almost every dramatized encounter with his family or ideological opponents. "With pitiless veracity Tolstoy shows the man's blindness, his egotism, and the ruthlessness which can inspire a prophet who believes himself entrusted with revelation.... Nowhere was Tolstoy more naked," Steiner concludes. "He presented the anti-Tolstoyan case with uncanny persuasiveness" (129).

In the light of the other writings and proclamations of Tolstoy during his final decades, this reading of the play is quite astonishing. For, however much we might wish to reassure ourselves, there is little indication that Tolstoy meant us to see Saryntsev, the light that shone in the darkness, as blind or ruthless. On the contrary, Saryntsev was making morally correct choices. The outer world—the outer darkness—would inevitably judge these acts in terms of the suffering they brought others and thus call them blind or cruel. That cruelty, however, is the inescapable byproduct of ethically consistent behavior and must be borne.

The dilemma here thus resembles the one surrounding Prince Myshkin in *The Idiot*: by his Christ-like goodness, the prince ruins every life he touches. How does Dostoevsky resolve this disagreeable truth? Steiner is very good on Myshkin in this regard: "The 'idiot' is love incarnate," Steiner writes, "but in him love itself is not made flesh.... Myshkin's 'crime' is the excess of compassion over love" (171). Such humility, alas, is not Tolstoy's. Tolstoy was unable to finish his final play, I suggest, not because he was embarrassed or stricken by the "pitiless veracity" of its hero's failure—but because Tolstoy, as playwright, had not yet found a way to make his point of view more irresistibly persuasive. Tolstoy was no advocate of the overly clever "problem play." Rather, he believed in the theater as a crucible for the right sort of "infection," one whose first task was to move human feelings. Mere outrageousness or run-of-the-mill unhappiness hardly mattered to the rightness of a moral position (witness Tolstoy's relish at the scandal over "The Kreutzer Sonata," and his subsequent insistence that he stood personally behind its plea for marital celibacy). In short, the unfinishedness of *The Light That Shines in the Darkness* can sooner be attributed to Tolstoy's frustration over the proper portrayal of his "positive hero"—in this sense, the parallels with Dostoevsky's quest are sharp and intriguing—than to any special discomfort on the part of Tolstoy at his own "nakedness" in a perfectly crafted self-parody.

In both these readings, Steiner reads and reacts as a sophisticated, culturally flexible European, a genuine comparativist. Inevitably, some of his balanced good sense and breadth rub off on his subject. For Slavists who read Tolstoy and Dostoevsky within these novelists' own more savage, insecure worlds, this can be an excellent and often enlightening corrective. In this connection we might note an instructive equivalent to Steiner among world-class scholars working on Russian themes today: Joseph Frank. Frank learned

Russian late, made a mid-career shift to Slavistics, and is currently completing this century's definitive biography of Dostoevsky.[14] In a territory dominated by mystic philosophy and messianic overstatement, the intricate, refined European underpinnings of the scholar are everywhere in evidence. "The Dostoevsky who emerges from Frank's pages is a man far less singular, impassioned, extreme than he is usually conceived to be," Donald Fanger has written in a review of the biography's third volume; scrupulous attention to evidence and sifting of legend brings the life story much more into the European mainstream, and what extremism there is finds its place "through a process of osmosis that lets Frank's own sovereign balance and reasonableness seep into the character he is recreating."[15] At crucial moments in his own essay, Steiner has much the same civilizing, almost "airbrushing" effect on the image of his two unruly Russian master novelists.

* * *

In conclusion let me return to the comparison, mentioned in the opening pages of this essay, between Steiner and Bakhtin. In Steiner's poetics, Tolstoy is at heart an epic writer, and Dostoevsky is a tragic dramatist. In Bakhtin's poetics, neither novelist by definition can be either of those things—because the essence of the novel lies, first, in transcending the stasis and impenetrable "absolute distance" of epic, and second, in surpassing the easy performability and mere "compositional dialogue" (almost always monologic) characteristic of drama. For Steiner, the "epic" aspects of Tolstoy are revealed in a lack of sentimentality, in a passion for the pitiless effect of circumstances and things on human beings, and in a pagan insistence that all moral dilemmas must be resolved in *this* world—without recourse to the miracles, mysteries, and authorities of God. Aspects of Tolstoyan aesthetics that do not fit the Homeric model (Tolstoy's rejection of heroism, for example) Steiner does not hide, but he also does not elaborate. Well he might not, because to a very large extent Tolstoy's militant antiheroicism is what makes the Tolstoyan novel what it is.

The case is more complex with the analogy between Dostoevsky and tragic drama. At the base of the problem is Steiner's rather uncomplicated notion of dialogue, which he sees as a continuum from its novelistic to its stage-drama poles. "It should be noted," Steiner remarks in his discussion of *The Idiot*, "that our difficulties in perceiving all the levels of action at a first reading [of this scene in the novel] are strictly comparable to the difficulties we experience when first hearing a complex piece of dramatic dialogue in the theater" (161). But they are not "strictly comparable" at all, if readers of the novel attend to the intricate layers and "voice zones" that permeate even the simplest narrative filler between slices of direct speech. Bakhtin's major concern—how words work in novels—is not Steiner's. That Steiner does not engage his texts at this level has little to do with the language barrier and much to do with the indwelling "unspeakability" of novelistic worlds (especially Dostoevsky's worlds), their potential to be several voices at once, and thus their resistance to even the most subtle intonation on stage—which would embody them too aggressively and thus flatten them out.

At several points, Steiner aligns Dostoevsky with the Aristotelian notions of dramatic catharsis (213) and a fusion of "'thought' with 'plot'" (228). Significantly, Bakhtin resists both these moves. "Tragic catharsis (in the Aristotelian sense) is not applicable to Dostoevsky," Bakhtin writes. "The catharsis that finalizes Dostoevsky's novels might be—of course inadequately and somewhat rationalistically—expressed this way: *nothing conclusive has yet taken place in the world, the ultimate word of the world and about the world has not yet been spoken, the world is open and free, everything is still in the future and will always be in the future.*"[16] Steiner intimates the radical freedom of Dostoevsky's characters, their freedom both from "their creator's will and our own previsions." He senses the polyphony that Bakhtin makes explicit, but then he attaches it to the dramatic, not to the novelistic.

There are advantages to Steiner's thesis. Among them is that his "dramatization" of Dostoevsky's verbal art can serve as robust corrective to some of Bakhtin's blind spots. One such spot shows up with special naivete in the latter's discussion of *Notes from Underground*, which Bakhtin reads rather benevolently in terms of "words with a loophole," the permanent noncoincidence of a self with itself, and the right of selves to counter every word cast in their direction with a new, fresh, free word.[17] Equipped with his less permeable definition of the word, Steiner sees the matter more darkly. In his reading—not an uncommon pattern for postwar readings of Dostoevsky—the mission of the Underground is to "lay bare the hypocrisies of high rhetoric" (218), and the failure of the Underground Man is connected not with the abused glory but with the shame of being human (225–26).

Here a return to Joseph Frank is in order, for he also resists Bakhtin, and in ways that Steiner would find compelling. The major difference between these two pan-European comparativists on this masterwork of Russian literature can be found in Frank's insistence that Dostoevsky, in giving voice to the dilemma of the Underground, is not an existentialist— that is, in no way does he endorse its dead ends and rhetorical traps as necessary complements to human freedom. Frank reads *Notes from Underground* as ice-cold Swiftian satire, as a deadly serious parody of certain patterns (absorbed naïvely and uncritically from the West) in Russian intellectual thought.[18]

According to Frank, some of these utopian patterns—such as the "rational egoism" of Chernyshevsky—are seductive, even compelling, but a head-on, negating resistance to them (the task of the Underground) is neither dialogic nor liberating. The Underground Man desperately seeks a moral anchor. Steiner misses the parody. He, too, posits the tragic nature of the Underground, but sees Dostoevsky buying in to it, sympathetic to its merciless "critique of reason" (227) and thus also to a human being's no-exit entrapment by this critique. Wedded as he is to the monologic notion of Dostoevsky as dramatic tragedian, Steiner has trouble detecting the independent—and polemically untrustworthy—voices of Dostoevsky's narrators.

To conclude, then. In this refitting of Tolstoy and Dostoevsky back into epic and tragedy, that is, into the two genres most central to a classical poetics, we feel most palpably the "oldness" of Steiner's Old Criticism. This sense of the richness of the old, its ever-present relevance, is surely one of the most liberating aspects of Steiner's essay. For in contrast to so much in modern critical practice that reduces the past to a pale, and always inadequate, reflection of the values and politics of the present moment, Steiner starts with the assumption that all great literature is richer than any single subsequent time could possibly appreciate in full.

Again, Bakhtin might be an appropriate guide to Steiner's larger intent. In 1970, near the end of his life, Bakhtin was invited by the editorial board of Russia's leading literary journal to comment on the future of Soviet literary studies. In his open letter Bakhtin wrote: "Authors and their contemporaries see, recognize and evaluate primarily that which is close to their own day. The author is a captive of his epoch, of his own present. Subsequent times liberate him from this captivity, and literary scholarship is called upon to assist in this liberation."[19] Now "liberation" is a fighting word. But in his letter Bakhtin intends the word in a sense quite contrary to the radical intent so commonly invested in it by radical critics. For Bakhtin, "liberation" meant a *suspicion* of the impulse to measure all of past culture by the social or political standards of the present day. Precisely that narrowing of vision makes an author—and a reader—a "captive of his or her own epoch." Releasing us from that captivity is the most important service that other times, past and future, can render us; this is *what great novels are for*. Thus to "liberate authors from their epochs" is not to read them into contexts that are immediately politically relevant. In Bakhtin's world view, more likely the opposite obtains: to liberate authors is to make them as open as possible to as many times as possible.

This conviction lies at the base of Steiner's critical world view as well. In *Real Presences* he takes severely to task the hardcore pretensions of literary theory—starting with the "absolutely decisive failing" that occurs when theoretical approaches attempt more than linguistic description and classification, "when such approaches seek to formalize meaning."[20] In *Tolstoy and Dostoevsky*, the ancient past is revealed as a richly surprising source for present relevance. Or, as Bakhtin put this point, "Dostoevsky has not yet become Dostoevsky, he is still becoming him."[21] More than anything, such faith qualifies George Steiner as a resident in his own republic of primary things.

NOTES

1. The book was first published in 1959. All citations for this essay are taken from George Steiner, *Tolstoy or Dostoevsky: An Essay in the Old Criticism* (New York: Dutton, 1971). Page numbers are included in parentheses in the text.

2. In his discussion of Tolstoy's religious beliefs, Steiner presciently notes what later scholars have amply documented, that despite Tolstoy's much-advertised "conversion" of 1881–82, continuity rather than break was the norm: "Actually, most of the ideas and beliefs expounded by the later Tolstoy appear in his earliest writings and the live substance of his morality was plainly discernible during the years of apprenticeship" (242). For a comprehensive exposition of this continuity thesis, see Richard F. Gustafson, *Leo Tolstoy: Resident and Stranger* (Princeton: Princeton University Press, 1986).

3. Gary Saul Morson, *Hidden in Plain View: Narrative and Creative Potentials in "War and Peace"* (Stanford: Stanford University Press, 1987).

4. Mikhail Bakhtin, "Epic and Novel," in *The Dialogic Imagination: Four Essays by M. M. Bakhtin*, ed. Michael Holquist (Austin: University of Texas Press, 1981), 37.

5. Leo Tolstoy to V. V. Stasov, 9 October 1903, *Tolstoy's Letters*, ed. and trans. R. F. Christian, 2 Vols., Vol. 2: *1880–1910* (New York: Scribner's Sons, 1978), 633.

6. The absurdity of Tolstoy's argument is clear in this crude form, but it is sobering—and not reassuring—to see how his idea (on the baleful

influence of fashionable critics and vogue) has resurfaced in current politicized theory of literary value.

7. In his "Preface" to the play, Camus reinforces much of the Steiner thesis: "For almost twenty years ... I have visualized its characters on the stage. Besides having the stature of dramatic characters, they have the appropriate behavior, the explosions, the swift and disconcerting gait. Moreover, Dostoevsky uses a theater technique in his novels: he works through dialogues with few indications as to place and action.... And yet I am well aware of all that separates the play from that amazing novel! I merely tried to follow the book's undercurrent and to proceed as it does from satiric comedy to drama and then to tragedy. Both the original and the dramatic adaptation start from a certain realism and end up in tragic stylization." For an English version, see Albert Camus, *The Possessed: A Play*, trans. Justin O'Brien (New York: Vintage Books, 1960).

8. Mikhail Bakhtin, *Problems of Dostoevsky's Poetics*, ed. and trans. Caryl Emerson (Minneapolis: University of Minnesota Press, 1984), 34. Later Bakhtin expands on the implications for stage performance: double-voiced language of the sort we get in dialogic novels "is difficult to speak aloud, for loud and living intonation excessively monologizes discourse and cannot do justice to the other person's voice present in it" (198).

9. The phrase is Aileen Kelly's. See her excellent essay "Dostoevsky and the Divided Conscience," *Slavic Review* 47, no. 2 (Summer 1988): 239–60, esp. 239.

10. D. S. Mirsky, "Some Remarks on Tolstoy," *London Mercury* 20 (1929): 167–75, reprinted in *D. S. Mirsky: Uncollected Writings on Russian Literature*, ed. G. S. Smith (Berkeley: Berkeley Slavic Specialties, 1989), 304.

11. One compromising side effect of Steiner's relentless pursuit of elegance, however, is a certain rhetorical imprecision: "railway yards" and "tentacular suburbs" are not really characteristic of Dostoevsky's cities, but rather of novels by Dickens or Zola set in Paris and London—or by an American novelist such as Theodore Dreiser.

12. Compare, for example, Nabokov's admiring discussions of *Anna Karenina*, "The Death of Ivan Ilych," and "The Lady with the Little Dog"— all annotated plot summaries—with his vituperative putdown of Dostoevsky's banal plots and "neurotic" heroes. Vladimir Nabokov, *Lectures on Russian Literature* (New York: Harcourt Brace, 1981).

13. It shows in conventions of Russian naming and address: discussing *The Idiot*, Steiner properly refers to "Gania" and "Aglaya," but does not sense why one must call the heroine (a well-bred woman of experience) "Nastasya

Filippovna," by name and patronymic as Dostoevsky always does, never just "Nastasya" as is Steiner's habit.

Only once does Steiner hazard an important thematic point based on an uncertain detail in translation. Nastasya Filippovna, having cast Rogozhin's one hundred thousand rubles into the flames and rejected Gania's suit, flees with Rogozhin. To Myshkin she shouts: "Farewell, Prince, for the first time I've seen a human being" [Prosh chai, kniaz, v pervyi raz ya cheloveka videla]. Working with an inadequate English version—"I have seen man for the first time in my life"—and unaware of Russian's lack of definite and indefinite articles, Steiner makes a questionable call. He wants to hear in Nastasya Filippovna's parting words to the Prince that she has seen "man" in all his "extremes of nobility and corruption" (168), but in Russian the addressee of her final cry is not "man" in general, but clearly the saintly person of Myshkin—to whom the heroine will compulsively return.

Imprecise labeling also somewhat miscasts discussion of *Notes from Underground* (20–28). Steiner refers to this work throughout as "Letters from the Underworld"—quite wrong. They are not letters but *zapiski*, "jottings" or "notes," an honorable nineteenth-century Russian genre with an important genealogy (Gogol, Turgenev, and Tolstoy all wrote works with that title). Not only is the Underground Man not composing an epistolary novel; part of his agony is precisely that he doubts he will have any addressees or readers at all. And—attending to the second half of the title—to render the Russian *podpol'e* ("underground" or "under the floorboards") as the "underworld" suggests Lucian ("Dialogues with the Dead") and other pagan satires. Steiner does indeed invoke this classical subtext (216), but it is arguably inappropriate to Dostoevsky's work, with its painful Christian genesis.

Likewise, in his treatment of the conflagration that closes *The Possessed*, Steiner begins at his own most "at-home" point, which is precise to the extent that it is Europe (i.e., Flaubert's reaction to the incendiarism of the Paris Commune) and increasingly blurred as we move closer to Russia itself. The fires that end the novel are indeed linked with "the traditional Russian theme of a fiery apocalypse" (183), but they were directly inspired by the real-life burning of Saint Petersburg in the spring of 1862. The nefarious campaign to pin blame for these events on the new generation of "nihilists" in the capital deeply agitated Dostoevsky.

14. Three volumes by Joseph Frank have so far appeared: *Dostoevsky: The Seeds of Revolt, 1821–1849* (1976); *Dostoevsky: The Years of Ordeal, 1850–1859* (1983); and *Dostoevsky: The Stir of Liberation, 1860–65* (1986), all by Princeton University Press.

15. Donald Fanger, "Turning Point" (a review of *Dostoevsky: The Stir of Liberation*), *New Republic* 196 (27 April 1987): 42.

16. Bakhtin, *Problems of Dostoevsky's Poetics*, 165–66. Emphasis in original.

17. Ibid., 50–54.

18. In an elaborate footnote near the end of chap. 21 in his *Dostoevsky: The Stir of Liberation* (346), very much in Steiner's capacious spirit, Joseph Frank comments on his own weaning from the Bakhtinian world view. There he resists two of Bakhtin's most colorful claims: first, that Dostoevsky was the founder of a "wholly new kind of polyphonic novel," and second, that Dostoevsky's novels are best understood as part of an ancient tradition of Menippean satire (the so-called carnivalesque) rather than the more accessible, and much more readily documented, tradition of eighteenth- and nineteenth-century European literature. In reading the *Notes from Underground* as satire, not as morbid philosophical truth, Frank cuts through a century of sentimentalism and existential despair. This satire has nothing to do with Menippean satire or carnival, with their rejuvenating guffaws, blasphemous mumbo jumbo, indestructible bodies, and easy exchange of masks; and it also is distant from the benign scenario in Bakhtin's Dostoevsky book, where even the tortured moves of the Underground Man come to represent a celebration of unrealized potential, the right to postpone forever the final word.

19. M. M. Bakhtin, "Reply to a Question from the *Novy Mir* Editorial Staff," in *Speech Genres and Other Late Essays*, trans. Vern W. McGee (Austin: University of Texas Press, 1986), 5.

20. George Steiner, *Real Presences* (Chicago: University of Chicago Press, 1989), 81. Steiner defines literature (and art and music as well) as "the maximalization of semantic incommensurability in respect of the formal means of expression" (83).

21. Mikhail Bakhtin, "Toward a Reworking of the Dostoevsky Book [1961]," in *Problems of Dostoevsky's Poetics*, 291.

W. GARETH JONES

A Man Speaking to Men:
The Narratives of War and Peace

I

Entranced by a night spent outside a military camp in the Caucasus in 1851, the twenty-three-year-old Tolstoy wrote in his diary, 'I thought—I'll go and describe what I see. But how to write it? One needs to go and sit down at an ink-stained desk, take some grey paper and ink; get one's fingers dirty and trace letters on the paper. The letters make up words, the words—sentences; but is it possible to convey the feeling? Is it not possible somehow to pour into another man one's view at the sight of nature?' (*J.E.*, vol. XLVI, p. 65). The young soldier was discomfited by the artificiality of writing, by an awareness of the fallibility of words. But in this jotting he had already signalled that the aim of writing for him went beyond composing something of intrinsic worth, poetry so well wrought that it could pretend to an independent existence. Parable would later be exalted by Tolstoy over poetry; not merely because the former carried a moral message, but because the parable was an art of performance, 'pouring one's view into another man', demanding an attentive and responsive listener. Writing for him, as for Wordsworth, meant 'a man speaking to men', and Tolstoy would occasionally enhance this sense of public performance by equating writing with singing to his fellow men. In the sketches for his *Childhood*, for example,

From *New Essays on Tolstoy*, edited by Malcolm Jones. © 1978 by Cambridge University Press.

it was to music that he turned for an analogy to explain his new kind of writing that would avoid stale convention in its direct 'anti-poetic' appeal to his reader. Significantly, it was not the musician as creative composer that suggested himself to Tolstoy but the *performing* artist; the image that he held of himself was not that of the song writer, but of the singer, intent on affecting his audience.

What is remarkable about Tolstoy is that he never saw himself as a solitary singer set apart from a world of passive listeners. His world's stage was peopled by men and women with their own voices, speaking and singing parts they had fashioned for themselves, listening as responsively as an audience for parables. So were his novels. For it was this Tolstoyan understanding that inspired his works: human society consisted of men, each pouring his feelings into another. His creatures live on the page because they too, like him, make sense of existence by narrating their experiences to each other. One must see *War and Peace* not as a single narrative issuing from one author, but as a dynamic pattern of many narratives, constantly varied and inter-reacting. To be Tolstoy's reader, so far as this novel is concerned, one's response must be not to the author's tale, but to the work's many narratives.

For Tolstoy was accustomed to imagine his fictional characters, like himself, as performers; often his creatures, in contrast to those of other novelists, do not engage in private conversation, cogitation or reflection but hold forth publicly, narrating, recounting or 'telling stories'—*rasskazyvat'* is the Russian verb for which it is difficult to find a single English equivalent. They speak to a company who respond as a distanced audience to a ritualised performance. So at the beginning of *War and Peace*, Prince Vasily talks 'like an actor speaking lines from an old play', Anna Scherer enthuses 'in order not to disappoint people's expectations' (I.i.1), the vicomte de Mortemart is introduced as 'un parfait conteur' (I.i.3). Much time and mental energy was spent by Tolstoy in the search for a beginning that would set his *War and Peace* in motion; over a dozen false starts are recorded. What is significant about the final choice—the description of a soirée at which the main protagonists are guests was hardly a fresh solution—is the way in which modes of narration, or communication between people, are presented and examined. It is as if Tolstoy, on the threshold of his own story-telling, wished to put his reader on his guard against its conventions and artifice by demonstrating to him different kinds of narration. First there is the polish and assurance of the vicomte de Mortemart's refined reciting of a scabrous anecdote about Napoleon and the duc d'Enghien, a piece of society gossip greeted with delight by his audience. Set against that, the earnest conversation of Pierre and the abbé Morio on the balance of power is shown, for all its sincerity, to be out of place and awkward. In Anna Scherer's salon, the *well told* anecdote, however superficial, always wins more attention than any attempt to bumble out the truth. Even a nonsensical buffoon's tale from Prince Hippolyte gains more respect than Pierre's honest theorising.

What is happening in these early scenes, as the reader commits himself to the long journey through Tolstoy's novel, is that the author is signalling to him some of the curious relationships between the man who tells the story and his listener. An attempt to tell the honest truth unconventionally, as by Pierre, is met with resistance; there may be more real communing, not only in the retailing of superficial gossip related with polished art, but even in twaddle such as Hippolyte's nonsense tale which makes everyone stop to listen and applaud (I.i.4).

Without making any separate declaration on the nature of his art, Tolstoy had embedded within his own narrative the awareness that had come to him under the Caucasian night sky: experience cannot be conveyed directly to another; the paraphernalia of art is necessary for any human communication. The same realisation had been fused into the narrative of *The Raid* (1853), where Captain Khlopov, so rich in life's experiences, can only seek to convey those experiences to a young volunteer by suggesting that he read the historian Mikhaylovsky-Danilevsky and chat to a young poet in the regiment (chapter 1). Aware that experienced truth was invariably modified by the artifices needed for its transmission, Tolstoy felt impelled to alert his reader to the extent to which he was being manipulated by fiction's conventions. So, as *War and Peace* was set in motion, its reader was warned to distrust its apparent solidity and fascination.

This insinuation into his fiction of passages that encouraged the reader to determine consciously his own attitude to narrative (whether to listen avidly along with most of Anna Scherer's guests, or turn away in disgust as Prince Andrey did from the anecdote about Napoleon) was not new for Tolstoy. If the examination of the relationship between narrator and audience is there at the beginning of *War and Peace* as it was in *The Raid*, it lay too at the foundation of Tolstoy's first published work, *Childhood*. In the sketches for that work, it is apparent how much more important enthralling and moving his reader was for Tolstoy than weaving verbal patterns. By the final version, a perusal of the bond between author and audience had been incorporated into the fiction in the central chapter 'Verses' where the boy, Nikolenka, faced with the task of producing a present for his grandmother's name-day, recites a poem for her. It is not as an entertainer that Nikolenka is presented but as an embryonic Tolstoyan narrator, beset with disgust and self-doubt, and fearful of his reception. In the boy's composing, Tolstoy revealed to his reader the inspiration, doggedness, plagiarism and posing involved in producing an inherently false communication to the listener of an initially sincere impulse.

There are times in *War and Peace* when Tolstoy becomes almost Brechtian in the relentless warning to his readers against being swept along by his narrative, particularly of the historical and military events. Again, however, no separate artistic manifesto is apparent; rather we are allowed, as in *Childhood*, to see the relationship between narrator and audience developing between the fictive characters. Inevitably, in such a work as *War and Peace*, with character and episodes embedded in a historical chronicle, the registering of event, time, place, conversation bears the novel along. Is Nikolay Rostov's arrival in Tilsit significant because he arrived there on 27 June 1807? Tolstoy's noting of that day is reminiscent of the conventional chronicler: 'That day, 27 June, the first conditions of peace were signed. The Emperors exchanged orders: Alexander received the Légion d'Honneur, and Napoleon the St Andrew 1st Class, and that day a dinner was arranged for the Preobrazhensky regiment given to it by a battalion of the French Guards' (II.i.19). Yet this sort of brisk narrative of Tolstoy's, making immediate the public, historical framework for private happenings, had just been put in question in the previous chapter where Boris Drubetskoy's habit of noting down particulars, even at the Tilsit meeting between the Emperors, had been mocked. It is Boris here who stands for the typical writer who stores up material with which he will later seek to affect an audience. Not only does he make a note of the persons present and their uniforms, but is meticulous about logging time: 'At the very moment when the emperors entered the pavilion, he looked at his watch and did not forget to look again at the moment when Alexander left the pavilion. The meeting had lasted 1 hour 53 minutes: that is what he noted that evening among other facts which he supposed had historical significance' (II.i.19). This ironic comment on memoir writing that concentrates on surface detail while telling nothing about the true condition of human relationship is again made through a narrating character, one of the 'performers' in the fiction, and not by Tolstoy himself. Ironically, it gives the reader an eloquent warning against narrative chronology used with effect by the author of *War and Peace*.

If Tolstoy wished to warn his reader against the conventional chronicling of diplomatic history, he was even more intent on setting him on guard against the narration of military exploits. And on guard against the reader's own craving for the conventional. It is through Nikolay Rostov—as much, surely, an emanation of Tolstoy's self as Prince Andrey and Pierre— and his recital of Schöngraben, that Tolstoy persuades his own reader to understand that however truthful a narrator would wish to be, he is swayed from the truth by his audience that is bound to rely on conventional signals. Transparent truth cannot be seen. Art's untruth springs not necessarily from the maliciousness of an embellishing narrator, but is demanded by an audience that relies on the conventional. So does Nikolay's audience: 'They expected an account of how he was all on fire, beside himself, how he rushed like a storm at the square; how he was hacked at, while striking to left and right; how a sabre cut into his flesh and he fell into oblivion, and so on. And he recounted all that for them' (I.iii.7). It is interesting that Tolstoy had once shared Rostov's feelings. In his note to the fourth volume of the Tolstoy Centenary Edition *Tales of Army Life*, Aylmer Maude recalled that 'One day, when talking about Sevastopol, he [Tolstoy] told me that when writing these sketches he was aware that, contending with his desire to tell the truth as he saw it, there was another feeling prompting him to say what was expected of him.' The point is made clearly to the reader of *War and Peace* that there are conventional ways of recounting battles that are inherently false; paradoxically it is only these false strokes that can shape an experience for an audience. Tolstoy does not propose to spurn these conventions, but would like his reader to be aware of them, and see *through* them to the real experience.

The lesson is well placed: the probing of Nikolay's 'imperceptible, involuntary and inevitable' slide into untruth must modify the reader's acceptance of the description of Andrey's wounding which follows shortly. At Austerlitz, from the moment that Prince Andrey shouts 'Hurrah!' and raises the standard to rally his men, the charge is recounted in a conventional manner. It is with the panache of jingoistic literature that the scene is told initially: the banner is held aloft, bullets whistle, men fall to left and right of our hero—it is as if we are listening again to Nikolay entertaining his audience. Already prepared by the insight into the gap between the conventional style of Nikolay's story of Schöngraben and the true experience which it obscured, the reader, following Andrey's charge, is swept along by the vigorous conventional description, but simultaneously suspects the truthfulness of the account. He may remember that it was this same Prince Andrey who had stemmed Nikolay's increasingly impassioned narrative, borne beyond convention into cliché, silencing him with his unexpected appearance. The reader is, therefore, prepared for the sudden dissolution of the conventional here as the same Andrey asks 'What are they doing?' on seeing the wordless but mortal tug-of-war between a French and Russian soldier. From that point on, we are subject to a new narrative technique—but not at the expense of old conventions.

If the experience of warfare, as indeed all human experience, was beyond man's ability to comprehend and narrate, why should Tolstoy have persisted so long with his writing? Tolstoy mediates his answer through a Nikolay Rostov made fully conscious of the perils of communication between men. After his experience of Austerlitz and the 1807 campaigns, Nikolay had realised that 'in recounting military events, men always lie, as he himself had lied while recounting' (III.i.12). So it is with shame that he listens to an overblown account of a patriotic exploit by General Rayevsky while providing his own debunking gloss to the narration in his mind. Yet he does not object to the narration. And the reason that Nikolay gives to himself might well be Tolstoy's apologia for continuing to write fiction, despite his rage for the truth. Such narration, he came to realise, even if it failed to communicate experience fully, had a particular justification: despite its falsity it exerted an independent moral force and enabled men to commune with each other in society. For Tolstoy this was no new revelation. The earlier Nikolenka of *Childhood* had also realised, as a consumer of literature, the way in which the lie of art enhanced the art of living. The vividness of the children's games was sharpened by their imitation of *Swiss Family Robinson*. Although Nikolenka knew as well as his supercilious elder brother Volodya that a stick was not a gun, his play was all the more intense if he pretended. The rhetorical question posed by the child to close the chapter 'Games' in *Childhood*, might still be the one for Nikolay Rostov to ponder over: 'If one is to judge by reality, then there would be no play. And without play, what would remain?' (chapter 8).

II

If the Nikolenka of *Childhood* was unsettled—and the reader in consequence—by his growing awareness of the fictive fluidity of verses, and story-based games, he was no more secure in the language, or it would be more correct to say languages, that shaped the expression of his experiences. *War and Peace*, which has been called a bilingual novel for its large use of French, was by no means the first work in which Tolstoy had troubled the reader with a foreign language. If *War and Peace* begins in French, then the first spoken dialogue in *Childhood* is in German between Karl Ivanich, the family tutor, and Nikolenka. While the use of German may be explained as historical colouring, as the work progresses we become aware that Tolstoy intended to present his child as one conscious of the lack of security afforded by human speech. Although the mother speaks Russian with the children, her own mother tongue, and the one she employs for her intimate thoughts, is German. The shift of language is noticed by the child as he perceives that French is used at the dinner table formally to exclude Grigory, the holy fool, from the community around the table. Foreign idiom was a means for Tolstoy to intimate to his reader his sense of the fragility of language as a means of communication.

The use of French, and to a lesser extent German, in *War and Peace* as well, is a means by which the reader is made aware of the linguistic texture of the fictional work. Too aware, perhaps, for many early reviewers—not only the young radical nationalist critics, but also Tolstoy's aristocratic friends—protested against an apparent over-indulgence in French. Indeed the novel begins with a sentence whose single Russian word is used as a calculated disparagement, 'Eh bien, mon prince, Gênes et Lucques ne sont plus que des apanages, des *pomest'ya*, de la famille Buonaparte' (i.i.1). Since it is Anna Scherer who speaks these words, it would seem natural for her to speak French and so it seemed to the editors of the jubilee Edition who maintained that *War and Peace* would make no sense without French since French was an 'integral accessory to the way of life of the upper class at the beginning of the nineteenth century'. Had they chosen to follow the 1873 edition in which the French had been translated, they argued, many of the characters, such as Anna Scherer, Hippolyte Kuragin, Bilibin, Napoleon, Kutuzov, Alexander I, would lose some of their individual quality. It was roughly these reasons—historical and dramatic—that Tolstoy himself gave as a rational justification for his apparently excessive use of French. Prompted by subsequent criticism from friends, however, Tolstoy allowed the 1873 edition to appear not only with the removal of his philosophical and historical discursions, but with all the French translated. This he did, however, with some regret. The use of French, despite what Tolstoy's editors and Tolstoy as editor of his own work suggested, goes far beyond the need for local colouring. Could he not have merely indicated the use of French, as contemporary critics suggested? There are times when Tolstoy does indeed state that his characters whose dialogue is given in Russian, are conversing in French; this is true even in the case of Andrey and Natasha. Furthermore the abundant gallicisms of the novel might have been sufficient to preserve the local historical colouring. However, French is not merely used for historical *vraisemblance*. Sometimes it would appear that French is used to stress artificiality of sentiment and attitude, as opposed to the genuineness of Russian: it is the language in which Pierre proposes to Hélène, the language in which Hélène addresses Natasha at the opera. For Andrey, it is not only Natasha's gaiety and shyness that are a mark of her naturalness, but her mistakes in French. However, some characters manage to be intensely Russian despite their French, such as Kutuzov with his fondness for Madame de Genlis' novels and French proverbs, or Bilibin who showed an 'exceptionally Russian fearlessness before self-judgement and self-mockery' in a long letter to Prince Andrey despite his writing it 'in French with French jokes and turns of phrase' (II.ii.8). Bilibin is one of the most conscious of Tolstoy's narrating characters, producing memorable phrases in his 'inner laboratory' that insignificant people could carry from drawing-room to drawing-room. And one of the features that ensures that the reader grasps the mechanical precision of Bilibin's narrations is his skill at mixing French and Russian, 'saying in Russian only those words which he wished to emphasise disparagingly' (I.ii.10).

It is this mingling of French with Russian which is met in the novel's first sentence, rather than the use of French itself that makes the reader linguistically unsettled, as were the early critics who would have felt more comfortable in the presence of *War and Peace* had Tolstoy spiked his Russian with less French. It was an experience that the English reader of Jane Austen, or even Dickens with his idiosyncratic idiom, never endured: English, the common mother tongue of writer and reader, ensured some stability in their relationship. Even this bedrock of communication was deliberately undermined by Tolstoy. The insidious French in his narrative is subversive, alerting the reader to the transience of language and the words used by the writer to communicate with him. In excusing his use of French in *A Few Words about 'War and Peace'*, Tolstoy drew an analogy with the formal texture of a painting. The French, he explained, was akin to the dark patches used by a painter: they may be perceived as shadows, but the naive eye sees them as black blobs. 'I would only wish that those who find it amusing that Napoleon speaks Russian and French in turn, would realise that they find it so only because they, like a man looking at a portrait, see not a face with light and shade, but a black patch under a nose' (*J.E.*, vol. XVI, pp. 8–9). However, what is striking about the analogy is how Tolstoy reveals his awareness that his use of French actually encouraged his reader to see through the conventional deceptive shadows of the artist to the dark, crude blobs of paint at the base of his craft. Language, too, may be as inexpressive as a paint pot.

Differing languages disturb the reader; he shares the experience of Prince Andrey, conscious of confusion on the battlefield when he hears the Babel of a multi-lingual exchange. 'Pfuel ... shouted angrily even at Wolzogen "Nun ja, was soll denn da noch expliziert werden?"—Paulucci and Michaud in a duet attacked Wolzogen in French. Armfelt addressed Pfuel in German. Tot explained it in Russian to Prince Bolkonsky. Prince Andrey listened in silence, and observed' (III.i.11).

III

It is that coolly observant listener, like Andrey, that Tolstoy would have liked his reader to be. Our discussion to this point has attempted to bring out the way in which, through his 'narrating' characters, Tolstoy has warned his reader against the deceit of story-telling. In wishing to make the reader aware in this way of the ritual of narration, Tolstoy seeks to elicit a special response from him, engaging him in the particular conspiracy in which the true novelist would wish to embroil his reader.

Readers of *War and Peace*, will, of course, object that they are surely not always treated by Tolstoy as cool, aristocratic observers of the world's stage. Sometimes there is a direct appeal to us as one of a mutinous mob. The coarse demagogic address is particularly apparent in Tolstoy's excursions into historiography. By showing the absurdity of other versions of historical events, he suggests that it must follow that 'ours'—that is, the author and reader in collusion—our version must be true. Dealing with the battle of Borodino, Tolstoy gave his own precis of the view of 'all historians' and then declared with the most conventional of debating ploys: 'That is what the histories say, and all that is completely unjust, which can easily be vouched for by anybody who wishes to look into the essentials of the matter' (III.ii.19). In then giving a revised account of Borodino, Tolstoy flatters the reader; we feel that we are privileged to know more about the battle than any learned historian. Again at the beginning of part iii we have the same tub-thumper's appeal to his audience: historians are wrong is the message, the implication being—and it is never more than an implication—that Tolstoy is right. And the debater's claim is supported by crude, simplistic mechanistic images: any fool can realise that it is not the hands of a clock that cause church bells to ring, nor is it its whistle that sets a locomotive running.

Yet even when his demagoguery is at its most effective, we find Tolstoy recoiling from it and subjecting it to the same criticism as other forms of conventional communication. One of the most effective of the scenes debunking historiography is that in which Lavrushka, Nikolay Rostov's servant, falls into the hands of the French. This interlude was based on a passage from Thiers' history which recounted the capture of a Russian whom the French took to be a Cossack, 'un enfant du Don', who showed a child-like wonder at being in the presence of the great Napoleon; the Emperor responded by freeing the Cossack and sending him back to the Russian lines, an action which is described by Thiers in an overblown, romantic and, consequently for Tolstoy, false phrase to which the reader's attention is drawn: 'Napoléon ... lui fit donner la liberté, comme à un oiseau qu'on rend aux champs qui l'ont vu naître' (III.ii.7). In reality Tolstoy would have us believe, it was not a noble savage of a Cossack that the French had captured, but Nikolay's wily lackey who, far from being impressed by Napoleon, realised that his role was to pretend astonishment and veneration. If the scene had ended there, then it would have been unconvincing, another example of Tolstoy's crude haranguing. Even if we are led to distrust Thiers' narrative, common sense suggests to us as we read the passage that there was little likelihood of Thiers' historical 'Cossack' being the fictional Lavrushka.

But the scene did not end with the freeing of Lavrushka. And as Lavrushka returns to the Russian lines, Tolstoy submits his own previous narrative to a critical appraisal through the mind of his character. Even more striking than Lavrushka's hoodwinking of Napoleon are his thoughts as he rides back: 'he galloped towards the forward posts, thinking up beforehand everything that had not been and that he would recount to his own side. Everything which had really happened to him, he did not wish to recount just because that seemed to him unworthy of a narrative' (III.ii.7).

As Lavrushka returns to his lines, the point is forcibly made strikingly soon after Tolstoy's attempt to 'tell the truth' by debunking Thiers and his 'enfant du Don'—that the substance of man's life is incommunicable. Lavrushka knows, as his master Nikolay did, that conventions which channel the flow of communication from narrator to listener will inevitably frustrate any stories he cares to tell based on perceived events. What he 'thinks up', or what comes to his mind, as he gallops back is a story to tell, not wholly unrelated to his experience, but 'worthy of being recounted'. Lavrushka and Nikolay like Nikolenka of *Childhood* and Captain Khlopov of *The Raid* before them are aware that what is recognised as 'worthy of recounting' is the only possible way for one person to communicate through speech with his fellows. Lavrushka is here, like his master previously, involuntarily and inevitably moved into untruth, despite his desire to tell things as they had happened.

For Tolstoy perhaps, Lavrushka could have only given voice to the truth through instinctive song—if he had been indeed Thiers, 'bird restored to its native fields'. Tolstoy had anticipated many writers who would feel how words are so much more haphazard and fugitive as a medium of expression compared with song. In the drafts for *Childhood* where he had sought an analogy for writing in music two types of singers were described—the 'head singer', bound by technique, and the 'chest singer', who sang more directly to his audience. The latter, the instinctive performer rather than the trained musician, reappears a number of times in *War and Peace*. So Natasha at the end of the second volume's first part is the typical, intuitively physical, 'chest singer':

> Natasha took her first note, her throat widened, her chest
> straightened, her eyes took on a serious expression. She did not
> think of anyone or anything at that moment, and from the lips,
> set in a smile, poured sounds, those sounds which anyone can
> produce at the same periods of time, the same intervals but which
> leave you a thousand times unmoved, and at the thousand and
> first make you shudder and weep.   (II.i.15)

Again it is not the beauty of Natasha's art that Tolstoy wished his reader to appreciate, since Natasha with her 'untrained voice, with her incorrect breathing and strained phrasing' (II.i.15) is as 'anti-poetic' as Tolstoy wished to be. But techniques can never be a substitute for sincere human expression such as the singing voice. 'Her voice had that virginal inviolability, that unawareness of its strength and that unpolished velvet quality which so merged with the mistakes in the art of singing that it seemed impossible to change anything in that voice without spoiling it' (II.i.15). There is an assurance in Natasha's singing, stressed by the set of her stride—a firm heel to toe movement—as she takes up her position. This same stride is repeated when she finds so much delight in the sound of her own voice as she goes through her singing exercises while waiting for Andrey: the rhythm of the voice exercises here gives way to the more elemental rhythm, in which she finds equal pleasure, of her heel and toe striking the parquet, 'just as joyfully as to the sounds of her voice, she listened intently to the measured tap of her heel and the squeak of the toe' (II.iii.23). Tolstoy was clearly fascinated by the primitive naive instinctive art of singing which somehow was not aimed at communication, was not therefore circumscribed by technique, yet somehow communicated directly with listeners—the type of folk singing practised by the Rostovs' uncle: 'Uncle sang as the peasant folk sing, in the full and naive conviction that in song all the meaning is in the words alone, that the tune comes of itself and that there is never a separate tune and that the tune is only there to hold it together' (II.iv.7). So the tune was unconscious, 'Like the tune of a bird.' The idea of song bursting forth from man's lips as from a bird's throat, as an unconscious affirmation of self, is again suggested in the description of Platon Karatayev's singing: 'He sang songs not like singers knowing that they are heard but sang, as birds sing, evidently because it was as necessary to emit these sounds, as it is necessary to join in song or break off' (IV.i.13). For Karatayev, and the uncle, for the people, singing is a means of self-affirmation and there need be no thought of the audience. It is not a prerogative of the common folk, however. It is the same unconscious delight that Natasha experiences in her voice exercises in the resonant drawing-room. For her, a failure to sing becomes a signal of her collapse after the break with Andrey; her restoration to health is marked by the renewal of the ability to sing. What Tolstoy shows in these singing passages is the necessity for human voicing of a reality which may be expressible but not wholly communicable. The listeners—one might even say the eavesdroppers on these naive, bird-like effusions—can only be stirred by the contagion with a deeper reality so distant from the surface manifestations of existence, such as those noted and registered by Boris Drubetskoy. Song is heard at climactic moments in *War and Peace*, and it would appear that Tolstoy was as taken by the idea of pure expression being possible through music as was Paul Valéry in his conviction that music was the ideal art.

Tolstoy's medium, however, was words, even if words did not spring so freshly from men's lips as song. Sometimes they may: they fell naturally from Platon Karatayev's lips so that he could not understand words taken in isolation, nor could he repeat what had been said. Language could, as in his case, flow along as an integral component of the life of the moment. Just as Natasha, unable to explain her experiences in words to Andrey when their love was at its most intense, made Andrey understand her despite the lack of articulation. As in love, so in war: Kutuzov at the height of battle does not rely on words alone but on the expression of the narrator and his tone. So the reader, following the words on the page, paradoxically is alerted to the dimness of words at climactic moments in man's life.

Thus, while using the full power of his rhetoric to sustain his fiction, Tolstoy intimates to his reader through Karatayev, Kutuzov and Bilibin, through the mingling of French with Russian, the insignificance and deception of words. In writing history with irony and persuasion, he alerts his reader, through Boris Drubetskoy, to distrust all historical narration. In reading Tolstoy's magnificent set pieces of adventure, heroism and love, the reader is reminded of Nikolay Rostov's and Lavrushka's realisation that it is only possible to mediate a modicum of true experience through narration. In the end, the reader puts his trust in Tolstoy, since he is being fashioned by an author who endeavours to let him take a critical stance. If Tolstoy as an omniscient narrator plays God with his creation, then he sets out not to predetermine his reader's responses but to endow him with critical free will.

IV

The passages where Tolstoy seems to reach out to his reader to alert and instruct him are remarkable for not being set apart from the main narrative. The problem of communication for Tolstoy was never reduced to a question of mere technique but was fully integrated into a particular Tolstoyan vision. So, although Tolstoy may use the chapter 'Verses' in *Childhood* to mediate his views on literary composition and its reception, that chapter is simultaneously a central scene in the work, placed at the point where a farewell has been sung to childhood as the boy became conscious of self in relation to others. Time after time, the reader finds that the characters' narrative performances within Tolstoy's main narrative are fused with emotional points of crisis in the novel. It is indeed a feature of Tolstoy's fictional universe to find characters at a high emotional pitch reading or writing, being in an audience or telling a story. At life's turning points, the art of narration intrudes. Two examples from the second volume of the second part will suffice: Pierre, on his way to Petersburg after his duel and break with his wife, is beset with nihilistic thoughts which are reinforced by his reading of an epistolary novel by Madame Suza (a writer despised by Tolstoy) which prompts him to compare his own situation and that of Hélène with the story of 'some Amélie de Mansfeld'. By the time Pierre arrives in Petersburg, after his conversion to freemasonry, he spends whole days reading Thomas à Kempis. From Madame Suza to Thomas à Kempis! Their narratives are shown to have influenced Pierre's life, revealed his instability and moved him from nihilistic despair to certitude. When shortly, in chapter 10, we cut to Prince Andrey at Bald Hills, *War and Peace* appears briefly to become an epistolary novel as Andrey opens two letters, one from his father and the other from Bilibin. Off stage, Andrey's son is hovering between life and death in the nursery. Yet Bilibin's letter, written in French, bristling with sardonic irony, consciously a literary creation aiming for effect, manages to capture Andrey's whole attention so that it is only with an effort of will that he can shake off his bondage to Bilibin's artificial narrating, and return to the solid reality of the nursery. Throughout the ensuing scene, the reader is conscious that this father, despite his deep feelings for his son, has been infected and somehow modified by his recent reading, so that he preserves— even in the private solitude of the nursery—some of Bilibin's diplomatic restraint: 'Prince Andrey wanted to seize, squeeze, press to his breast this small helpless being; he did not dare do it' (II.ii.9).

What we should recognise is that the narrative mode itself is often employed to precipitate feelings. In both the above cases we have stock figures from fiction: the despairing cuckold of a cold wife, the distressed father of a dying son. The reader would expect the conventional novelist to limit himself to a description or dramatisation of that despair, of that distress. Tolstoy, however, does not attempt to describe these states directly; the ultimate reality of distress, pain or joy is indescribable. They are too complex. Mingled with Pierre's despair unto death is an irritating enjoyment of his emotional state; with Andrey's brimming paternal love, there is an admixture of cold aloofness and male exasperation at being shackled to domesticity. These complexes of emotion may be vented in such acts as intuitive song, or mutely in a brisk walk, such as Natasha's heeling and toeing in her drawing-room. But if they are to be cast into words, then such states are best given shape through the medium of some formal address or narration which may well be tangential to the real experience. So the nature of Pierre's *pleasurable* despair is made evident in his reading of Madame Suza. It is Bilibin's letter, exquisite in its artificiality, that brings out the full complexity of Andrey's genuine emotional state.

The second volume from which the above examples are taken is a section of *War and Peace* where the love affairs of the novel are developed, if not resolved: Pierre is reunited with Hélène, Prince Andrey asks for Natasha's hand in marriage, Nikolay declares his love for Sonya, Boris Drubetskoy and Julie Karagina make their match, and Natasha is seduced by Anatole. It appears that Tolstoy had set out to examine the thousand faces of love in tracing these matches and mismatches. Again a framework of novelistic convention can be seen around each affair: faithful love being put to the test of absence, love triumphing over impediments of social station, a marriage of convenience, a conventional seduction. However, once more Tolstoy shows how rapport is made not in discussion or even conversation, but emerges through men's use of those many forms of narrative that have been elaborated in human culture. Before following these manifestations of love it is worth noting at the outset that the reader is reminded of the futility of trying to transfer one's vision directly to another. During Pierre's address to his brother freemasons on a way of regenerating the world, the reader is told that Pierre was driven by the need 'to convey his thought to another exactly as he understood it' (II.iii.7). That, for Tolstoy, is the impossibility. The lodge reacts as negatively to Pierre's honesty as Anna Scherer's salon had: not only those opposed to his views reject him, but even those in general agreement misunderstand him. The result of this confusion is that Pierre is awkwardly reunited with his wife. The awkwardness of that dutiful cohabitation is, of course, an unstable foundation for the love affairs that follow. If the cohabitation had been made possible by a rational address, then it is other forms of narrative—song, mumming, sentimental literature, music, opera and dramatic readings—that determine the relationships that ensue. Their common feature is that they are all addressed to an audience. They are all performances.

Without being informed by the narrator, the reader realises that Prince Andrey comes to full realisation of his love for Natasha when she sings at the clavichord. His falling in love is fixed in time and place as if it were a religious conversion. One is reminded of Paul Claudel's memory of his own conversion, so rooted in the Christmas of 1886 in Notre Dame 'on the right, opposite the vestry by the second pillar before the choir'[1] as he responded to the singing.

> Prince Andrey stood at the window, conversing with the ladies and listening to her. In the middle of a phrase Prince Andrey fell silent and had a sudden feeling that his throat was filling with tears whose possibility he had not known in himself. He looked at the singing Natasha, and something new and joyful happened in his soul. He was happy, and also he was sad. He had nothing to cry about, but he was ready to cry. For what? His earlier love? The little princess? His disappointments? His hopes for the future? ... Yes and no. The main thing that he wished to cry for was his sudden vivid awareness of the terrible contrast between something infinitely great and indefinable within him and something narrow and corporeal which he was himself and even she was. This contrast brought him distress and joy during her singing.   (II.iii.18)

Again the response to the song has allowed Tolstoy to transform a conventional love scene into a searching examination of a complex of emotions.

Some time later the apparent superior naturalness of a Russian national life, uncontaminated by Western ways, is conveyed to Natasha during her visit to her uncle after the hunt, mainly through the music of balalaika and guitar, and the Russian dance, the instinctive movements for which had not been stifled by the *pas de châle*. It is this music that first causes doubts and worries about her relationship with Andrey to come to Natasha. Would *he* appreciate this music-making that she so enjoys? The refrain of that music, now linked with worrying thoughts about Andrey, re-echoes in the Rostovs' drawing-room. It is the picking out on her uncle's folk guitar of a phrase she had heard in a St Petersburg opera with Prince Andrey that ushers back first memories of her distant betrothed, and then, when she plays for Sonya, the despair at her enforced parting from him.

The examination of the love relationship between Andrey and Natasha continues with music. Even the mother's complicated response to her daughter's match is brought out by music. The mood of that scene is set by

Dimmler playing Countess Rostova's favourite Field nocturne on the harp by
moonlight (there is no indication that 'European' music is any less potent
than Russian folk music in its ability to promote the transference of thought
and emotion). Then Natasha sings at the clavichord her mother's favourite
song to the assembled gathering. Again it is the complexity of the listener's
emotion, in this case, that of the old countess, that resonates to the formal
song. Feelings are apprehended which could not be expressed in any
conversation with her daughter or in cogitation.

> The old Countess sat with a happily melancholic smile and tears
> in her eyes, shaking her head from time to time. She thought of
> Natasha, and of her youth, and that there was something
> unnatural and frightful in Natasha's forthcoming marriage with
> Prince Andrey ... Her mother's intuition told her that Natasha
> had too much of something and consequently would not be
> happy.   (II.iv.10)

The ominous feelings called forth by the resonance of the singing voice
are interrupted by the sudden arrival of the domestics as mummers who
launch into their traditional songs, dances, choruses and games. Drawing-
room music yields to the rude gaiety of folk traditions: yet the mumming
provides the same type of artificial background fostering human intercourse
as Field's nocturnes. The only difference is in a register of culture. Yet it is
through these artificial conventions alone, however varied they may be, that
Tolstoy informs his reader that men may communicate. Despite their living
closely together, Nikolay had found it impossible to declare his love for
Sonya. It is only when released by the grotesque artificiality of the mumming
from their conventional selves that Nikolay, in an elderly lady's farthingale,
and Sonya, as a moustachioed Circassian, seal their love with a kiss redolent
of burnt cork from Sonya's mock moustache.

    That their love was not expressed sufficiently in truth, but in the
rigmarole of mumming, does of course suggest its instability. Yet the
mumming is not treated by Tolstoy in as harsh a fashion as the rigmarole of
sentimentalism through which Boris and Julie have to arrange their match.
The sentimental verses with their melancholic descriptions of gloamings and
graveyards, penned in Julie's album, the doleful nocturnes on the harp, the
emotional reading of Karamzin's *Poor Liza* together, all necessary signals in
Boris's plan to make a rich match—but the literature of sentimentalism had
fooled neither Boris nor Julie. Whereas in the previous chapters artificialities
had managed to crystallise human relationships which were dimly felt but

had not found their expression, here there was an emotional emptiness between Boris and Julie that not even the heightened emotionality of a forced sentimentalism could fill. Despite the album verses and the harp's nocturnes, the marriage would remain one of cool convenience: 'The betrothed, without further mention of the trees plunging them in gloom and melancholy, made plans for the future setting up of a splendid home in Petersburg, went visiting and made full preparation for a splendid wedding' (II.v.5).

With the excesses of sentimental literature apparently mocked, it would not seem strange for Tolstoy to find operatic conventions more laughable. Towards the end of this volume, there is the passage describing Natasha's visit to the opera which has become a classical reference in Tolstoy criticism. Yet our response to that opera visit may be distorted if we peruse that performance in isolation from the preceding ones. The fresh young girl from the country is apparently made to see through artificial staginess.

> They all sang something. When they finished their song, the girl in white went up to the prompter's box and was approached by a man in tight silk trousers over his plump legs, with a plume and dagger who began to sing and wave his arms.
>
> The man in the tight trousers sang alone, then she sang. Then both fell silent, the music struck up and the man began to finger the arm of the girl in the white dress, evidently waiting for the beat again in order to begin a new duct with her. They sang together and everyone in the theatre clapped and shouted and the man and woman on the stage who represented lovers, took their bows, smiling and extending their arms.   (II.v.8)

The visit to the opera has often been quoted in support of the view that central to Tolstoy's method was *ostraneniye* 'estrangement' or 'making strange', a term coined by Shklovsky to define Tolstoy's specific ironic detachment, a view as piercingly fresh as that of the boy who refused to see the Emperor's clothes. Yet here, it is not Tolstoy but Natasha who refuses to form the opera in her mind, from her perception of its conventions. There is no reason to suppose that Natasha was incapable of grasping the peculiarities of the opera: although fresh from the country, she had received voice training, had been credited by Dimmler with 'a real European talent', and had lovingly recalled a visit to the opera in St Petersburg with Prince Andrey. What causes her to reject the opera is not so much its absurdity—if ironic detachment had been rigorously applied, the folksy balalaika strumming at the uncle's could be made equally absurd. Tolstoy does not grade the ritual ways of communication into ones which are more or less artificial, or more or less genuine. It is the reaction of the audience to a performance that for him is crucial: a melancholy nocturne played at the Rostovs' can elicit real feelings, whereas the same nocturne played by Julie Karagina for Boris would echo in the emptiness of their relationship. The opera is another 'performance' in the series of performances which have illuminated the variety of sexual bonding in this part of the novel. The description of the opera in that context is not intended mainly to show the absurdity of artifice, or the superiority of Natasha's naive vision. Her failure to take in the opera results from the cruel rebuff she has just experienced from the Bolkonskys and the impossibility of having any reassurance from the absent Andrey: her rejection by them is turned into her rejection of the opera. The highly-strung Natasha, put more on edge by the tension of the operatic event, becomes hysterical: 'She looked and thought, and the strangest thoughts suddenly, without cause, flashed through her head. Now the thought presented itself of jumping behind the footlights to sing the aria which the *artiste* was singing, now she wanted to flick the old man sitting near her with her fan, lean over towards Hélène and tickle her' (II.v.8). It is at this moment that Anatole Kuragin, her seducer, makes his appearance in the theatre: one might almost see it as a dramatic operatic entry. Motivating the seduction of Natasha by Anatole and making it plausible was undoubtedly difficult. Again though, as with all the other sexual bondings in this part of the novel, it is the ritual performance that acts as a catalyst: slowly Natasha begins to accommodate the conventions of the opera, and eventually as she begins to be fascinated by the male peacockery of Kuragin, she joins in the mass hysteria for the male dancer Dupport. That the final storm is an artificial creation of chromatic scales and diminished seventh chords is no longer a barrier: 'Natasha no longer found it strange. She looked around her with pleasure and a joyful smile' (II.v.9). By accepting the star performer, she had shown herself ready to accept Kuragin. And Natasha's new response to the final act is what informs us of the strength of the bond forged between her and Anatole Kuragin during the interval:

> Again the curtain rose. Anatole left the box composed and happy. Natasha returned to her father's box completely subject to the world in which she found herself. Everything which took place before her already seemed completely natural; but on the other

hand all her previous thoughts about her betrothed, Princess
Marya, life in the country not once entered her head, as if all that
was in the distant, distant past.   (II.v.9)

On the next occasion when Natasha meets Anatole at a soirée at Hélène's, it
is again a performance, this time a declamation by Mademoiselle Georges of
some French verse 'about her criminal love for her son', presumably from
Phèdre, that causes Natasha to return to the 'strange, senseless world, so far
removed from her previous one' (II.v.12), where she is open to Anatole's
advances. Finally the seduction is completed by Natasha's trusting
acceptance of a letter from Anatole. From all the artful performances the
reader has witnessed, the truthfulness of the written word, carefully weighed
for the benefit of the audience—we may remember Natasha's own letters to
Andrey written almost as school compositions with the spelling mistakes
corrected by her mother—cannot be trusted. Ironically, Marya's sincere
letter of apology to Natasha does not find any response in its addressee,
rather as Pierre's honesty is invariably misunderstood. What Natasha accepts
as the truth is a letter apparently from a passionate lover, but in fact
composed for Anatole by Dolokhov: yet it is in that sham that she finds
'echoes of all that she thought she had felt herself'. It is the literary fake that
turns Natasha: '"Yes, yes, I love him!"—thought Natasha rereading the
letter for the twentieth time and searching for some special deep meaning in
its every word' (II.v.14).

   From the above, we see that 'performances' by their inherent
fraudulence pervert human relationships and particularly sexual bondings.
Honest, straightforward communication on the other hand—such as Pierre's
address to his masonic lodge or Marya's letter to Natasha—do not find a
receptive audience. For Tolstoy, communicability is possible only when
narrator and listener both understand the futility of transferring thought and
emotion through words alone. And of course, this is the accord that he would
wish to make with his reader. Again such understandings, brought about by
the recognition that full communication is not possible, occur at high points
in the novel such as Andrey's recollection of a communion with Natasha on
the eve of the Battle of Borodino. For Andrey to admit to such
understanding is particularly remarkable since throughout the novel he is
one who spurns vain attempts at relating experience from the moment when
he shies away from the anecdotes in Anna Scherer's salon. He is the one who
brings Nikolay's tale of Schöngraben to an end, and the most poignant
example of his failure to relate to others through 'performance' is his
breaking off the tale of Bluebeard to his son. Yet on the eve of Borodino,

unable to sleep, he remembers Natasha recounting the story of being lost in the forest while mushrooming. Exasperated by her apparent failure to tell her story, Natasha keeps explaining this to Andrey: 'Natasha was not content with her words—she felt that the passionately poetic experience which she had felt that day and which she wished to bring to the surface was not coming out' (III.ii.25). Yet in her failure to tell it as it was, Natasha communicated with Andrey. He consequently understood and loved her. But the man of war only came to understand this as his final battle approached.

<h2 style="text-align:center">V</h2>

All these narratives and performances are, of course, enfolded within Tolstoy's own great narrative which holds forth to an audience in the same way. It is remarkable to find as the novel is brought to a resolution that the story of *War and Peace* is, as it were, retold within the novel. And it is retold through the mouth of Pierre who eventually is able, through the reprise, to achieve real communicability while preserving his honesty. Central to the resolution of the novel is the fact that the Pierre who, throughout the course of the novel found his rage for honesty an impediment to communication, is at last able to transfer his thoughts to another in his love for Natasha.

In the treatment of Pierre's realisation of his love for Natasha Tolstoy demonstrated in a powerfully ironic way the force of an insincere tangential narrative in crystallising real emotions. Pierre's full understanding of his love comes when he acts as an audience to Captain Ramballe's risqué recital of his amorous adventures: nothing could be more absurd than that the tipsy captain's recital should bring Pierre to a realisation of love. Pierre reciprocates with a telling of his own story—which in a way is a retelling of the story that the readers of *War and Peace* know—and again Pierre fails to communicate (III.iii.29). What Ramballe grasps as the main import is not the essence of Pierre's love for Natasha, but that he was rich with two palaces in Moscow. Ramballe is made to appear as a comically misunderstanding audience with which the reader of the novel can compare himself to his own advantage.

If his story told to Ramballe ends in a fiasco of non-comprehension, Pierre finally is able to achieve communication when in chapter 17 of the last volume he tells his story—again a reprise of what we have learnt from the novel itself—to Marya and Natasha. Pierre begins by giving expression to all those problems of evaluating experience and communicating it, which we have discussed: 'I am told about such miracles which I have not dreamt of.

Marya Abramovna invited me to her house and kept on telling me what happened to me or what should have happened. Stepan Stepanych also taught me how I should tell my stories' (IV.iv.17). Repetition, as R. F. Christian has demonstrated, is one of Tolstoy's most powerful techniques,[2] and this chapter reverberates with the repetition of the verb *rasskazyvat'* (to narrate) and its cognate noun *rasskaz*. Pierre is being importuned to tell a conventional story (what should have happened) in conventional terms (Stepan Stepanych taught me how I should tell my stories). But at last Pierre is able to turn away from self-mockery and tell of *real experiences* naturally; what had made his narrations so awkward previously, from the first one in Anna Scherer's salon, was that he had been only able to speak honestly of abstractions or, at best, of half-digested experiences. Now he began to speak 'with the restrained enthusiasm of a man experiencing strong impressions in his recollections'. Pierre at last understands that true communication, 'man speaking to man', is akin to Wordsworth's celebrated understanding of poetry, originating in 'emotion recollected in tranquillity ... till by a species of reaction, all tranquillity gradually disappears, and an emotion, kindred to that which was before the subject of contemplation, is gradually produced and does itself actually exist in the mind'. Again, of course, the act of narration, the 'performance', marks a climactic moment in the novel. Whereas previously the performances were flawed and the accompanying sexual bondings insecure, finally, in the closure of *War and Peace*, we find that the union of Pierre and Natasha is made manifest by a perfected narration fused with a most sympathetic reception. What effects the union is not eloquence (even at this moment Tolstoy launched into a scathing aside at *intelligent* women who listen to words to retell them or to use them as starting points for their little 'laboratorial' thoughts), but the whole narrating experience whose significance Pierre had grasped with Platon Karatayev whose stories were told with the naturalness of a singing bird.

And in this new-found way of telling, he finds his ideal listener in Natasha, who responds in the way that Tolstoy would probably have wished any reader of his to react. By look and gesture she indicates to him that 'she understood exactly what he wished to transmit'; and more than that, 'It was evident that she understood not only what he was telling but also what he would wish to tell but could not express in words' (IV.iv.17). It is in the telling itself that Pierre became fully aware of the significance of experience—as Tolstoy himself had become aware of the significance of his own experiences during the long writing of *War and Peace*—and Natasha in her reaction personified the ideal reader that Tolstoy would have wished to reach out for: 'Natasha, without knowing it, was all attention: she did not let slip a word, a tremor of the voice, a look, a shudder of a facial muscle, nor a gesture of Pierre's. She caught in flight the as yet unexpressed word and carried it straight into her open heart, guessing the secret significance of Pierre's whole spiritual world.'

At the novel's end, having pleaded with his reader and hectored him, having shown him the futility of seeking to transmit experience, and the fluidity of human language, and having also demonstrated to him that only in his narrations and performances to his fellows could man hope to give form to his existence, Tolstoy too, through Pierre, rests content in the knowledge that in making *War and Peace*, he had also made his reader.

NOTES

1. Paul Claudel, *Oeuvres en prose* (Paris, 1965), pp. 1009–10.
2. R. F. Christian, *Tolstoy's 'War and Peace': A Study* (Oxford, 1962), pp. 148–54.

MARTIN BIDNEY

Water, Movement, Roundness: Epiphanies and History in Tolstoy's War and Peace

War and Peace is incomparably more than merely an attempted refutation of Carlyle's *Heroes* in a contest of rival epiphanies of history. Yet it provocatively plays that role among the other things it does. The extensive authorial disquisitions on history that are inserted into (or appended at the conclusion of) Tolstoy's massive narration could be collectively entitled *On the Nullity of Heroes and the Vanity of Hero Worship*. These authorial essays contain counter-Carlylean epiphanies. (Indeed, no epiphanies could possibly be more counter-Carlylean, even though Tolstoy does not explicitly invoke the name of Carlyle as representative of the theoretical position he is attacking.) To Carlyle's clamant historical hero-fires upbursting from a central heart into a surrounding darkness Tolstoy replies, as it were, with visions of historical tides and currents into which individuals willy-nilly merge or blend—the wiser ones gladly. If Carlyle's Napoleon is at least a flash of gunpowder, Tolstoy's is nothing but an arrogant drop in an historic wave. In staging a phenomenological debate of epiphanists of history by juxtaposing *War and Peace* and *Heroes*, we will have to neglect many of the features that make the former work one of the world's best novels. But we will be doing something interesting and useful nonetheless, for in highlighting the epiphanic pattern of *War and Peace* we will find its imaginative center.

From *Patterns of Epiphany: From Wordsworth to Tolstoy, Pater, and Barrett Browning* by Martin Bidney. © 1997 by Southern Illinois University Press.

147

War and Peace is an uncommonly rich phenomenological lode for the Bachelardian seeker of epiphanic patterns, particularly as these relate to the envisioning of a model of historical meaning. For in *War and Peace* Tolstoy achieves (among other goals) an ambitious threefold purpose. First, he vividly evokes the epiphanies—the intense, expansive, mysterious moments—experienced by five very different but (in their contrasting ways) appealing and sensitive seekers or seers: Pierre, Platon Karatayev, Prince Andrei, Petya, Nikolai Rostov. Second, Tolstoy expounds his own (that is, the narrator-persona's) comprehensive theory of history. Finally, he conveys to the reader the pervasive sense of an intimate connection between the seers' visions and the historical destiny of which, according to Tolstoy's theory, these people's lives are a part. The way Tolstoy makes this connection imaginatively powerful is by presenting an epiphanic vision through his own authorial persona in his remarks on history, an authorial epiphany of historical process that shows the same basic element–motion–shape pattern as do the epiphanies of the five seers. The Tolstoy persona becomes, as it were, the sixth seer, the sixth envisioner[1] of the recurrent epiphanic pattern, which we are now given to understand is nothing less than the pattern of history itself.

Gary Saul Morson's *Hidden in Plain View* is the best presentation we have of Tolstoy's many strategies for endowing *War and Peace* with its extraordinarily lifelike open-endedness in character creation and plot structure. For Tolstoy, as Morson shows, individual selves are in some ways really aggregates, multiplicities; incidents and entire characters may fall to realize their potential in the overall "plot" of *War and Peace*, yet such failed potentials are themselves intended to be an important part of the novel, for they are part of human life.[2] In these and other respects the openness of the book's structure is indeed unprecedented.

But Morson goes too far when he calls *War and Peace* a "book with an absent center."[3] Emphasizing the polyphonies, the dialogic interchanges, the pluralism and relativism of the novel, Morson runs into difficulty in dealing with the emphatic pronouncements of the narrator-persona regarding the theory of history. Tolstoy's attempt to make absolute "statements that are completely non-novelistic, that is, both nonfictive and nondialogized" is an attempt that, in Morson's view, "ultimately fails" because the reader is conditioned by the book itself—a "book with an absent center"—to see events as open-ended and open to multiple perspectives.[4]

But *War and Peace* is not, in fact, centerless, and in demonstrating this fact we will be obliged to argue against Morson's influential presentation. For there is a central link between Tolstoy's lectures on the theory of history and the complex lives of seekers within the Tolstoyan tale. That link is a *shared pattern of epiphanic vision*. Tolstoy is a seer, even in the midst of his abstract-sounding declarations of alleged historical principle, he uses metaphors with vivid imagery—elemental, epiphanic imagery that acquires a life of its own. Tolstoy—or his narrative persona—actually presents an epiphany as the basis for his (and the novel's) vision of history. And Tolstoyan characters are seers too; they, too, experience epiphanies, whose powerful oneiric imagery varies that of the narrator-persona himself. Each Tolstoyan quester is multifarious, many-sided, but the pattern of the questers' epiphanies, taken together, turns out to be surprisingly unitary.

War and Peace, then, *does have a center*: it is the shared pattern that links all the Tolstoyan questers' epiphanies and connects each of them with the narrator-persona's own epiphany of history. Neo-Bachelardian phenomenological analysis will enable us to discover the genuine imaginative center of Tolstoy's massive work. And in doing so it will aid our understanding of Tolstoy's problems as polemical novelist in two additional ways. (1) We will see how the vision of history that Tolstoy derives from his epiphanic material contradicts troublingly the ethical doctrines that he also wants to teach. (2) Since Tolstoy's epiphanic pattern unites his own vision of history as author-persona with the several epiphanies of his fictional questers, this overall pattern reveals a strong totalizing tendency quite at variance with any Bakhtinian dialogism that *War and Peace* may otherwise exhibit. We shall thus be shedding light both on the book's unacknowledged inner contradictoriness and on its unsuspectedly powerful—even willful—tendency to offer an epiphanic viewpoint that will see all individual lives and visions as part of a vast historical unifying scheme.

To isolate the epiphanic image-pattern of *War and Peace* seems at first a tricky undertaking. The distinctive material element, form of motion, and type of shape in the Tolstoyan seekers' visions and in the interpolated essays on history's meaning usually occur only individually or in partial combinations. Indeed, they all appear simultaneously only once (though that single appearance is decidedly the central epiphany of the book: Pierre Bezukhov's dream about Platon Karatayev). But the component images[5] of Tolstoy's element–motion–shape pattern, even when they occur only singly or two together, never serve simply to illustrate an idea. Because they take on a life of their own and attain a surreal emotional strength, they lend unity to the mixture of poetry and polemic, of individual experience and speculative exploring, that animates the book.

To analyze *War and Peace* from this point of view, the following method will be used. First, element, motion, and shape will be studied together in

Pierre's central dream-vision, an explicitly labeled "vision" or "dream" to serve as paradigm, in intensity and completeness, for more fragmentary versions of the epiphanic pattern. Pierre's dream plays the same paradigmatic role in *War and Peace* that Carlyle's vision or epiphany of Odin played in *Heroes*.

Once the paradigmatic epiphany offered by Pierre's dream has been analyzed, other epiphanic passages will be examined in which the three components of Pierre's paradigm appear only one or two at a time. The first group of passages describes the personally experienced epiphanies of individual seers or questers; the second group conveys Tolstoy's (that is, the narrator-persona's) own epiphany of history. Both sets of epiphanies, the personal and the historical, express the same fundamental mood or experience as does Pierre's dream of Platon Karatayev: the sense of living in a harmonious, rhythmic unity with an encompassing cosmic totality. Element, motion, and shape—water, rhythmic motion, and sphere—will be seen as the vehicles of this vision, the components of the recurrent epiphanic pattern, throughout the whole of Tolstoy's masterpiece.

Because he is the chief quester in *War and Peace*, Pierre Bezukhov's dream-epiphany is crucial. Platon Karatayev, peasant sage, is Pierre's spiritual mentor. After Platon's death Pierre has a dream in which the meaning of Platon's life and death becomes clear and by implication the meaning of Pierre's own destiny is revealed. As Pierre sinks into slumber, he hears a voice—his own or someone else's, he cannot tell—saying,

> "Life is everything, Life is God. Everything changes and moves, and that movement is God. And while there is life there is joy in the consciousness of the divine. To love life is to love God. Harder and more blessed than all else is to love this life in one's sufferings, in undeserved sufferings."
>
> "Karatayev!" came to Pierre's mind.
>
> And suddenly there rose before him, as though alive, a long-forgotten, gentle old man who had given him geography lessons in Switzerland. "Wait," said the little old man. And he showed Pierre a globe. The globe was an animate, vibrating ban with no fixed dimensions. Its whole surface consisted of drops closely pressed together. These drops moved, changed, several merging into one, or one splitting into many. Each drop tended to expand, to occupy as much space as possible, but others, with a like tendency, compressed it, sometimes destroying it, sometimes merging with it.
>
> "That is life," said the teacher.

"How simple and clear it is," thought Pierre. "How is it that I did not know this before?"

"In the center is God, and each drop strives to expand so as to reflect Him to the greatest extent. And it grows, merges, disappears from the surface, sinks to the depths, and again emerges. That's how it was with Karatayev: he expanded and disappeared. Do you understand, my child?" said the teacher.[6]

Emerging at birth from total unity with God, Platon Karatayev had gradually risen to the surface of the sphere of life as he advanced toward the self-consciousness and discrete individuality of adulthood. Even as he strove to perfect his own powers, however, Platon only reflected the central power of God. A water drop reflecting the round ocean that is God, Platon Karatayev had no qualms about dying: for Platon dying simply meant regaining the center so as to merge completely with the sphere of which he had always been, consciously or unconsciously, a part. Such is the dream-lesson taught to Pierre.

It is worth pausing here to note the likely presence of an intertextual determinant in Pierre's dream: the *sphaera cuius centrum ubique* or divine sphere whose center is everywhere, an epiphanic component we earlier found adapted in Wordsworth's "Pilgrim's Dream" narrative. Like Wordsworth, Tolstoy as epiphanist participates in a tradition that allows certain intertextual constants to recur in new visionary variants.

All components of the fundamental Tolstoyan epiphanic element–motion–shape pattern come together in Pierre's paradigmatic experience. The element is water. The shape is the sphere. And the type of movement is regular, gradual, rhythmic. Each "drop strives to expand" and "grows, merges, disappears from the surface, sinks to the depths, and again emerges." The sphere is womblike in its liquidity, heartlike in its systolic–diastolic motion: movements from center to surface and back again are as rhythmically regular as breathing. In this passage the motions are chiefly up and down, elsewhere in *War and Peace* they may also be horizontal, like ocean currents; or else regularly repeated mergers and separations, like those of the drops on the sphere's surface, are simply rhythmic in a general way, without any specified direction ("These drops moved, changed, several merging into one, or one splitting into many"). But all Tolstoyan visionary motion is instantly recognizable because these diverse sorts of movement always share one basic quality: regular, unforced, natural rhythm, steady and constant.

Element, motion, and shape—water, gradual rhythmic motion, and sphere—are almost equally distributed among the epiphanies of all the major male questers in the book. Sphericity marks Pierre's early impressions of Platon. Harmonious, unforced rhythmic motion characterizes the central epiphanies of Prince Andrei and Petya Rostov (indeed, the rhythm in both cases is even combined with a sort of "music"). Water appears in the "sea" metaphor with which Tolstoy describes the ecstatic transport of Petya's brother Nikolai. We shall treat each of these visions in turn, showing their links to Pierre's water–sphere dream of the motion of souls. This analysis win demonstrate the kinship of all Tolstoyan epiphanies, their underlying similarity to the illuminating experience of Pierre, and the meaning they all share with Pierre's dream. This meaning is always the same: the harmonious, unforced unity of the individual with the rhythms of the greater cosmic totality.

Pierre's early impressions of Platon introduce the theme of roundness, and this theme constitutes their chief link with the later dream-epiphany of the water-sphere. The roundness of Platon, as Pierre first describes him, troubles most readers of *War and Peace*. We are reluctant to imagine Pierre's spiritual guide as a Dickensian roly-poly caricature; such grotesqueness is unexpected. As Pierre later recalls his fellow prisoners,

> they were all dim figures to him, all except Platon Karatayev, who always remained in his heart as a vivid, precious memory, the personification of everything Russian, kindly, and round. When at dawn the next morning Pierre looked at his neighbor, his first impression of him as something round was fully confirmed: Platon's whole figure in his French military coat belted with a piece of rope, his cap, and bast shoes, was round; his head was perfectly round; his back, chest, shoulders, and even his arms, which he always held as if about to embrace something, were round, and his friendly smile and large, tender brown eyes were round. (*WP* 1161; *SS* 7:58)

The impression is grotesque because Tolstoy is trying to transpose onto the plane of naturalistic description an epiphanic intuition mystical or pantheistic like Platon's, or like the one expressed in Pierre's later water-sphere dream. Other passages make it clear that Platon's roundness, here expressed rather naïvely as a physical quality, is really a metaphysical one, like the roundness of Being according to Parmenides, or the metaphorical roundness of God in the traditional image of the sphere whose center is everywhere. The reason why, in Pierre's mind, Platon "always remained what he had seemed that first night; an unfathomable, round everlasting personification of the spirit of simplicity and truth" (*WP* 1163; *SS* 7:60), is that Platon's rounded simplicity is absolute, it is Truth. Indeed, it stems from the Absolute, from something "unfathomable" and "everlasting," from a larger whole of which, like Pierre's water droplets in the dream, Platon is always a part:

> Every utterance, every action of his, was the manifestation of a force unknown to him, which was his life. But his life, as he saw it, had no meaning as a separate entity. It had meaning only as a part of a whole of which he was at all times conscious. His words and actions flowed from him as smoothly, spontaneously, and inevitably as fragrance emanates from a flower. He could not understand the value or significance of any word or deed taken separately. (*WP* 1163; *SS* 7:60)

Pierre's dream-sphere and Platon's roundness mean the same thing: the sense of an individual life as intuitively conscious of the larger unknown life it reflects. Kindred shape, kindred insight.

By contrast, Prince Andrei's epiphany shares with Pierre's water-sphere dream not a shape but a pattern of motion: an up-and-down rhythm, a sequence of harmonious, regular rises and falls. Note also the motion of "expanding and spreading out," like that of the water drops on the surface of Pierre's sphere:

> Prince Andrei heard (without knowing whether it was delusion or reality) a soft, whispering voice repeating over and over again in a steady rhythm: "piti-piti-piti,"[7] and then "ti-ti," and again "piti-piti-piti" and "ti-ti." And to the sound of this whispering music Prince Andrei felt that over his face, from the very center of it, a strange ethereal structure of delicate needles or splinters was being erected. He felt that he must carefully maintain his balance (though this was exceedingly difficult) so that the rising edifice should not collapse; nevertheless it kept falling to pieces and slowly rising again to the sound of the rhythmical, whispered music. "It is growing, extending! It keeps expanding and spreading out!" said Prince Andrei to himself. While he listened to the whispered sounds and felt the sensation of the edifice of needles rising and expanding, every now and then the red halo of the light around the candle caught his eyes, and he heard the

rustle of cockroaches and the buzzing of the fly that plopped
against his pillow and his face. (*WP* 1101–2; *SS* 6:431–32)

While keeping track of the regular rising and falling movements of this
melodious, rhythmic structure, Prince Andrei at the same time notes a white
sphinxlike shape by the door. For a while the whole mélange of perceptions
seems too much to take in, but just as Prince Andrei is about to give up
exhaustedly, "all at once feeling and thought floated to the surface of his
mind with extraordinary power and clarity" (*WP* 1102; *SS* 6:432)—just like
an ascending drop within Pierre's water-sphere. While in this elevated state,
Prince Andrei experiences "that feeling of love which is the very essence of
the soul and which requires no object"; he knows the "bliss" of loving "God
and all his manifestations" (*WP* 1102; *SS* 6:432). Filled also with new love for
Natasha, Prince Andrei feels the need to forgive her for her earlier attempted
betrayal. And now, to the earlier white sphinx (just a shirt transformed by
Prince Andrei's semidelirium) is suddenly added a "new white sphinx," as
Natasha herself approaches the sickbed. At this point, "like a man plunged
into water," Prince Andrei loses consciousness (*WP* 1103; *SS* 6:433).

The ascent–descent pattern of the epiphany is complete, as in Pierre's
water-sphere paradigm; water is even mentioned to reinforce the parallel.
The love–death of Prince Andrei, after his rise to unusual clarity of
consciousness, precisely parallels Platon's descent as a water drop, his
regaining of the center after initially rising to the surface of Pierre's liquid
globe. Prince Andrei has learned from his epiphany the power of "divine
love" to help him see another creature as God's manifestation: "for the first
time he imagined her soul" (*WP* 1102; *SS* 6:432). Rhythmic risings and
fallings, symbolizing an intimate, harmonious bond between an ascent to
conscious clarity and a descent to unconscious communion, ally Prince
Andrei's elemental epiphany of love and transcendent unity with the
epiphanies of Platon and Pierre. All three seers make us recall the
Heraclitean maxim (epigraph to Eliot's "Burnt Norton") that "The way up
and the way down are one and the same."[8]

Like Prince Andrei's vision, young Petya Rostov's epiphany of the
musical fugue carries over the pattern of motion from Pierre's water-sphere
dream. We see the same successive, regular, harmonious blendings and
separations as in Pierre's globe of droplets, together with the "rhythmical,
whispered music" from Andrei's experience of the rising and falling structure
of needles. This harmony–epiphany of Petya's begins as the sky clears after a
storm. The heavens seem to participate in an up-and-down rhythmic
motion: "At ... times the sky seemed to rise high overhead, then to sink so

low that one could have reached out and touched it. Petya's eyes began to close and he swayed slightly" (*WP* 1260; *SS* 7:168-69). The up-and-down rhythm helps set a mood quite reminiscent of Pierre's dream.

> The trees were dripping. There was a low hum of talk. The horses neighed and jostled one another. Someone snored. *Ozheeg-zheeg, ozheeg-zheeg* ... hissed the saber on the whetstone, and an at once Petya heard a melodious orchestra playing some unfamiliar, sweetly solemn hymn.... The music swelled, the melody developing and passing from one instrument to another. What was playing was a fugue—though Petya had not the slightest idea what a fugue was. Each instrument ... played its own part, and before it had finished the motif, merged with another instrument that began almost the same air, then with a third, and a fourth; and they all blended into one, and again separated, and again blended, now into solemn church music, now into some resplendent and triumphal air.[9]
>
> "Oh, but I must have been dreaming," Petya said to himself as he lurched forward. "It's only in my ears. Perhaps it's music of my own making. Well, go on, my music. Now! ... "
>
> He closed his eyes. And on all sides, as from a distance, the notes vibrated, swelling into harmonies, dispersing and mingling again. (*WP* 1260; *SS* 7:169)

Petya wonders if it is he or someone else who is making the music, just as Pierre was unable to tell whose voice was saying, "Everything changes and moves, and that movement is God" ("someone, he or another, articulated his thoughts" [*WP* 1272; *SS* 7:181]). Indeed, Petya's and Pierre's epiphanies are separated by barely a dozen pages in the novel, and their strong typological similarity makes it clear why Tolstoy felt no need to provide any additional interpretive commentary for Petya's. Both epiphanies also share with Prince Andrei's dream the connection of a rising with a contrasting but interfused sense of depth:

> And from unknown depths rose the swelling, exultant sound. "Now, voices join in!" Petya commanded. At first, from afar, he heard men's, then women's voices steadily mounting in a rhapsodic crescendo. Awed and elated, Petya listened to their wondrous beauty.

The voices blended with the triumphal victory march, the
dripping of the trees, the *ozheeg-zheeg-zheeg* of hissing saber ...
and again the horses jostled and neighed, not disturbing the
harmony, but becoming part of it [literally, "entering into it,"
"vkhodia v nego"]. (*WP* 1261; *SS* 7:169–70)

All three epiphanies—Pierre's, Andrei's, Petya's—affirm a serene
consciousness of, and a blending with, a harmonious cosmic totality. The
three visions achieve this through rhythmic motions of rising and of
"mingling again," "entering into it."

The final epiphany of a Tolstoyan quester to be looked at here—the
reaction of Petya's brother Nikolai to an imperial review of troops—is
patriotic rather than cosmic. Merger with a nation is a far different thing
from merger with the cosmos. For this reason, Nikolai's experience cannot
be regarded as quite analogous with the visions of Pierre, Platon, Andrei, and
Petya. Yet it too is an experience of love and a reverie of merger in a
mysterious larger unity. As such, it shares with Pierre's water-sphere dream-
epiphany the metaphoric use of the element water: "Every general and
soldier felt his own insignificance, was conscious of being a grain of sand in
that sea of men, and at the same time felt his own might, being conscious of
himself as part of that great whole"; Nikolai's own feeling is one of
"tenderness and ecstasy such as he had never before known" (*WP* 301, 303;
SS 4:331, 332–33). Nikolai is even ready to cry at his inability to express his
exultant surge of love for the czar, and he thinks that if the latter should speak
to him, "I should die of happiness" (*WP* 303; *SS* 4:333)—a striking
modification of the love–death motif from Andrei's and Pierre's dreams.

The element of water is just as important as round shapes and
rhythmical, regular motions to Tolstoy's vision of unity in multiplicity. Only
the nonentities in *War and Peace*, the petty egotists Boris Drubetskoy and
Julie Karagina, deeming themselves a "breed apart," cannot identify with the
great metaphoric sea of the one life within us and abroad: "Meeting at large
gatherings Julie and Boris gazed at each other like kindred souls in a sea of
prosaic people" (*WP* 665; *SS* 5:346). Unlike even the relatively limited
Nikolai, they can never become conscious of themselves as "part of that great
whole"; unlike Andrei (and Platon and Pierre), they can never understand
that "Love is God, and to die means that I, a particle of love, shall return to
the universal and eternal source" (*WP* 1175; *SS* 7:74).

Study of the epiphanic element–motion–shape pattern of *War and Peace*
has revealed the unity of the Tolstoyan questers' individual intuitions of
themselves as partakers of a love that passes understanding. But this same

image pattern is equally basic to Tolstoy's own meditations on the nature and meaning of human history as a whole. For Tolstoy, the age-long process of human activity that constitutes history could take on the same resonant unity, the same symbolic cohesiveness and visionary immediacy as the epiphanies of a Pierre, a Petya, or a Prince Andrei. Moreover, Tolstoy as historian and Platon Karatayev as spiritual master teach the same lessons, which may be grasped through the same visionary, epiphanic expressions: water, regular rhythmic motion, and spheres.

Tolstoy's incorporation of this element–motion–shape pattern into his own epiphany of history begins with a strong emphasis on the "motion" part of the pattern. After listing, for more than four paragraphs, the "myriads of causes" that have been adduced by one historian or another, or that might hypothetically be adduced, to account for Napoleon's invasion of Russia, and after making sure these causes have been enumerated in as dull a style as possible in order to show how monotonously alike are their insubstantial claims to our attention, Tolstoy offers the following conclusion, which merits study:

> There was no single cause for the war, but it happened simply because it had to happen. Millions of men, renouncing human feelings and reason, had to move from west to east to slay their fellows, just as some centuries earlier hordes of men had moved from east to west slaying their fellows. (*WP* 731; *SS* 6:9)

In other words, no single factor caused the war except some principle of reciprocal motion, of pendular rhythmic movement—an epiphanic pattern exemplified by vast surges or sweeping movements of large masses of men. The rhythm of movement pattern is introduced seemingly quite casually and briefly, as if the second sentence quoted above were simply a more or less obvious implication of the first. Tolstoy is saying: (1) the war happened because it had to happen, and (2) this means that it was part of an eastward movement that had to happen in order to counterbalance an earlier westward movement that had to happen. But the second statement implies a principle that Tolstoy never proves, though it undeniably held a strong grip on his epiphanic imagination—namely, the principle that mutually counterbalancing large-scale movements of people somehow "have to happen." Tolstoy never offers any proof of his conviction that the Napoleonic eastward onrush was a necessary counterpart to the westward sweep of the Golden Horde in the thirteenth century. But he does very tellingly refer, at one point, to Attila's invasion and to the Crusades, which are clearly to be construed as another pair of westward and eastward counterbalancing movements. The "movement of the peoples at the time of the Crusades," described as a "movement of peoples from west to east," is juxtaposed to the "migration" in the reverse direction led earlier by Attila (*WP* 1427, 1445; *SS* 7:349, 370). Tolstoy does not elaborate, however, on this solitary additional example, so the rhythmic principle that westward and eastward pendular movements are the essential stuff of history (i.e., that they are what simply "has to happen") remains the unproved axiom of Tolstoy's theory of history. Its grounding or support is an imaginative one. And once it is assumed, the inevitability of all else follows. If we admit

> that the purpose of the upheavals of European nations is unknown to us, that we know only the facts—the murders, first in France, then in Italy, in Africa, in Prussia, in Austria, in Spain, and in Russia—and that *the movements from west to east and from east to west comprise the essence and end of these events*.... [then] it will be clear that all those minor events were inevitable. (*WP* 1355; *SS* 7:269, emphasis added)

Compared with these massive, reciprocal, rhythmic motions, which constitute the *essence* of historical reality (note Tolstoy's word "essence," "sushchnost'") and which provide history's underlying pattern, various political murders in seven countries are merely minor events. Tolstoy insists upon the *absolute formal symmetry, the rhythmic regularity, of eastward and westward movements*:

> The fundamental and essential significance of the European events at the beginning of the nineteenth century lies in the bellicose movement of the mass of European peoples from west to east and then from east to west. This was instigated by the movement from west to east. (*WP* 1356; *SS* 7:269)

For Tolstoy's epiphanic imagination, this principle or pattern of rhythmic movement is vividly compelling. But the imaginative appeal of such movements for Tolstoy cannot be fully understood apart from the "element" and "shape" constituents of his pattern of historical epiphany. Rhythmic motion, water, and spheres mean as much to Tolstoy the epiphanic historian as they did to Pierre the epiphanic dreamer.

First, the element: water. History is like a sea and behaves as a sea does:

Seven years had passed since the war of 1812. The storm-tossed sea of European history had subsided within its shores and seemed to be calm; but the mysterious forces that move humanity (mysterious because the laws determining their actions are unknown to us) continued to operate.

Though the surface of the sea of history appeared to be motionless, the movement of humanity went on as unceasingly as the flow of time. Various groups of people formed and dissolved; the causes that would bring about the formation and dissolution of kingdoms and the displacement of peoples were in the course of preparation.

The sea of history was not driven by gales from one shore to another as before: it seethed in its depths. Historical figures were not borne by the waves from one shore to another as before. (*WP* 1351; *SS* 7:264)

The "sea of history" in this Tolstoyan epiphany is driven by gales from one shore to another, with lulls (such as the period of "reaction" after the victory of the Holy Alliance) when it seethes in its depths. The horizontal wave motions of large-scale invasions and migrations bring about the "formation and dissolution of kingdoms and the displacement of peoples." Napoleon, according to Tolstoy, was a bad philosopher precisely because he failed to realize this. Like King Canute, Napoleon thought he could direct the sea, whereas he was but "the figurehead on the prow of a ship," and even his startling return from exile was but the "last backwash" of an eastward wave (*WP* 1203, 1360; *SS* 7:107, 274).

But horizontal currents are not the only indicators of changing movement in the historical sea: vertical motions are also crucial, as in Pierre's paradigmatic epiphany, his water-sphere dream. During the lulls between major horizontal sweeps, upward surges from below, mysterious seethings of the sea from its "depths," cause diverse groups of people to be successively "formed and dissolved." Each new horizontal movement, westward or eastward, is initiated by a preparatory stage of vertical surgings from below. These seethings from the depths provide the crucial link between Tolstoy's ocean-epiphany of history and Pierre's water-sphere epiphany of "life." "Groups of people" form and dissolve as a result of seethings originating in the depths of the historical sea, just as individuals rise to the surface and dissolve back to the center of Pierre's water-sphere. (Recall also the description of drops that "moved, changed, several merging into one, or one splitting into many," on the surface of the sphere.) Moreover, just as Pierre

learns that "in the center is God," so likewise Tolstoy learns from his vision
of history that "*only the Deity*, prompted by no temporal agency, can *by His
sole will* determine the direction of mankind's movement" (*WP* 1431; *SS*
7:353, emphasis added).

Tolstoy does not introduce the epiphanic image of the sphere or globe
as explicitly into his discussions of historical pattern as he does in Pierre's
dream, but implicitly the notion of the Newtonian earthly sphere pervades
these historical discussions, which abound in references to Newton's laws of
gravity. The "force of free will" is as subject to the "laws of necessity" as the
"force of gravitation" is to "Newton's law" (*WP* 1450; *SS* 7:376). "As with the
law of gravity," the "enormous mass" of the retreating French armies attracts
"the discrete atoms [individual soldiers] to itself," thus ensuring its
cohesiveness (*WP* 1228–29; *SS* 7:134). Commander Kutuzov knows it is
pointless to pursue the French, for "the apple must not be picked while it is
still green. It will fall of itself when ripe" (*WP* 1223; *SS* 7:129). Kutuzov, like
Tolstoy himself, uses Newtonian metaphors to show his intuitive grasp of the
laws of historical gravity.

These gravitational laws of our earthly sphere—laws central to
Tolstoy's and Commander Kutuzov's shared epiphany of history—derive
from God; they describe God's direction of history ("only the Deity ... can by
His sole will determine the direction of mankind's movement"). Platon
Karatayev believes that "Man proposes, but God disposes": Platon's example
provides Pierre with what is specifically labeled a "center of gravity," namely,
a spiritual and psychological sense that he too, like Platon, has a "judge
within him who by some rule unknown to him" decides "what should and
should not be done" (*WP* 1158, 1324; *SS* 7:53, 239). The feeling of a center
of gravity that Pierre acquires from Platon is a sense of contact with the
"center" of our earthly sphere, that center that is God. God controls the laws
of motion of our individual and collective life-sphere; indeed, as we learned
from Pierre's dream, in a larger mystical or pantheist or epiphanic sense, God
is the sphere. Tolstoy, as historian, likewise teaches that God controls the
laws of motion of our life-sphere: "only the Deity ... can by His sole will
determine the direction of mankind's movement."

From Platon, Pierre learns the Tolstoyan lesson that only receptive,
intuitive, or unconscious thought—wise passiveness—can put one in touch
with the mystery at the "center of gravity" of our historical sphere. The laws
of gravity that govern the movements of droplets and currents, of individuals
and societies, are at bottom spiritual laws, beyond reason. But these spiritual
laws of individual and social life share the inevitability of the laws of natural
and even of divine life.

In sum, as presented to us by the unifying element–motion–shape pattern of *War and Peace*, Tolstoyan reality, in the realms both of personal epiphany and of historical epiphanic pattern, is a round and centered thing, composed of symmetrical, harmonious, mutually counterbalancing motions in accord with an inner law like the control of gravitational forces over water. People without awareness of holistic reality, people who feel no oneness with the great oceanic swells and lulls of our life-sphere (St. Petersburg nobles are good examples of such people), live in a world of unreality, "phantoms and echoes," "form" not "substance" (*WP* 850, 1117; *SS* 6:145, 7:7). Their thoughts belong to maya, illusion, not to the rounded, rhythmic reality of the encompassing ocean.

We have been led to an epiphanic justification of History's ways to humanity.[10] I would be tempted to call the total experience a theophany except that the element–motion–shape pattern seems much more deeply rooted in Tolstoy's imaginings than the very loosely defined "God" it is said to manifest. (In any case, I see a continuum leading from theophanies to epiphanies, and [as noted in my introduction] the distinction in any given case may be nearly impossible to make.) Spheres, pendular or symmetric motion of drops or tides or currents or waves, even of aery needlelike structures or musical sound waves—these have a hallucinatory force in *War and Peace*, a dreamlike power that carries conviction. Pierre Bezukhov's water-sphere dream and all the closely related epiphanies of Prince Andrei, Petya, Nikolai, Kutuzov, and Tolstoy himself express a serene and meditative calm that could hardly offer a more marked contrast to Carlyle's flaming Odin, a seer who in vision recreates himself as human-divine epiphany of eruptive, flashing Fire.

Yet Tolstoy and Carlyle are alike in that neither can escape the distortions, the hazards, of trying to force history into the bounds of an elemental epiphany. Carlylean heroes all emulate Odin, but Odin is an unhistorical imagining of Carlyle's; it turns out, moreover, that when we look at history we find Odin's would-be emulators to be rather poor copies, anyway—poorer and poorer as history proceeds. Teufelsdröckh reimagines the Odin-style fire force rather well, but he too fails to embody it in his own life story. Carlyle's epiphany-inspired theory of historical heroism is called radically into question by history not just by history as we might see it, but even by history as Carlyle himself sees it. Tolstoy's problems as epiphanist of history are no less severe.

These problems are threefold. First, of course, the assumption that eastward and westward movements constitute the essential stuff of history is unproved, and many readers will doubt its validity. Second, it is unprovable that such movements are divinely caused, no matter how vaguely divinity is defined. And finally, even if God's purposes, as ultimate efficient and final causes of history's formal movements, are ultimately inscrutable, there is still the problem that these purposes come into open conflict with the Christian ethics Tolstoy would also like to teach. Tolstoy emphasizes that "with the standard of good and evil given us by Christ," we know that greatness requires "simplicity, goodness, and truth" (*WP* 1279; *SS* 7:190). Yet Tolstoy's God disregards these Christian criteria in appointing historical leaders, for Napoleon's "cruel, grievous, harsh, and inhuman role" was "predestined for him" when "providence" chose him specifically "for the deplorable ineluctable role of executioner of peoples" (*WP* 980–81; *SS* 6:293, 295). Dunnigan's translation is fairly accurate, but it is misleading to write "deplorable" (suggesting moral disapproval) where Tolstoy says merely "sad"—a word that indicates no moral judgment. The depressing bleakness of Tolstoy's utterance is inescapable: Napoleon is described as "prednaznachennyi provideniem na pechal'nuiu, nesvobodnuiu rol' palacha narodov"—literally, "pre-appointed by providence for the sad, unfree role of executioner of peoples."

It is astonishing that Tolstoy can bring himself to make such a claim as he does here: only his deep imaginative commitment to his epiphany of historical "currents" and "waves" can explain it. If Napoleon is but a drop in a divine historical current or wave, subject to those ineluctable laws of "gravity" that govern the movement of historical waters over the surface of our earthly sphere, then Napoleon's tragic actions may seem justifiable to Tolstoy (that is, providentially approved, divinely predestined) by the "logic" of the image pattern that Tolstoy invokes as an epiphany of history. But twentieth-century readers will have no less difficulty with this extraordinary providential or divine appointment of an "executioner of peoples" than did Tolstoy's nineteenth-century critics.

Tolstoy's totalizing tendencies get him into an unfortunate position— that of invoking an epiphany-based image of history whose implications conflict very disturbingly with the humane values we may legitimately derive from the equally epiphanic experiences of his privileged fictional questers. Morson's description of Tolstoy's novel as "a book with an absent center" cannot be maintained in view of our findings here, for the pattern uniting Tolstoy's own epiphany of history with the epiphanies of his fictional seers functions as a powerful—perhaps too powerful—unifying center of *War and Peace*.

NOTES

1. The number of questers or seers or seekers will depend on one's criteria for counting. I have included Platon Karatayev as a visionary on the assumption that if he *embodies* epiphanic truth (as he evidently does—we shall learn—through his metaphysical or ontological "roundness") he has presumably somehow "seen" that truth. Clearly, though, Platon is to be regarded as having basically found the truth he embodies (or else it somehow found him), so he is in that sense no longer a visionary seeker or quester—if indeed he ever was.

2. Gary Saul Morson, *Hidden in Plain View: Narrative and Creative Potentials in "War and Peace"*; see, for example, 205–10 on self as aggregate, 147–53 on "unnecessary" incidents and characters. In opposition to E. E. Zaidenshnur and R. P. Christian, who saw Tolstoy's creative process in producing *War and Peace* as fundamentally unified and coherent, and to Viktor Shklovsky and Boris Eikhenbaum, who viewed that process as conflicted and contradictory, Morson seeks to show that Tolstoy deliberately set out to discover the book's structure in the act of making it, to let the book "shape itself" as it was "being written" (see 173–82). "Round Table: Five Critiques and a Reply," an extensive discussion of Morson's work (critiques by Freeman Dyson, Alfred J. Rieber, Cathy Popkin, Carol Any, Anna A. Tavis, reply by Morson), appears in *Tolstoy Studies Journal* 2 (1989): 1–40.

3. Morson 143.

4. Morson 19. In Bakhtinian fashion, Morson argues that "there is no way to speak completely noncontextually in a novel," that since a novel is a dialogical form of literature, even a statement intended to be taken as absolute is contextualized, relativized by the reader who is cognizant of "novelistic tradition"; Morson calls this "metacontextualization" (19–20).

5. James M. Curtis, "The Function of Imagery in *War and Peace*," *Slavic Review* 29 (1970): 460–80, divides the imagery of the novel into "organic and inorganic—that is, images which refer to animals and plants and those which refer to machines and inanimate objects" (462). But the element–motion–shape pattern I discern in the book's epiphanies (water, symmetric or pendular motion, and the sphere) escapes both of Curtis' categories. Curtis suggests that water "links the organic and inorganic similes" (470) he has studied, but the instances of water imagery he quotes are not analyzed, so their linkage value remains unproved.

Though I can find in the criticism no systematic phenomenological studies of the epiphanic pattern in *War and Peace*, there are certain phenomenological qualities in John Weeks, "Love, Death, and Cricketsong:

Prince Andrei at Mytishchi," *In the Shade of the Giant: Essays on Tolstoy*, ed. Hugh McLean, 61–83, an attempt to account for Andrei's "extraordinary psychological state" prior to his death by looking at Tolstoy's use of "aural texture" (61).

6. Leo Tolstoy, *War and Peace*, trans. Ann Dunnigan, 1272; L. N. Tolstoi, *Voina i mir* (*War and Peace*) vols. 4–7 in *Sobranie sochinenij*, 20 vols., 7:181–82. All Tolstoy citations (hereafter *WP* and *SS* respectively with volume and page numbers in parentheses) refer to these editions.

7. Weeks speculates that an echo of this "piti-piti-piti" may be audible in the "regular tattoo of *'ljubit'-ljubit'-ljubit'*" ("to love, to love, to love") that forms part of the sound texture of Prince Andrei's meditations later on in the passage (77).

8. Eliot gives it in Greek; see T. S. Eliot, *Collected Poems, 1909–1962* 175.

9. Weeks says since "Andrei and Petya are about to die" they are "given dispensation to hear the music of the spheres" (79).

10. For landmark discussions of Tolstoy on history from non-phenomenological viewpoints, see Boris Eikhenbaum, *Lev Tolstoi*, 3 vols.; Isaiah Berlin, *The Hedgehog and the Fox*, Paul Debreczeny, "Freedom and Necessity: A Reconsideration of *War and Peace*," *Papers on Literature and Language* 7 (1971): 185–98; Edward Wasiolek, "The Theory of History in *War and Peace*," *Midway* 9, No. 2 (1968): 117–35; F. F. Seeley, "Tolstoy's Philosophy of History" in *New Essays on Tolstoy*, ed. Malcolm Jones, 175–93; Andrew Baruch Wachtel, *An Obsession with History: Russian Writers Confront the Past* 88–122; Wachtel's dialogic and decentered approach, like Morson's in *Hidden in Plain View* and in his more recent *Narrative and Freedom: The Shadows of Time*, finds no epiphanic center in *War and Peace*.

FELICIA GORDON

Legitimation and Irony
in Tolstoy and Fontane

—what was being said of the rights and education of women should have interested Kitty. How often had she considered the question ... how often had she wondered what would be her own fate if she did not marry and how many times had she argued with her sister on the subject. But now it did not interest her in the least.[1]

One way of reading novels of adultery, which combine social and psychological realism with melodramatic and exemplary punishments of the adulterous wife, is in relation to the issue of democratic legitimacy. In the late eighteenth and through most of the nineteenth centuries, democratic or quasi-democratic civil societies relied on some form of public consent, whilst they simultaneously excluded women from the democratic process.[2] One function of novels of adultery, it will be argued, was to legitimise women's exclusion from the public sphere by demonstrating that marriage was their only safe haven and that outside marriage they were doomed. Novelists as disparate as Flaubert and Tolstoy represent women's lapse from marital fidelity as deserving the most severe form of punishment, if not by stoning as decreed in the Old Testament, then by the death, often suicide, of the adulterous wife. In examining the philosophic subtext of *Anna Karenina*, *The*

From *Scarlett Letters: Fictions of Adultery from Antiquity to the 1990s*, edited by Nicholas White and Naomi Segal. © 1997 Nicholas White and Naomi Segal.

Kreutzer Sonata and *Effi Briest*, it will be suggested that one phenomenon novels of adultery may reflect is a transformation of the ancient legally sanctioned historic violence of husbands towards wives into an internally assumed violence of women towards themselves. At the very moment when in many European countries, laws affecting women were either becoming or threatening to become more liberal, novels of adultery showed the law of the father internalised in the feminine subject.[3] Tolstoy's Kitty Shcherbatsky, the dutiful daughter soon to become the good wife, has lost all interest in 'the woman question'.

Geneviève Fraisse (*Reason's Muse*) has suggested that democratic cultures faced a new crisis of gender definition.[4] Self-evidently democracy, by its claim that legitimacy rested on the consent of the governed, raised the question of women's inclusion in the sphere of citizenship. To deny women participation in civic life required a renewed theorising of sexual differences. The idea of the moral life associated with male-only participation in the public sphere (citizenship) meant that women were necessarily excluded from the ethical realm in its highest form. This move, extensively theorised in Rousseau, Kant and Hegel produced a circular reasoning by which women were self-evidently unfit for citizenship, because they lacked the highest moral sense.

In spite of such philosophic legitimation, this visible inconsistency between democratic theory and political practice did not disappear. Even in autocratic cultures like Russia and Prussia the problem was not eliminated, since the heritage of the Enlightenment ensured that 'women's place' formed part of any discussion of social reform. Yet the gap between progressive legislation and the fictional representation of marriage is striking. For example, although Prussia had the most liberal divorce laws in Europe, the dramatic requirement for the adulterous heroine's social ostracism and early death in Fontane's *Effi Briest* remained intact.[5] Tolstoy in *Anna Karenina* ensures that his plot precludes divorce as a solution to marital breakdown, although it was permitted in law. Novels of adultery which dramatised the interplay between the private and the public sphere both legitimated women's place in the scheme of things but also, as we shall argue, served to undermine philosophic certainties.

Women were still, as Hegel suggested, tied to the old laws of the 'nether world', a necessary reminder of divinity but incomplete without male self-consciousness.[6] In a century where theories of change were identified with progress, a negative attitude towards women's participation required that inequality be figured as naturally rather than socially constructed. If women were not to function as members of the polity, arguments needed to be based on incapacity, not exclusion but on an incapacity paradoxically affirming women's special and semi-divine status. Thus from the dawn of the democratic era in philosophic discourse, as Fraisse demonstrates, women were consigned to the realm of nature. Simultaneously however, marriage and the family became a central focus of bourgeois moral orthodoxy. The citizen was to be nurtured in the moral family. The question then arose as to how amoral or pre-moral persons, normally women, could incarnate the moral core of a society from which they were excluded. In Kant and Hegel the problem was resolved via the idea of a bridge of mutual recognition.

Kant in his *Observations on the Feeling of the Beautiful and the Sublime* (1763) and Hegel in his *The Philosophy of Right* (1817) and *The Phenomenology of Mind* (1830) attempted to wrest the institution of marriage from either the purely religious (a sacrament) or the largely material (property) to allow it to function within the ethical realm as an instrument of culture.[7] Such ideas can be clearly traced in Tolstoy, where in *Anna Karenina* the three marriages: Dolly and Stiva Oblonsky's which nearly fails but is repaired thanks to Dolly's forbearance, Anna and Karenin's which does fail thanks to her adultery and Kitty and Levin's which is difficult but successful, show Tolstoy, like Kant and Hegel, searching for an ethical bridge between the sexes. In *The Kreutzer Sonata* on the other hand Tolstoy abandons the idea that nature and culture can be harmonised, particularly as nature in the form of sexuality is figured as irredeemably evil. Marriage founded on desire becomes the destroyer of the ethical personality in husband and wife.

In both novels Tolstoy shows himself conversant with and preoccupied by the 'condition of woman question'.[8] John Stuart Mill's *The Subjection of Women* (1869) is explicitly satirised in *Anna Karenina* in a multi-layered conversation in which the proponent of liberalism is shown as irascible and foolish and the supposed beneficiary of women's emancipation (Kitty) is not able to feet any interest in the subject.[9] (See opening quotation.) Tolstoy's attacks on women's emancipation in *Anna Karenina* and *The Kreutzer Sonata* may be linked to related anxieties about the loss of faith and certainty in the post-Darwinian world.[10] He focuses on marriage as representative of the 'condition of Russia question', arguing that the problem of Russia is not primarily one of economic backwardness as the liberal or socialist reformers claimed, but a question of ethics.[11] He seeks to demonstrate that ethics are not culturally relative but universal. So in *Anna Karenina*, marriage and adultery are intended to exemplify the workings of a universal moral law. Tolstoy's abandonment of the ideal of marriage in *The Kreutzer Sonata*, however, can be seen as a logical development of the early themes associated with sexuality and desire.

In *Anna Karenina*, Levin is deeply ashamed of his early sexual adventures and wishes to marry in order to give his sexuality a moral framework. His preoccupations appear to echo Hegelian descriptions of the marriage state.[12] For Hegel, the family rescues sexual relations from the purely natural, particular and contingent, and links them to the ethical and the universal. While all human beings desire full ethical self-consciousness which is achieved by the recognition of others, for men this recognition is achieved in the public sphere and for women in the family. The family forms part of the ethical life, but on a lower plane, being tied to nature. Yet to the extent that it is ethical, family life is intrinsically universal. Hegel, like Tolstoy, wished the family to represent more than mere nature (sex) but also to represent more than a contract of material convenience (property).[13]

> In a household of the ethical kind, a woman's relationships are not based on a reference to this particular husband, this particular child, but to *a* husband, to children *in general*,—not to feeling, but to the universal. The distinction between her ethical life [*Sittlichkeit*] (while it determines her particular existence and brings her pleasure) and that of her husband consists just in this, that it has always a directly universal significance for her, and is quite alien to the impulsive condition of mere particular desire. On the other hand, in the husband these two aspects get separated; and since he possesses, as a citizen, the self-conscious power belonging to the universal life, the life of the social whole, he acquires thereby the rights of desire, and keeps himself at the same time in detachment from it.[14]

What happens to women in the ethical household who do demonstrate particularity of desire? Considering Anna Karenina, one can appreciate how she violates the Hegelian ethical model. Not only does Anna desire a particular man, Vronsky, who is not her husband, she is physically repelled by her husband, Alexei Karenin, as a particular individual. She fails to love her husband as a Hegelian universal and wishes, but fails, to love him as a particular individual. Nor is desire validated as either authentic or happy in the novel. Kitty and Levin's honeymoon 'remained in the memories of both of them as the bitterest and most humiliating period of their lives'.[15] The consummation scene between Vronsky and Anna shows him distraught with 'lower jaw trembling' and Anna grovelling on the floor in the classic pose of the woman taken in adultery.[16] This scene, far from representing pleasure, is equated with shame and guilt, which Anna internalises, begging forgiveness from the only representative of male culture present, her lover/seducer, Vronsky. 'She had no one in the world now but him, and so to him she even addressed her prayer for forgiveness.'[17]

A further important distinction emerges between men and women in what Hegel calls the particularity of desire. Women can only have access to the ethical realm within the family and through the mediation of the husband who participates in the universal concerns of the community. Women derive their meaning from their husbands, who function not as individual objects of desire, but in their role as ethical exemplars for the family. It follows that a wife's particular feelings of love or aversion for any particular husband are irrelevant. The husband, however, who derives his ethical significance from the public sphere, has the right to feel particularity of desire for this or that woman.

Anna Karenina's destruction is shown to proceed from her social exclusion, which in turn leads her to depend ever more heavily on Vronsky, to become pathologically jealous of him and to imagine suicide as a form of revenge. But social pressures in themselves are inadequate to explain the process of Anna's deconstruction from confident magnificence at the novel's opening to querulous misery at the end. Tolstoy demonstrates that the consequences of female adultery (male adultery is notoriously not punished in Anna's brother, Stiva Oblonsky) are not merely social ostracism or personal misery within the family. The double sexual standard is not shown to be socially just, but to exist as a transcendental law. By betraying her husband, Anna denies the universal ethical principle represented by the husband and through him, civil society.[18] In Hegelian terms, Anna loses all possibility of significant Being when she abandons her role as wife, since Being flows from the husband. Outside of marriage there is nowhere for Anna to go. She enters a parody of marriage as Vronsky's mistress but her self-confidence, warmth, and vitality vanish. As Hegel puts it: 'The individual, when not a citizen, and belonging to the family, is merely unreal insubstantial shadow.'[19] Tolstoy's ideological message is that the heroine's nemesis is the outcome, not of husbandly outrage or even of social disapprobation but of the inexorable workings of the moral law. Dolly, on the other hand, who forgives her erring husband, devotes herself to her family and rejects Anna's suggestion of birth control methods with horror, takes on added stature. However, Tolstoy, a realist as well as an ideologue, does not suggest that the good Hegelian wife will necessarily be a happy one.

Anna Karenina juxtaposes Anna's failure in marriage and adultery with Levin's successful achievement of marriage and a family. The novel closes with a return to the land and the establishment of a patriarchal family. Kitty becomes the Rousseauistic mother. Here ethics seem grounded in nature, not culture, where in St Petersburg, aristocratic life had encouraged the Anna/Vronsky liaison. But Levin's (and Tolstoy's) admiration for Kitty's spontaneous ability to respond to the realities of life and death is heavily charged with condescension as well as envy. Apart from Tolstoy's own marital difficulties, it is unsurprising that marriage which was to provide ethical salvation is subsequently denounced in *The Kreutzer Sonata* as being a gross deception. Whereas critics often focus on the overtly personal nature of this story, it is worth emphasising its consistencies with *Anna Karenina*. In both, sexuality is terrifying and distasteful. But for the later Tolstoy there is no possible bridge between nature and culture; the only mutual recognition between the sexes becomes that of hostility.

Pozdnyshev, the tormented husband, follows through the logic of those Hegelian contradictions in marriage suggested in *Anna Karenina*. The narrator's discovery that marriage encompasses nature (sex) and that even a woman's love for her children has a sensuous element, invalidates the idea that marriage can attain any degree of ethical universality. Thus the Rousseauistic family is construed as evil. Women, because they inflame men's sensuality, are also evil. It does not matter whether Pozdnyshev's wife has taken the musician as her lover or not; she is guilty on either count. Tolstoy logically undermines the very married state which had been the ethical cornerstone of *Anna Karenina*. The private sphere of the family becomes a hell from which there is no transcendence. All relations between the sexes are doomed. Tolstoy has constructed a parody of Hegel's master/slave relationship whereby each player in the dyad attained self-consciousness through the recognition of the other. In *The Kreutzer Sonata* the slave is degraded and so is the master. 'And there she is, still the same humiliated and debauched slave, while men continue to be the same debauched slave-masters.'[20] The very fact that Pozdnyshev recognises the alterity of his wife, that she is another person and in spite of his best efforts cannot simply be reduced to an object, leads him to kill her. *The Kreutzer Sonata* could be read as an ironic post-lude to *Anna Karenina* but the conflicts it treats as insoluble save through murder are already suggested in the former work.[21]

Anna Karenina while acknowledging the tragedies of the female condition, legitimates women's subjection by convincingly dramatising the horrors of social, spiritual and mental exclusion. The novel validates female oppression not by approving of it, but by suggesting that no other existence is available to women, save the even worse one of perpetual exile from the world of self-conscious Being. *The Kreutzer Sonata* legitimates oppression in another sense, by logically demonstrating the impossibility of ethical relations between the sexes. The corollary must be the requirement to contain the 'weaker' sex because, paradoxically, Pozdnyshev asserts that women are the dominant sex:

> The way things are at present, the woman is deprived of the rights possessed by the man. And, in order to compensate for this, she acts on the man's sensuality, forces him into subjection by means of sensuality, so that he's only formally the one who chooses—in actual fact it's she who does the choosing. And once she has mastered this technique, she abuses it and acquires a terrible power over men.[22]

Pozdnyshev echoes Rousseau's fear that if women had the rights of desire, 'the men, tyrannised over by the women, would at last become their victims and would be dragged to their death without the least chance of escape'.[23]

Though faithful to the traditional plot of novels of adultery which requires the punishment of the wife, Theodor Fontane in *Effi Briest* (1895) offers a devastating indictment of the bankrupt nature of sexual relations based on separate spheres theory.[24] As Roy Pascal has observed, *Effi Briest*, in its account of the breakdown of a marriage, represents the 'general contradictions of the whole of civil society'.[25] The disillusionment of the deceived husband, Innstetten, with the Hegelian ethos of public service is often focused upon by critics as demonstrating the bankruptcy of the Junker class and of the Prussian State founded on Hegelian principles.[26] Effi is sometimes understood as a shallow character, demonstrating Fontane's inability, unlike Tolstoy, to portray passionate natures. I will be arguing, however, that her supposed limitations are central to Fontane's critique of separate spheres. Far from showing his incapacity to depict passionate natures, his portrayal of Effi, like that of Innstetten, represents an accurate expression of Kantian gender categories operating in this novel in the context of the Hegelian State.

Kant's *Observations on the Feeling of the Beautiful and the Sublime* (1763) was an early text, preceding his analytic works and indebted to Rousseau's *Emile* (1762) and in it Rousseau's portrait of the ideal girl/wife, Sophie.[27] In the *Observations* Kant contends that aesthetics and ethics divide on gender lines. Women have an instinctive feeling for the beautiful, men have a spontaneous facility for the understanding of principles and for the sublime. Thus women have 'a strong *inborn feeling* for all that is beautiful, elegant and decorated ... They have many sympathetic sensations, good heartedness and compassion, [they] prefer the beautiful to the useful.'[28] It follows that virtue is different according to gender: 'the virtue of a woman is a beautiful virtue. That of the male sex should be a noble virtue. Women will avoid the wicked not because it is unright, but because it is ugly ... I hardly believe that the fair sex is capable of principles.'[29]

Effi Briest as a young girl is the personification of the Rousseauistic/ Kantian ideal. Seen first in the tamed nature of her parents' garden, she is eager to marry and to marry well. She has no hesitation in accepting a husband who is to be her mentor in the world of culture, the role Innstetten appropriately adopts. A spontaneously Kantian woman, she prefers the beautiful to the useful. In buying her trousseau, Effi would rather go without than not have the best and most luxurious items. Effi enters upon a marriage where, in a Hegelian sense, she should derive maximum significance. Her husband is the embodiment of the Hegelian commitment to the public sphere (or the Kantian sublime). In Effi, Fontane has hit on a gender stereotype which will illuminate the contradictions inherent in the gender relations implied by it.

Effi rightly senses the unbridgeable gap between herself and Innstetten even before their marriage. She remarks to her mother: 'And I think Niemeyer even said later that he was a man of fundamental principles, too ... And I'm afraid that I ... that I haven't got any ... He's so kind and good to me and so considerate but ... I'm scared of him.'[30] Kant, we remember, hardly believed 'that the fair sex is capable of principles'. Effi bears him out.

The chasm between Effi and her husband is the Kantian one of the feminine deriving spontaneous pleasure from beauty and the masculine which through laborious effort attains an abstract universality of principle, or the sublime. In Hegelian terms it is the gap between female and male, the family and the state. How is marriage supposed to allow individuals to bridge this gulf, to move from one state of being or consciousness to another? Kant's answer is that each individual recognises the qualities of the beautiful or the sublime in the other. 'Woman has a superior feeling for the beautiful, so far as it pertains to herself; but for the noble so far as it is encountered in the male sex ...'[31]

In Fontane, this ideal of spontaneous recognition founders on the misery and loneliness of Effi, the beautiful artefact. The man of principle seeks to control the woman without principles by fear, already noted in the passage quoted above, and orchestrated with gothic embellishment by the device of the Chinaman's ghost. Innstetten's cruelty in manipulating Effi's fears, as well as his detachment, link him to the Kantian sublime: 'A man who grounds his actions on the principle of justice, for example, will subordinate all other actions and impulses to it. Love for another may still remain, but from a higher standpoint one sees it in relation to one's total duty. As soon as this feeling has arisen to its proper universality, it has become sublime, but also colder.'[32] Effi recognises this coldness in her final judgement on Innstetten's 'rightness'. Like Alexei Karenin, he is a good man, who, as she puts it 'doesn't really love'. From a Kantian perspective, the inability to love deeply is what makes him a good man.

In killing off Effi, Fontane writes the obverse of his novel *L'Adultera* (1882) where the adulterous couple are shown succeeding in an arduous but satisfying life. Yet Fontane, while offering a plot which appears to endorse Kantian and Hegelian gender prescriptions, ironically chronicles the collapse of belief systems, an almost universal breakdown in strategies for living. The sense of unease pervading all personal and social relationships relates to a sense of inauthenticity in public roles. Innstetten who goes through the motions of the code of honour knowing it to be bogus and who admits that his commitment to public service is hollow, is representative of the emptiness of social life grounded on no ability to feel or as Effi says, to love. The world of the novel is like the empty rooms in Innstetten's Kessin house, full of nothing but whispers.

Fontane exudes scepticism about the ideological structures to which his characters attempt to conform. Innstetten and Crampas, both a generation older than Effi, subscribe to the same unbending code of honour. Husband and lover equally attempt to 'educate' Effi with their fictions, Innstetten with his tale of the Chinaman and Crampas with that of Don Pedro. They are parodies of the Kantian husband-educator. Nor are their fictions shown as having a sustaining virtue. Passion seems bloodless in this novel; Crampas dies for nothing; Innstetten decides he has killed a friend for nothing. Wüllersdorf's 'auxiliary constructions', another name for sustaining fictions, seem equally fragile. The rigidity of abstract universality and its divorce from life is ironically exposed in Effi's mother, a woman who holds to the doctrine of social acceptability above that of family affection. It is her husband, lacking any grasp of theory or principles, who affirms his right to love his daughter. In the paradise of Hohen-Cremmen, gender roles are reversed and the father, far from being a figure of patriarchal severity, exudes a kind of muddled, *unprincipled* goodness. Unlike his wife and son-in-law, he is not concerned by social status, but like Fontane, who he may resemble, he is past the age of ambition.

The fate of the adulteress in novels of adultery arguably betrays an underlying anxiety. Women, thanks to their civic exclusion, are a source of instability: they enact the revenge of the repressed. The bourgeois novel of adultery may be read simultaneously as a construction of legitimation or an ironic undermining of the ethical double standard on which marriage depended. At the very moment when women's emancipation threatened to become an historical reality and when divorce and the dissolution of marriage became a practical possibility, such novels acted as powerful agents of denial. Female adultery could be figured as calamitous, not because it caused pain and misery to individuals, not because betrayal and deceit are ethically obnoxious, but because it denied the power of abstract universality on which the very concept of ethical life was held to depend, a universality which turned out not to be universal at all, but masculine. Whether approached from a standpoint of Tolstoy's moral absolutism, or Fontane's scepticism, female adultery was an instance of reality breaking through ideology. Neither Anna nor Effi can be construed as social rebels or feminists *manquées*. They largely accept the foundational masculinist assumptions of their culture. One is reminded of the dead Emma Bovary, watched over by those two ideologically opposed individuals, whom Flaubert parodies as symptomatic of the political divisions of nineteenth-century France, the anti-clerical chemist, Homais, and the priest, Bournisien. Superficially in conflict, they speak the same language, as do the uncomprehending husbands and lovers of the novels of adultery, a language of abstract universality from which women are excluded. The nineteenth-century novels of adultery can be read as Tolstoyan didactic warnings— 'vengeance *is* mine, and I will repay'—as efforts to legitimate and to render 'natural' the sexual double standard upon which all other social inequalities depended or as ironic deconstructions of the murderous artificiality inherent in gender prescriptions.

NOTES

1. Leo Tolstoy, *Anna Karenin* (sic) (1878), trans. by Rosemary Edmonds (Harmondsworth: Penguin, 1978), p. 415. All subsequent references will be to this edition.

2. For a wide ranging discussion on women's exclusion from citizenship in the post-revolutionary settlement see Geneviève Fraisse, *Reason's Muse: Sexual Difference and the Birth of Democracy*, trans. by Jane Marie Todd (London: University of Chicago Press, 1994), to which this paper is much indebted.

3. For a comparison of laws relating to marriage and divorce see Roderick Phillips, *Putting Asunder: A History of Divorce in Western Society* (Cambridge: Cambridge University Press, 1988), pp. 403–73. On the

legitimacy of domestic violence see Carole Pateman, *The Sexual Contract* (Cambridge: Polity Press, 1988).

4. Fraisse, 'Introduction: Troubled Reason', pp. xiii–xviii.

5. Prussia was relatively liberal on the question of divorce which was sanctioned on a wide variety of grounds including adultery, desertion and insurmountable aversion (Imperial Divorce Law, 1875). The Russian Code of 1836, on the other hand, legalised women's obedience in marriage where women had a serf-like status. Adultery was the only admissable grounds for divorce and needed eye-witness, third party testimony. See Phillips, *Putting Asunder*, pp. 428–39 and Richard Stites, *The Women's Liberation Movement in Nineteenth-century Russia* (Princeton: Princeton University Press, 1978), p. 182.

6. 'Just as the family thereby finds in the community its universal substance and subsistence, conversely the community finds in the family the formal element of its own realisation, and in the divine law its power and confirmation. Neither of the two is alone self-complete. Human law as a living and active principle proceeds from the divine, the law holding on earth from that of the *nether world* [my italics], the conscious from the unconscious, mediation from immediacy; and returns to whence it came. The power of the nether world, on the other hand, finds its realisation upon earth; it comes through consciousness to have existence and efficacy.' Georg Wilhelm Friedrich Hegel, *Phenomenology of Mind* (1830), trans. by J. Baillie (New York: 1967), pp. 478–9.

7. Kant, *Observations on the Feeling of the Beautiful and the Sublime* (1763), trans. by John T. Goldthwaite (Berkeley: University of California Press, 1960); Georg Wilhelm Friedrich Hegel, *The Philosophy of Right* (1817), trans. by T. M. Knox (New York: 1967), *The Phenomenology of Mind* (1830), trans. by J. Baillie (New York: 1967).

8. Leo Tolstoy, *Anna Karenina*, pp. 411–14. On Tolstoy's anti-feminism see Richard Stites, *The Women's Liberation Movement in Nineteenth-century Russia*, pp. 159 and 177–8.

9. J. S. Mill's, *The Subjection of Women* (1869) had an enormous European-wide readership and was translated into most European languages (though not Russian). Russians probably read it in French. See Richard J. Evans, *The Feminists* (London: Croom Helm, 1977), pp. 18–21 and note 16, p. 40.

10. Leo Tolstoy, *The Kreutzer Sonata and Other Stories* (1889), trans. David McDuff (Harmondsworth: Penguin, 1983). All subsequent references will be to this edition.

11. Levin is much troubled by the implications of materialism (see Part 1, Ch. 7, *Anna Karenina*). Tolstoy, like Dostoevsky, took issue with the utopian and materialistic vision of social and sexual emancipation developed in Cherneshevsky's *What is to be Done* (1863).

12. For extended discussions of Hegel and the family see: Genevieve Lloyd, *The Man of Reason: Male and Female in Western Philosophy* (London: Methuen, 1984), Carole Pateman, *The Sexual Contract*, especially Chapter 5, Diane Coole, *Women in Political Theory*, (Brighton: Harvester, Wheatsheaf, 1988), Chapter 8.

13. Hegel, *Phenomenology of Mind*, 'The Ethical Life', p. 112, paragraph 163 and p. 114, paragraph 166.

14. Hegel, *Phenomenology of Mind*, pp. 476–7.

15. *Anna Karenina*, p. 509.

16. *Anna Karenina*, pp. 165–6.

17. *Anna Karenina*, p. 165.

18. The logic of Hegel's position tends to equate adultery to treason, as in English law it was once 'petit treason'). See Roderick Phillips, *Putting Asunder*, p. 130.

19. Hegel, *Phenomenology of Mind*, p. 470.

20. Tolstoy, *The Kreutzer Sonata*, p. 64.

21. See Roderick Phillips on spouse murder as a solution to marital problems, pp. 307–9.

22. Tolstoy, *The Kreutzer Sonata*, p. 49.

23. Jean-Jacques Rousseau, *Emile* (1762) trans. by Barbara Foxley (London: J.M. Dent and Sons Ltd, 1974), p. 322.

24. All references to this novel are to Theodore Fontane, *Effi Briest*, trans. by Douglas Parmée (Harmondsworth: Penguin, 1967).

25. Roy Pascal, *The German Novel* (Manchester: Manchester University Press, 1956), p. 201.

26. See: Erika Swales, 'Private Mythologies and Public Unease: On Fontane's *Effi Briest*', *Modern Language Review* (75, 1980), pp. 114–23, Stanley Radcliffe, *Fontane's 'Effi Briest'* (London: Grant and Cutler, 1986), J. P. Stern, *Reinterpretations* (Cambridge: Cambridge University Press, 1964), Henry Garland, *The Berlin Novels of Theodore Fontane* (Oxford: Clarendon Press, 1986), J. M. Ritchie, 'Embarrassment, Ambiguity and Ambivalence in Fontane's *Effi Briest*', in Jörg Thunecke (ed.) *Formen realisticher Erzählkunst* (Nottingham, 1979), pp. 563–9.

27. Immanuel Kant, *Observations on the Feeling of the Beautiful and the Sublime*, Introduction by John T. Goldthwaite, pp. 1–8.

28. Kant, *Observations*, p. 77.

29. Kant, *Observations*, p. 81.
30. Fontane, *Effi Briest*, p. 39.
31. Kant, *Observations*, pp. 93–4.
32. Kant, *Observations*, p. 58.

A. GALKIN

Death or Immortality?:
Dostoevsky Versus Tolstoy

La Rochefoucauld, true to his skeptical rationalism, believed that it was meaningless to think about death, if only on account of the impossibility of avoiding it. Montaigne, on the contrary, maintained that philosophizing meant learning how to die. Moreover, he cites an aphorism of Pliny that is striking in its laconicism: "An instantaneous death is the height of happiness in man's life."[1] Indeed, would it not be happiness to be killed suddenly by an exploding cannon ball without even having the time to realize that you have been killed?!

Three hundred years later, another outstanding thinker, Leo Tolstoy, who, incidentally, deeply respected and loved Montaigne, would describe as if by chance a death caused by a shell splinter. Here, despite Montaigne's view, the consciousness reacts in a heightened way to what is occurring and fades in a deliberately delayed manner, snatching thousands of trivial details from its memory, illuminating a whirlwind of thoughts, images, and actions with an instantaneous light:

"Whom will it kill, me or Mikhailov? Or both of us? If it's me, where will it hit? In the head? Then, it's all over. But if it hits me in the leg, they'll amputate it, and I'll ask them to make sure

From *Russian Studies in Literature* 34, no. 4 (Fall 1998). © 1999 by M.E. Sharpe, Inc. English translation © 1999 by M.E. Sharpe, Inc. Translated from the Russian text © 1993 by "Voprosy literatury," "Smert' ili bessmertie? (Dostoevskii protiv Tolstogo)," *Voprosy literatury*, 1993, no. 1, pp. 157–72. Translated by Laura Givens.

they give me chloroform. And I just might pull through. Maybe it'll just kill Mikhailov. Then I'll tell them about how we were walking along side by side and how it killed him and I got all splattered with his blood. No, it's closer to me—I'm the one it'll get."

At this point he remembered the twelve rubles he owed Mikhailov, he remembered a debt in Petersburg that he should have paid long ago, and the Gypsy melody he had sung in the evening came to his mind. The woman he loved appeared in his imagination wearing a cap with lilac ribbons; he remembered a man who had insulted him five years earlier and whom he had not yet paid back for the insult ... ("Sevastopol' in May" [Sevastopol' v mae])

The theme of death troubled the work and personal life of Tolstoy with a penetratingly disturbing dissonance. A frenzied fear of death seems to haunt the artist persistently. Tolstoy's dead heroes (Nikolen'ka Irten'ev's mother, Andrei Bolkonskii, Nikolai Levin, Ivan Il'ich) surround him, as it were, from all sides: they draw near him, crowd him, stretch toward him their withered fingers with joints showing through; they question him about the secret of death, turning the soul of the writer to ice with some otherworldly, inhuman horror. Finally, they dart a parting, fading glance at Tolstoy, as if their eyes were already covered with the haze of decay. A sense of squeamishness fills Tolstoy the artist when he, with his characteristic pedantry, reproduces the stages of the putrefaction of the flesh, records the process of the inexorable dying away of the tissues of the human body, a body whose terrible stench assaults the nose and that shows off its sores and sicknesses, a body out of which the immortal spirit seems to have been pressed. This is how Tolstoy depicts the final days of Ivan Il'ich:

Special accommodations had also been made for his, excrements, and each time it was torture. Torture due to his uncleanliness, unseemliness, and smell, and due to the consciousness that another person must take part in it.... On one occasion, when he got up off the chamber pot too weak to pull up his trousers, he sank down into a stuffed armchair and looked with horror at his bare, debilitated thighs with their sharply delineated muscles. (*The Death of Ivan Il'ich* [Smert' Ivana ll'icha])

As a rule, Tolstoy's dying hero loses all grace: he becomes capricious, malicious, and irritable; he shamefully and fussily clutches at life and is sometimes even imbued with a hatred for the health of those around him. They, in turn, respond in kind: in their thoughts they hasten his death, wishing to be freed as soon as possible from his tiresome moaning.

In order for Tolstoy to put an end to this—both semantically and compositionally—he depicts the actual demise as a moment of liberation, the longed-for crossing over into the Christian state of eternal bliss. Finally, at the moment of death, the hero finds the sought-after meaning of life.

> They both [Natasha Rostova and Mar'ia Bolkonskaia—A.G.] saw him [Andrei Bolkonskii—A.G.] sink deeper and deeper, slowly and peacefully leaving them for some other place. And they both knew that this was how it should be and that this was good. (*War and Peace* [Voina i mir])

> Before the priest had finished the prayer, the dying man (Nikolai Levin—A.G.] stretched, sighed, and opened his eyes.... And a moment later his face became radiant, a smile appeared under his moustache, and the women who had assembled busily set about laying out the body. (*Anna Karenina*)

> At that very moment, Ivan Il'ich fell through and saw the light, and it was revealed to him that his life was not what it should have been, but that it could still be put to right.

However, this way of understanding death is so traditional that it is clearly not in keeping with Tolstoy's consistent negativism with respect to any type of generally accepted social or religious directives, which he subjected to review and furious criticism with all the frenzy of a fanatic. Might Tolstoy have been insincere in his depiction of death? Hardly likely. Most probably, Tolstoy *wished* with all his might for death to be purifying, joyful, meaningful. He very much *wanted to believe* in such an ideal death.

Nevertheless, Tolstoy's strength lies not in the fact that he strives, rationally and dogmatically, to grasp the irrational and to pin it down with a word, but rather in the fact that he admits how much the irrational is stupefyingly not subject to his meticulous rationalness. Little by little *the irrational* creeps with its swirling poisonous fog into the consciousness and completely engulfs the individual, dragging him into the pitch-dark, mystical abyss. The dream Andrei Bolkonskii has just prior to his death, besides everything else, graphically illustrates Tolstoy's complexes as a writer. Long before Freud, the strength of artistry demonstrated the power of thoughts about death, a power that is stubbornly forced into the subconscious but that bursts out into the open, if only in the form of a literary hero's internal monologue:

> Little by little, imperceptibly, all these people begin to disappear, and everything is supplanted by a single question about the closed door. He arises and goes toward the door to bolt and lock it. Everything depends upon whether he can lock it in time. He goes, he hurries, but his legs refuse to move, and he knows that he will not be able to lock the door in time. Still, he painfully strains every nerve. And he is seized by an agonizing fear. And this fear is the fear of death: it stands behind the door. But while he is feebly and awkwardly crawling toward the door, that dreadful something is already pressing on the other side and forcing it open. Something inhuman—death—is forcing the door, and he must hold it back. (*War and Peace*)

Later on, Ivan Il'ich's wild cry "Oh! O-oh!" and the way he "struggled about in that black bag"—lacking the strength to climb into the black hole that would bring an end to his torments—would become the crowning moment of Tolstoy's meditations on death. He does not see light in it but darkness, terror, savage fear, nothing, nonexistence—in a word, emptiness and godlessness.

In this sense, Tolstoy's own death strangely resembles the death of his heroes. The Buddhist ideals of "nonaction" and passivity that he proclaimed enigmatically contradicted his own demise and his demonstrative departure from his home, which made him a laughing stock among his enemies and brought reproach from his friends. Was his death pretty? Hardly. Rather, the death that overcame the genius was incomplete, as if it had come about suddenly—it was like a careless dot or even a drop that fell from the tip of a pen and ran across a white sheet of paper.

Why did Tolstoy fear death in such a mystical way? There is a direct link between his thoughts on death and his squeamish depiction of the debilitated flesh of the dying. Tolstoy sets himself the fantastical goal of destroying all flesh; he tries to extract the spirit from the body and, in so doing immortalize the spirit. But what, then, is left for the body that has been abandoned by the spirit? An agonizing death! And the spirit, all alone, pines and annihilates itself, not having the power to resist death's attraction.

Hatred for one's own body leads to an unbearable fear of death, that is, of capitulation to life. It would appear that God turns away from Tolstoy at the moment of his demise, leaving him alone with his fear of death in revenge for his lack of true faith, which he had falsely replaced with impetuous attacks on the church and traditional Christianity.

A different kind of departure awaited his great contemporary and constant opponent, F. Dostoevsky. Everything began as it had with Tolstoy: with scandal, insults, and the bitterness of misunderstanding. A heated conversation with his sister Vera about the inheritance from their aunt, A. F. Kumanina, hastened Dostoevsky's death. Vera Mikhailovna Ivanova, the writer's sister, came to Dostoevsky requesting that he relinquish his rights to the Riazan estate left to him by his wealthy aunt, the wife of a merchant in favor of his sisters. The artist was ever in need and had dreamed all his life of leaving his children at least something; indeed, only a year prior to his death he had paid off all his debts thanks to the efforts of his wife. And now this blow! And from whom? His beloved sisters.

Even after receiving the Eucharist, the dying Dostoevsky could not forgive the injustice of his sisters. During the night of the twenty-fifth and the morning of the twenty-sixth of January 1881, he suffered a hemorrhage after moving a heavy bookcase to find a pen. An artery in his lungs burst and flooded his lungs with blood. A second hemorrhage followed the first. Early in the morning Dostoevsky awakened his wife and told her: "Ania, I've been lying here thinking, unable to sleep for the past three hours, and I've only now come to the realization that I will die today."[2] He asked for the copy of the Gospels that was given him by the wives of the Decembrists when he went to the labor camp and that he would often open randomly as a means of guidance. The Gospels opened up to a passage from the third chapter of Matthew. Anna Grigor'evna read it out loud: "But John forbad him, saying, I have need to be baptized of thee, and comest thou to me? And Jesus answering said unto him, "Suffer it to be so now." "Did you hear it says 'suffer it to be so'? That means I will die," said her husband and closed the book. "Remember, Ania, I always loved you dearly and was never unfaithful to you."[3]

Why did Dostoevsky have such an easy time leaving this life? Because all his life he preached the idea of the immortality of the soul, and, unlike Tolstoy, he truly believed in it. This idea is so all-embracing that it grants the person who believes in it the ability to love and feel compassion while giving him the meaning of life. "Real life" [*zhivaia zhizn'*] is what the writer calls the love that penetrates an individual causing him to pour out this love, like Christ, into the world and imbue it with a warm light and joy. "Real life" nourishes man: he puts down deep roots, and unbounded strength, both spiritual and material, flows up to him from the depths of the earth, his Motherland, the "soil."

On the contrary, the loss of the idea of the soul's immortality entails the devaluation of the meaning of life, hence the breaking of the law of compassion and love, moral nihilism, and, as a result, inevitable suicide:

> love for mankind is even absolutely inconceivable, incomprehensible, and *absolutely impossible without a combined belief in the immortality of the human soul....* When the idea of immortality is lost, suicide becomes a perfect and even inescapable necessity for every man, who is just a little more highly developed than the beasts. On the contrary, immortality with its promise of eternal life binds man more firmly to the earth ... for it is only with faith in his own immortality that man comprehends his entire rational purpose on earth. When man is not convinced of his immortality, his connections to earth snap, become more slender, more rotten, and the loss of a higher meaning in life (which is felt, even if only in the form of a most unconscious sadness) undoubtedly leads to suicide. Hence, we have the moral teaching that views this in reverse: "If a conviction of immortality is so necessary for human existence, then it would seem to be a normal state of mankind, and if that is so, then the immortality of the human soul *undoubtedly exists.*" In a word, the idea of immortality is life itself, real life, its definitive formula and chief source of truth and correct consciousness for Mankind.[4]

Dostoevsky's suicides, like Tolstoy's heroes and, obviously, like Tolstoy himself, are convinced that there can be nothing after death other than decomposition. Their thought is entirely focused on the mortal flesh, on the absolute recognition of matter and its primacy over the spirit. The suicide Kirillov (*The Devils* [Besy]) believes that merciless laws of nature operate in the world and that they even ruthlessly destroyed their own miracle—Christ. If this is so, then the phenomenon of Christ and his crucifixion were a tragic mistake. Kirillov confesses in a frenzy to Petr Verkhovenskii: "There was a day on earth, and in the middle of the earth stood three crosses. One man hanging on the cross believed so strongly that he said to another: 'This day you will be with me in paradise.' The day ended, they both died, and they left this world and found neither paradise nor resurrection. His words did not come true."

A. G. Dostoevskaia recalled that one time in Basel Dostoevsky caught sight of Hans Holbein's painting *The Dead Christ in the Tomb*. The writer was so struck by the representation of Christ on the canvas that he began to have an attack of epilepsy, and it was with great difficulty that Anna Grigor'evna led him away from the painting. "A painting like that could make one lose one's faith,"[5] Dostoevsky said when he came to his senses. He subsequently gave these words to Prince Myshkin, who saw a copy of the Holbein in Rogozhin's house.

Unlike many representations of this traditional subject—"The Deposition"—in which the figure of Christ is surrounded by the disciples, the Madonna, and Mary Magdalene, *only the dead body* of Christ is depicted in Holbein's painting. His body—covered with bruises that have already gone blue, his dead blue-gray lips, and the frozen expression on his face of unbearable *physical* pain—all give the sensation of the visible reality of death. The laws of nature seem to have triumphed over the radiant, luminous spirituality of the Savior. This is apparently what stunned Dostoevsky.

If one were to dwell on the terrifying thought that had completely taken possession of Kirillov's consciousness causing him to rave, laugh hysterically, and in a burst of animal rage *bite* Petr Verkhovenskii on the finger at the moment of his suicide, if one were to dwell on the thought of the physical death of Christ, who has not risen from the dead after his crucifixion, then everything in this world is justified: murder, debauchery, and outrages against children. "If there is no God, then all is permitted," according to Dostoevsky's idea. This is when "the laws of nature" prove to be an ominous symbol of unbelief and immorality. They take moral responsibility away from the individual. (While Rogozhin, Nastas'ia Filippovna's murderer, looked at Holbein's *The Dead Christ in the Tomb* with his decomposing flesh, he fostered within himself the idea of the crime.)

What then is the meaning of human life? What is man's purpose on the earth? These are the questions Dostoevsky suddenly resolves before the coffin of his first wife ("Masha is lying on the table"). He agonizes over Christ's commandment to "love thy neighbor as thyself" and writes: "The highest use to which a man may put his person, and the full development of his own I, is the destruction, as it were, of that I, to give it entirely to the service of each and everyone, selflessly and wholeheartedly" (15:365). Christ alone succeeded in such boundless self-sacrifice. Dostoevsky believed that man must strive toward this ideal. Herein lies the meaning of his sojourn on earth and his spiritual debt to the generations.

It is true, in the words of Ivan Karamazov, that Christ "was God. But we are not gods." Did Christ leave even the least guidance showing how people are to follow him, the Savior, along the spiritual path? According to Dostoevsky, when Christ rejected the three temptations of the devil, he delineated the contours of human behavior and outlined three points of support that describe to each person the meaning of life.

The first temptation of the devil is "to turn stones into bread." What does this symbolic image mean to Dostoevsky? The artist himself explained it in a letter to V. A. Alekseev. The evil spirit, tempting Christ, seems to say: "Command that henceforth the earth bring forth fruit without labor; give people the knowledge or teach them the order of things so that they henceforth will live without want. Do you not believe that man's chief vices and troubles come from cold, hunger, and poverty and from the impossible struggle for existence?" (15:408). Socialism in Europe and Russia "eliminates Christ and, first and foremost, concerns itself with *bread*, calls upon science and maintains that poverty, the struggle for existence, 'the corrupting environment,' is the sole cause of human misfortunes" (ibid.).

Indeed, if one were to assign primary importance to the physical nature of man ("hunger, cold, and poverty"), then the theory of "the environment," which the writer found so abhorrent, would triumph. This theory attributes everything to unsatisfactory social conditions and completely removes personal moral responsibility from man. It can be argued logically that the theory of the environment may easily be united with Darwin's theory and that the laws of the animal kingdom and its struggle for existence can be transferred to human interrelations. In such a case the thesis of the "corrupting environment" justifies even murder. Thus, Ivan Karamazov speaks with hatred of his father and his brother Dmitri: "One viper will devour the other—it serves them both right!" Once a man has been completely determined by his environment, then, in essence, he loses freedom of choice and is like an animal, something that inevitably legitimizes the idea of the brutish baseness of human nature. All tyrannies and despotic regimes arise from and are supported by this. Here we locate the root of the Grand Inquisitor's conviction that man is a weak, defenseless animal craving a "community of worship," as well as his conviction that the coming of Christ with His unshakable faith in the greatness and the chosenness: [*izbrannichestvo*] of each person is a mad undertaking that has been disproved by world history. In keeping with Dostoevsky's idea, Christ responds:

> "Man does not live by bread alone," that is, he stated the axiom about man's spiritual origin as well. The devil's idea could only approach man as beast. Christ knew that bread alone would not give man life. If, besides bread, he has no spiritual life, no

ideal of Beauty, man will begin to pine, will die, go mad, kill himself, or indulge in pagan fantasies....

But what if Beauty and Bread were given together? Then labor, *individuality, the self-sacrifice of one's own good for the sake of a neighbor*—in a word, all of life, the ideal of life, would be taken away. And therefore it is better to proclaim the spiritual ideal alone. (15:408)

To put it differently, the indisputable value of human life, its creative enthusiasm, love for others, and the feeling of responsibility, or, to be more precise, the recognition of one's own mission on earth, are all determined by one thing alone—the priority of the spirit over the flesh, over the physical nature of man. He who fails to see or does not wish to see anything around him other than vulgar materiality, who scoffs at this ideal or thinks it beneath him, sooner or later loses the main feeling that is primordially inherent in man—the feeling of love; he becomes embittered and emits hatred into the world. Moreover, this hatred destroys him from within. One could say that Smerdiakov "hanged himself maliciously," whereas Stavrogin put an end to his life because depravity and the murders he had committed robbed him of the ability to love. Svidrigailov alone makes the desperate attempt to bring back his human face: he sacrifices his voluptuousness in the name of his love for Dunia Raskol'nikova—he releases his beloved as soon as she confesses to him her inability to love him. But even in this, the hero is poisoned by his *lack of ideals*, insofar as, without belief in Christ and God, he sees eternity as something like "a sooty village bathhouse with spiders in all its corners—that's all there is to heaven." It is not without reason that the Elder Zosima's homilies include the notion that hell is "suffering from no longer being able to love" and that sinners are those who are deprived of the ability to love.

Indeed, if eternity is a "bathhouse with spiders," then *what* is life here on earth? It goes without saying that it is nonsense, foolishness, absurdity; moreover, there neither is nor can be anything *there* because there is no such thing as immortality. Such is the conviction of *real* suicides whose suicide notes Dostoevsky analyzes in *Diary of a Writer* [Dnevnik pisatelia].

The suicide Pisareva, who is "tired of living," is in a terrible hurry and becomes quarrelsome in her impatience. She demands that they "pull off" (not take off) her stockings and shirt, peevishly asks that *no one wail*, certain that, with her, nothing "*besides laughter*" will likely come of it. However, just before her death she is endlessly occupied with money questions. She divides her tiny sum of money among her acquaintances and relatives. This fact forces Dostoevsky to write again and again "about stones turned into bread" and about the "main prejudice of all of life," when it is thought that

> if all were provided for, if all were happy, then there would be no poor among us and there would be no crime.... Herein lies all that little everyday, dreadfully typical and consummate catechism of those convictions to which they devote themselves in life with such faith (despite how soon everyone grows tired of both their faith and life) and that they substitute for everything: real life, connection to the earth, belief in the truth—everything, absolutely everything. (23:25)

The writer debunks anew the theory of the "environment" and on the rebound lashes out at socialism, whose main doctrine consists in the goal of bringing "bread to mankind" on wagons, as Stepan Trofimovich Verkhovenskii, the hero of *The Devils*, aptly puts it. On the contrary, like Christ, in the name of the ideal, mankind must renounce the love of money (*the second temptation of the devil*). Dostoevsky believed that the Roman Catholic Church yielded to this temptation in precisely the same way that socialism did.

The second case of suicide is the death of Herzen's seventeen-year-old daughter, who poisoned herself with chloroform. In her suicide note, she mentions, with the intonation of a reprobate, the champagne with which her resurrection from the dead will be toasted if suddenly her suicide attempt is unsuccessful and, with that in mind, requests that "they bury me only after they are absolutely certain that I am dead, because it would be thoroughly unpleasant to wake up in a coffin underground. *It would even come off very very un-chic!*" (23:145).

Unlike Pisareva, who put an end to her life because she was "tired of living" and not because of some clear ideological causes, Herzen's daughter had a grudge against the absurd order of life, against the laws of nature that, by the immutable condition of existence, dictate inevitable death. Dostoevsky sees in her suicide the very same philosophical reasons that underlie that of his fictional "logical" suicide. His fictional suicide is "of course a materialist" (23:146), and the writer even quotes him in the chapter "A Sentence" [Prigovor] (*Diary of a Writer*). In turn, this suicide is very reminiscent of Kirillov and Ivan Karamazov in the method and tone of his arguments:

Tomorrow all this will be destroyed. I, and all this happiness, and all love, and all mankind will revert to nothing, to the chaos of old. And under such conditions I cannot accept any happiness on any account.... Well, if I were to die and mankind were to remain in my place eternally, then perhaps I would find consolation in it. But our planet, after all, is not eternal, and mankind is granted no more than the instant I have been granted. And no matter how intelligently, joyously, justly, and piously mankind has arranged things on earth, it will all be as naught tomorrow. And even if this is necessary for some reason, in accordance with some all-powerful, eternal, and dead *laws of nature*, believe me, this idea contains a very profound disrespect for mankind that I find deeply offensive and particularly unbearable because there *is no one to blame here* [my emphasis—A.G.]. (23:147)

The logic of the "logical" suicide reminds one a great deal of the logic of Leo Tolstoy's reasoning when he began thinking about committing suicide and then told about it in his *Confession* [Ispoved']. At the age of fifty, Tolstoy was faced with unanswerable questions: Why? And what then? "Why should I go on living? Why should I desire anything? Why should I do anything?" the writer racked his brain. "Fine, so you'll be more famous than Gogol, Pushkin, Shakespeare, Molière, and all the writers in the world—well what of it?" Such logic leads him to an idea that is inevitable (according to this very logic): life is evil, and one must save oneself from it (from life). The escape of "strength and energy," as determined by Tolstoy, is suicide—at the very moment the individual realizes that life is evil and an absurdity. This is the path that strong and consistent people take—moreover, they take it while in the prime of life. Others either choose the escape of "weakness," continuing to toil away in life, knowing that nothing good will come of it, or the escape of "Epicureanism," which consists in "knowing the hopelessness of life, yet enjoying, for the time being, the blessings one has." Finally there is the escape of "ignorance" about these questions, the way out unconsciously chosen by women, by the very young, or by very stupid people. The idea of the meaning of life can be doubted because meaning is too unsteady, whereas death, on the contrary, seems absolute and unavoidable to the artist. "Is there any meaning in my life that will not inevitably be destroyed by my imminent death?" Tolstoy asks himself and is unable to answer since a picture of an execution rises before him, when "the head was detached from the body, and both the one and the other knocked into each other in the box." It is as though death is laughing at the meaning of life and at Tolstoy's agonizing thoughts.

Trying to find his way out of this dead end (after all, my mind can make a mistake and all the others, millions and millions of them, are alive), Tolstoy repudiates logic just as categorically as he once followed it. In exchange for it he finds faith to be "the knowledge of the meaning of human life." What meaning is not destroyed by death? Union with the everlasting God and paradise, replies Tolstoy. In the same *strong-willed* way that he had earlier sought the meaning of life without finding it, Tolstoy, like a true solipsist, *forces* himself to believe in God, finds him in his own soul, and orders himself to believe:

> I have only to know about God and I am alive; I have only to forget and not believe in him and I die. What are these revivings and dyings? You see, I am not alive when I lose faith in the existence of God; indeed, I would have killed myself long ago were it not for my dim hope of finding Him. You see, I am alive, truly alive, only when I sense Him and seek Him. So what else am I seeking? ... God is life.

In essence, Tolstoy did not answer any of the questions he posed. Hypnotized by the insurmountable inevitability of death, he simply closed his eyes to these unanswerable questions. When Gorky tells K. Chukovskii about Tolstoy, he suddenly—by a law of associations that is mysterious and *cruel* in its precision—seems to bring together by chance the fear of death, with which Tolstoy was as familiar as with his own alter ego, and the immortality of Christ, in which the preacher refused to believe at one time:

> For him, death was more terrible than anything else—it tormented him his entire life. Death—and womankind.
> Chaliapin once exchanged the Easter kiss and greeting with him: Christ is risen! Tolstoy remained silent, allowing Chaliapin to kiss him on the cheek, and then he said, "Christ is not risen, Fedor Mikhailovich."[6]

Dostoevsky goes about things differently: from the viewpoint of the immortality of the soul, he values not only the meaning of life but also the meaning of death. The third case of suicide analyzed by Dostoevsky is that of a peasant woman who threw herself from a window "with an icon in her hand." At a later date, the writer uses this incident in his story "A Gentle Creature" [Krotkaia]. But for now he is stunned by the "gentle" soul that has destroyed itself and submissively accepted death because, as the writer sees it, "she simply could no longer go on living, 'God did not wish it,' and so she died, praying" (23:146). Even suicide—an act that is an offense to God according to the teachings of the Orthodox faith—is, for the writer, a confirmation of his idea about the immortality of the soul and of Christ's truth. He contrasts this death with the death of Herzen's daughter: "Two different creatures, just as if they were from two different planets! And two very different deaths!" (23:146). Two antithetical deaths hold antithetical meanings: the death of unbelief and the death of belief. The death of the peasant woman is tragic but not dismal: it is "gentle" and "radiant." The death of Herzen's daughter, a theomachist and a blasphemer, rejects any hope in resurrection.

In his philosophy of a common cause, N. Fedorov dreams of the resurrection of mankind in which the dead will also regain the bodies that formerly belonged to them. At the end of his life, Dostoevsky also found himself under the influence of Fedorov's ideas (as retold by N. Peterson). It is precisely during the period of his work on *The Brothers Karamazov* that Dostoevsky wrote to Peterson: "I believe in a real resurrection, literal and personal, and I believe that it will come to pass on earth" (15:470). Despite this, in the novel we find a strange episode: the saintly elder Zosima, a righteous man and a teacher, "began to stink" immediately after his death. Alesha Karamazov, who expected divine miracles and signs, suddenly found only the stench of a corpse issuing from his preceptor. Truly, the temptation of expecting a miracle is the most difficult of the temptations.

Alesha clearly forgot the gospel of Christ, who refuted the devil's third temptation and did not cast himself from the roof of the temple in order to experience the power of the love of God the Father, because his faith was strong without it. "Not faith because of miracles but miracles because of faith" was Dostoevsky's immutable dogma. People are willing to believe only if they are offered *material* proofs of the existence of God.[7] So it is with Alesha Karamazov: when he does not receive visual confirmation of Zosima's saintliness, he intends to cast himself into the abyss of sin, to fall into the embraces of the voluptuous Grushen'ka. The hero wishes to drown his sense of grievance toward God and the improper structuring of the world in the pleasures of the body—in a word, he wishes to supplant the stinking spirit with the spiritless flesh. Dostoevsky senses very profoundly the alternative to the immortality of the soul—it is voluptuousness without love, in which the harmony of the bodily and the spiritual is disrupted, the moral criteria in relations between people are lost, and all that remains is the desire for a *boundless* debauchery without shores, for the sweet sensation of falling deeper and deeper, ever more unstoppably.

"This moment" of Alesha Karamazov's unexpectedly coincides with Grushen'ka's "moment." She is not in the mood for voluptuousness: the man who had wronged her, who had seduced and abandoned her many years earlier, is coming to her at last. On the contrary, a tangle of contradictory feelings propels her toward Alesha, and she extends to him the hand of brotherly love. She gives him an "onion," as in the parable of the sinful woman, which Grushen'ka then relates to Alesha. In it, an angel, wishing to save a very wicked woman from the lake of fire, suddenly remembers that she had once given a beggar an onion. The angel holds out an onion to her and she grabs onto it, but the other sinners also wish to be saved and so they grab onto the woman's legs, and she begins to kick and shout that *she* was the one who had given the onion. At this, she falls back into the fire, while the angel moves away, weeping. Christian brotherhood consists in compassion. Grushen'ka saves Alesha, turning into his *sister*; he becomes her *brother* and also gives her an "onion," supporting her in a painful moment of emotional disturbance.

This is the moment when the Christian miracle comes! Alesha dreams of Cana of Galilee next to the coffin of the elder Zosima. It is as though heavenly strength fills his soul; he throws himself to the ground and kisses it ecstatically. The heavenly vault, strewn with stars, seems to be parting and rushing toward him. He falls to the ground a weak youth and arises a Christian warrior.

An unselfish prayer relegating present miracles to oblivion grants a real miracle—the inner change of the entire makeup of the human body, of that very dream of Dostoevsky's in which people "will be changed physically." Faith gives birth to miracles: the tragedy of death is overcome by faith in immortality. After crossing the boundary of despair, the person grieving over the death of a loved one enters into the kingdom of love. The inspired Christian ecstasy that unexpectedly appears to Alesha Karamazov was most likely experienced by Dostoevsky himself. This took place at Optina Pustynia [Monastery], where he went with Vl. Solov'ev after the death of his beloved son Alesha. Three-year-old Alesha died of epilepsy. Dostoevsky blamed himself for the death of his son. The elder Amvrosii comforted the writer. Perhaps those words of comfort were the very ones used by the elder Zosima in addressing the inconsolable mother who had lost her three-year-old son: "Rejoice, woman, and weep no more, for your babe is now with the Lord, abiding in the assembly of His angels."

The beginning of the transfiguration of the flesh lies in the mortal life of man. Man receives the freedom of choosing good or evil. Herein lies the grace of God, in Dostoevsky's view. However, all that is dark is by no means born of the flesh but rather in the human soul, *in thought*.

Criminal thought (about murder, debauchery, violence, lies) blocks the human spirit. Man is forced to remain alone with his flesh without any supporting principle, and, as a rule, he is unable to sustain this opposition. Stavrogin, Svidrigailov, Smerdiakov, and Raskol'nikov fall seriously ill and suffer from hallucinations because their spirit is ill ("not the flesh but the spirit was corrupted in our day," wrote Tiutchev). The spirit spurs the ceaseless recollections of crimes, comes down into the body, and corrupts it, acting as God's punishment brought on by man himself. He is *unable to stop remembering* his sin, he *himself* calls it forth within him, according to Stavrogin in his murderous confession.

Tolstoy's mistake consisted in his attempting, with all the ardor of a fanatic, to kill the flesh as such when it would have behooved him to investigate how one could *breathe the spirit* into the flesh. This is the path Dostoevsky took. Pushkin and Gogol logically traversed this path as well, from the former's *Gabrieliade* [Gavriiliada] and "Hermit Priests and Chaste Wives" [Otsy-pustynniki i zheny neporochny] to the latter's *Dead Souls* [Mertvye dushi] and the transubstantiation of the body of Christ in his "Reflections on the Divine Liturgy" [Razmyshlenia o Bozhestvennoi liturgii].

* * *

The entire twentieth century is marked by a lack of ideals, and therefore by suicide. Jack London, Hemingway, Esenin, Mayakovsky, Tsvetaeva, and thousands upon thousands more settle their score with life. Maupassant, the bard of the flesh, dies in agony. Nietzsche, who proclaimed that God is dead, gains the ecstasies of inspiration from illness. In this day and age, illness is not looked upon as it once was—as retribution or as one of life's trials that must be endured with a sense of humility and submissiveness to one's fate.

In contrast, illness and suffering appear on the pages of the existentialist novels of the twentieth century as absurdity and the spiteful mockery of a meaningless world. God the Creator is entirely out of the question. And death, for its part, is only the final point of this absurd life, the logical conclusion to the accident of birth. A. Camus's reinterpretation of the myth of Sisyphus—in which the hero rolls a stone up a hill and, knowing that it will roll back down the moment he reaches the top, rolls the stone back up anyway, contrary to all common sense—this tragic myth that symbolizes life crowns the intellectual quest of twentieth-century philosophy. The Nitzschean "murder" of God brought about universal despair among those in the arts. An enormous number of Western writers, even those who were not admirers of Nitzsche, could still subscribe to the words of Dante posted at the gates of hell: "Abandon hope, all ye who enter here" (*The Divine Comedy*), having in mind that hell is life on earth.

Remarque, a spontaneous existentialist and therefore a more vigorous existentialist than the estheticized philosophers Camus and Sartre, unveils a sequence of novels of despair in which the "lost" generation perishes, spiritually maimed by the war of 1914. Those not killed in the bloody war live for the moment, take pleasure in the moment. Food, wine, golden rum, the random woman, the shoulder of a friend—these are the delicate threads that bind them to life. The love of Pat Hollmann and Robert Lohkamp (*Three Comrades*) is a small, unlawful respite before the now battle with life; it is an unearned brief happiness that must give way to the inevitable reckoning—sickness and death. The love of Remarque's heroes is but a small rivulet in a raging ocean of hatred. But this makes it possible to understand the words of Robert Lohkamp, who says in a fit of anger as his sweetheart is dying, "At that moment I could have killed Roth without a second thought if I knew it would make Pat well again." Without faith in God, there is no love for people, and love for one person is also doomed. The end of the novel staggers one with its black despair. "Then I washed the blood off her. I became numb. I combed her hair. She grew cold. I laid her in my bed and covered her with blankets.... I saw Pat's face change. I couldn't do anything. I could only sit there, devastated, and look at her. Then morning came, and she was no more."

Today despair and the fear of death govern the world. Unfortunately, beauty is not saving the world; the world is destroying beauty. Nevertheless, the idea of immortality—which Dostoevsky defends in each of his works and which he believes will sooner or later take possession of the human mind— is already sending out a tender and delicate shoot in people's consciousness. One would like to hope that Tolstoy's and Dostoevsky's frenzied enthusiasm, their passionate yearning to save mankind and set it on the path of truth, will not have been in vain and that each person, like Nekhliudov, will find his own *Resurrection* [Voskresenie] and, like Alesha Karamazov, will see universal brotherhood.

NOTES

1. M. Montaigne, *Opyty*, vol. 2 (Moscow-Leningrad, 1958), p. 326.

2. See S. Belov, *Zhena pisatelia* (Moscow, 1986), pp. 151–54.

3. A. G. Dostoevskaia, *Vospominaniia* (Moscow, 1987), pp. 396–97.

4. F. M. Dostoevskii, *Polnoe sobranie sochinenii v 30-i tomakh*, vol. 24 (Leningrad, 1982), pp. 49–50. Further references to this edition will be given in the text [by volume and page number].

5. Dostoevskaia, *Vospominaniia*, pp. 186, 458.

6. Kornei Chukovskii, *Dnevnik, Novyi mir*, 1990, no. 7:155.

7. Even Fedor Pavlovich Karamazov scoffed at material representations of hell. He asserted that, if the devils drag sinners into a boiling cauldron with *iron* hooks, then there must be an iron foundry in hell, something in which he refused to believe.

VLADIMIR GOLSTEIN

Anna Karenina's
Peter Pan Syndrome

To Grow Up or Not To Grow Up

"When I was a child, I spoke as a child, I understood as a child, I thought as a child; but when I became a man, I put away childish things" (I Corinthians: xiii, 11),—writes St. Paul, a person who had the first-hand experience of conversion, that is, of the drastic expansion of understanding and growth. Tolstoy shares St. Paul's conviction that a grown-up needs to put away childish things. As early as 1853 Tolstoy remarks in his diary:

> One of the main mistakes of the wealthy is that we are too slow to realize that we are grown-ups. All our life's experience till the age of twenty-five, and sometimes beyond, precludes us from understanding it. It is quite the opposite of what happens with peasants, among whom a fifteen-year-old marries and becomes fully in charge. I am frequently surprised by the independence and self-confidence of a peasant lad. (*PSS* 46: 188–189).*

In other words, whatever views Tolstoy held about the nature of historical progress, or the charm, joy, and truth of childhood, he never questioned the value and direction of individual growth. Those who know

From *Tolstoy Studies Journal* 10. © 1998 by *Tolstoy Studies Journal*.

how seriously the early Tolstoy took marriage will appreciate his 1865
notebook entry: "The difference between a bachelor and a married man: the
former just gets old, the latter grows" (*PSS* 48: 115).[1] This view of marriage
as a process of initiation pervades the pages of *Anna Karenina*. On one
occasion, Koznyshev and Varen'ka, who failed to transform their mutual
sympathy into a marriage proposal, are compared to school children: "they
both experienced what is felt by a pupil who has failed in an examination and
has to remain in the same class or be finally expelled from the school" (Part
VI, ch. vi). On another occasion, when Dolly visits Anna at Vronsky's estate,
she is struck by its light-hearted, "childish" atmosphere—so removed from
her usual family concerns. Observing an after-dinner game of lawn tennis;
Dolly registers "the unnaturalness of grown-up people when they play
childish games in the absence of children" (Part VI, ch. xxii).

Tolstoy's own desire for growth and self-perfection remained the
driving force behind his personal life. Therefore it is hardly surprising that
his diaries and notebooks are filled with proverbs and statements on the need
to correct and rectify former sins and mistakes. Compare, for example,
"*umnyi i sogreshit i popravit*" (the clever one will both sin and correct it) (*PSS*
48: 339); "*umei zatevat', umei i rasputyvat'*" (if you want to entangle, know
how to untangle) (*PSS* 48: 356); or "*umei oshibit'sia, umei i popravit'sia*" (if you
make a mistake, know how to correct it); "*chto dokuchaet, to i nauchaet*" (what
gets you teaches you) or "*ne isportiv dela, masterom ne budesh*" (you'll never
become a master until you break things first) (*PSS* 48: 340)—this list can
obviously go on, but the tenor of these proverbs is clear: only by trial and
error can one grow up. Or, in the words of Milton's *Areopagitica*: "that which
purifies us is trial, and trial is by what is contrary .... for God sure esteems the
growth and compleating of one virtuous person, more than the restraint
often vicious."

Since in *Anna Karenina* Tolstoy presents this paradigm of growth
within the context of a fallen world, neither its articulation, nor the
circumstances in which it is articulated can be perfect; thus Tolstoy's
introduction of this paradigm in an unlikely setting, that of Princess Betsy
Tverskaia's tea party. In fact, the setting would appear less arbitrary if we
keep in mind that the scene at Betsy's was the first scene that Tolstoy drafted
for his novel.[2]

Betsy, who can hardly be suspected of being a mouthpiece for Tolstoy,
pronounces a statement, which—she insists—is more serious than her usual
small talk: "No, joking apart, I believe that to understand love one must first
make a mistake and then correct it" (Part II, ch. vi i). When one of the guests
inquires whether one should make and correct this mistake before or after

marriage, another responds with an English proverb: "it is never too late to mend." This proverb, as well as those compiled by Tolstoy in his notebooks; hardly encourages sin, but points rather to how one should behave after a transgression has occurred. One has to correct it in order to understand and to grow.

"One has to make mistakes and correct them,"—repeats Betsy and addresses these words to Anna, requesting her commentary. Anna, however, brushes off this question, and offers instead a pseudo-profound statement on the diversity of ways in which people think and express their love: "I think ... if it is true that there are as many minds as there are heads, then there are as many kinds of love as there are hearts" (*ibid*).[3] By refusing to view the passion that breaks families as a mistake that should be either avoided or corrected, Anna indicates her willingness to embrace it. Vronsky recognizes this and immediately charges ahead: "Friends we shall not be ... but whether we shall be the happiest or the most miserable of human beings ... rests with you" (*ibid*). While the previous conversation stresses the need to change and mature, Vronsky instead aspires to be locked in the timeless dichotomy of paradise/hell which passionate love so idolizes. Anna will later insist on a similar embrace of stasis: "if I could be anything but his mistress ... but I cannot and do not want to be anything else" (Part VII, ch. xxx).

When at the close of the party Betsy addresses Anna again, she encounters the following emblematic reaction: "'... oh yes!' said Anna, radiant with a smile of happiness and not understanding a single word of what Betsy was saying" (Part II, ch. vii). Anna thus avoids the recipe for growth offered to her.

Anna's observation, that neither thinking nor love obey general rules and instead depend on a particular mind or heart, is clearly correct, even if too general to contain any heuristic value. In fact, the presentation of various minds and hearts in the diversity of their expression seems to be a unifying theme of the novel: Koznyshev and Sviazhsky, Russian peasants and a foreign prince—all think and love differently. Yet, regardless of such a variety, there seems to be only one way to grow: the way suggested by Betsy Tverskaia, and followed in the novel by Kitty and Levin. They indeed grow up, and accomplish it by making mistakes and correcting them.

Anna's refusal to learn from her mistakes and correct the situation, that is to grow and develop, inevitably leads to the circularity of her physical and emotional existence. Thus, when on one occasion Vronsky is surprised by Anna's refusal to understand him, the narrator draws our attention to the already familiar nature of that situation: "'For God's sake, Anna, what is the matter with you?',—said Vronsky, awakening her as did her husband some time ago." Yet, Anna replies in a manner familiar to us from her treatment of Alexei Karenin: "I don't understand what are you asking me about" (Part V, ch. xxxii). The fact that Anna herself emphasizes the identity of her husband's and her lover's first name, Alexei, suggests that she views her relationship to them as being in some sense equivalent. Both Vronsky and Karenin encounter the same wall when dealing with Anna. *Cf.* "He [Karenin] saw that the depths of her soul, till now always open, were closed to him. More than that ... [she] seemed to be saying frankly: 'Yes, it is closed, and so it should be and will be in the future'" (Part II, ch. ix). Only a few chapters later, Vronsky encounters a similar resistance:

> Vronsky had tried several times before ... to lead her on to the discussion of her position, and had always encountered the same superficiality and lightness of judgment ... It was as if... as soon as she began to speak about this matter, she, the real Anna, withdrew into herself and another woman appeared who was strange and alien to him ... and who resisted him. (Part II, ch. xxiii)

Since she refuses to change and correct her circumstances, Anna is bound to experience recurrent psychological conflicts. She continues to shed tears as a way of avoiding choices, and repeatedly resorts to the same magical phrase "It is all over" (*vse koncheno*)—used on at least four different occasions. The circular movement of her emotional responses becomes evident even to Anna herself: after one of her fights with Vronsky she realizes: "that in the attempt to quiet herself she had again completed the circle she had already gone round so often, and had returned to her former cause of irritation, she was horror-struck at herself" (Part VII, ch. xxiii).

Anna's struggle with Vronsky becomes a vicious circle. In fact, the circle motif arises throughout the novel in connection with Anna, be it the curls of her unruly hair, or her circular palindromatic name, Anna. One can also recall the circularity of her pre-suicidal gesture of kissing her own hand (*cf.* Rancour-Laferriere 40; Herman 8). It is only fitting that the last physical image that Anna sees before death is the circular movement of the train's wheels under which she jumps. Furthermore, before her death she sums up her life experience by invoking another image of circularity: "*vint svintilsia*" (the bolt unbolted itself; Part VII, ch. xxx). This striking image conveys the circular movement both metaphorically and even acoustically. Whether consciously or not, Anna envisions her life as the circular movement of a bolt (a simplified, mechanical version of the wheel of fortune); it comes to an end when the further possibility of turning the bolt is exhausted.[4]

Tolstoy's suspicion of circular, repetitive activity becomes obvious when one considers the following comment from his 1867 letter to Slavophile thinker and journalist, Iuri Samarin. Invoking the image of a horse forced to turn a millstone, he condemns Samarin's involvement in journalistic polemics:

> Let old mares move this destructive wheel, but you are pulling this wheel consciously, you, who like a good horse, could have galloped in the fields, you join the wheel, walk slowly with mares and say to yourself. "I will walk like that so that the flour will come out fine." Yet, the flour will be the same as when it is produced by the horses who naively think that they can go very far while tied to this wheel. Explain this to me. (61, 158)[5]

The recurrent, circular character of Anna's existence points unequivocally to her dominant feature—her failure to introduce changes, corrections, and modifications of her conduct, that is, her inability or refusal to grow. I suggest that Anna is clearly a victim of what has now become known in psychology as the Peter Pan Syndrome. Dan Kiley, the author of the study, *The Peter Pan Syndrome* (1983), comments that the "Peter Pan Syndrome is not a fatal affliction (although some victims commit suicide)" (Kiley 35). Yet. "when the Peter Pan Syndrome is in its fully developed form, the victim's path to adulthood is blocked by fatalistic procrastination, irrational and magical thinking and a denial system that borders on the bizarre" (*ibid.*).[6]

The irresponsibility, anxiety, and fatalistic procrastination of the syndrome's victims are features long familiar to any reader of Tolstoy's novel. Anna refuses to think about her situation, she insists that Vronsky stop reminding her about it and finally decides to take morphine in order to avoid facing it. Kiley describes such behaviour as resorting to "magical thinking": "if I don't think about it, it will go away"; "If I think it will be different, then it will be" (Kiley 10).

Anna shares her child-like qualities, including her spontaneity, sincerity, and openness, with her immature brother, Stiva Oblonsky. The narrator stresses how both brother and sister—similar to children—provoke involuntary smiles from other people. The novel contains, however, one more grown-up character, who is explicitly compared to a child and therefore illuminates an important dimension of Anna's personality. I refer to

Liza Merkalova: "The weary yet passionate look of those eyes ... was striking in its perfect sincerity. Looking into those eyes everyone felt as if they knew her perfectly, and knowing her could not help loving her. At the sight of Anna her whole face lit up with a joyful smile" (Part III, ch. xviii). Anna shares with Liza more than a charming smile. They also share a feature that might be called a militant sincerity.[7] "Why should I work ... I cannot and I do not want to do it just for a pretense" (*narochno pritvoriat'sia ia ne umeiu i ne khochu*) claims Liza, echoing Anna's refusal to do anything that is not based on love (Part VII, ch. x). Liza's lover, Stremov, is correct in his assessment of Liza: "You are incorrigible." Yet Liza is what she is. She is an ingenuous, irresponsible person and this does not bother her: "Betsy ... had said that Lisa was playing the role of an ingenuous child (*nevedaiushchii rebenok*), but when Anna saw her she knew that this was untrue. She was really ingenuous, and a perverted but a sweet and irresponsible woman" (Part III, ch. xviii).

Both Liza and Stiva possess a certain organicity and integrity. They remain psychologically immature, yet, oblivious of being so. As Donna Orwin puts it: "What Stiva totally lacks is moral freedom, the freedom to make moral choices among competing influences" (Orwin 176). We do not know much about Stiva's inner struggle and his "denial system," for example. Rather conveniently for himself Stiva forgets about anything unpleasant, be it Dolly's misery, or the pain of the crushed railroad guard. Anna, however, does not forget. She has therefore to resort to what Kiley' describes as "fatalistic procrastination, irrational and magical thinking and a denial system that borders on the bizarre." It is this acute awareness of a grown-up predicament coupled with a conscious refusal to resort to the grown-up ways of solving it that makes Anna's Peter Pan syndrome so pronounced.[8]

ANNA AND NIKOLENKA IRTENEV

Tolstoy's own work frequently explores the dynamics of immature behaviour. In *Boyhood*, Nikolenka Irtenev confronts such universal aspects of moral life as guilt, shame, fear, pity, and self-pity. The way he resolves the conflict of these complex emotions is rather childish—which in his case is hardly surprising, given his age. It becomes more disturbing, however, when grown-ups, like Anna, follow the pattern of responses delineated by a young boy.

In *Leo Tolstoy: Resident and Stranger*, Richard F. Gustafson points to a similarity of a rhythm between *Anna Karenina* and *Boyhood*: "both works ... begin with the hope of love. They culminate in despair over sin which leads the central characters in each into a world of solitary confinement filled with thoughts of revenge" (Gustafson 44). The reason for this despair and solitude lies in the childish way in which both characters deal with their predicament.

Let us explore Nikolenka's behaviour and compare it to Anna's way of resolving moral conflicts. I propose to consider the events of central chapters entitled respectively, "The Bad Mark," "The Little Key," "The Traitress," "Eclipse," "Imaginings," "It Will all Come Right in the End," and, finally, "Hatred." As my discussion unfolds it will become clear that the dynamics of Nikolenka's behaviour foreshadows not only that of Anna Karenina, but also other grownup Tolstoy characters, such as Pozdnyshev (*The Kreutzer Sonata*) and Evgenii Irtenev (*The Devil*). In the latter case, Tolstoy himself signals this similarity by endowing the protagonist of *The Devil* with the same last name as that of his young Nikolenka. I suggest, in other words, that it is the adolescent and immature ways of these protagonists that result in the movement from the hope of love to despair, solitude, and crime characteristic of these narratives.

We first see Nikolenka as he experiences the fear engendered by the prospect of punishment for bad grades. His irritation and fear increase as he knows that he is not ready for class. Similar to Anna, he resorts to magical thinking. As he puts it: "the comforting thought occurred to me that the whole thing was over now (*vse koncheno*) and they would forget about me" (137). Yet, he is called on and gets a failing grade, which only increases his irritation and despair. Nikolenka compares his state to that of a gambler who has lost so much that he continues to gamble in order not to deal with his loss. He thus embarks on a series of new misdemeanors that only irritate him more. One such action includes a deception of his father; another, a physical attack on his teacher, St. Jerome. From this avalanche of shameful actions, the protagonist graduates into self-pity and the general dismissal of everyone around him: "Leave me alone!—I shrieked through my tears. 'You don't any of you love me or understand how miserable I am. You are all horrid and disgusting!'" (144). Nikolenka, similar to Anna on her carriage ride to suicide, views the world as consisting of revolting and disgusting people created only to torment him.

As punishment for his transgressions the boy is now locked in the cellar, where his thoughts form a recurrent pattern: "and again and again I would enter a hopeless (*bezvykhodnyi*) maze of uncertainty as to the fate in store for me, of despair and of dread" (145). For the boy, the maze has no exit, since he refuses to entertain the idea of his own guilt. Instead he prefers to imagine himself a victim, an illegitimate son of his parents: "I like to think that I was unhappy not through any fault of mine but because I was fated to be so from the day of my birth" (*ibid.*).

When he is later summoned to his grandmother, he bursts into tears, yet refuses to acknowledge his guilt. Tolstoy suggests here that tears in response to a moral predicament are caused by the refusal to accept one's guilt, that they represent a childish way of avoidance. Because of this, the conflict is bound to recur. Anna—we recall—bursts into tears periodically, while the narrator frequently compares her crying to that of a child. *Cf.* "Darling, little one!' said Anna, and began to cry in the same weak and childlike way as he [Serezha]" (Part V, ch. xxx). Describing another such outburst, Tolstoy observes: "she ... began to cry, sobbing with her whole bosom heaving, as a child cries," and echoes it in the next paragraph: "and she cried, without restraint, like a punished child" (Part III, ch. xvi).

Surrendering to his next impulse, Nikolenka rushes madly downstairs. Luckily for him he is caught by his father who pulls his ear; yet regardless of his pain, the boy does not cry this time, says that he is sorry, and feels that the punishment is just: "although my ear hurt very badly I did not cry but experienced an agreeable feeling of moral relief" (150). This moral relief, however, is not experienced because the boy comes to terms with his guilt. He, in fact, avoids dealing with it by attributing it to some mysterious cause: "I don't know what possessed me" (*ibid.*). Nikolenka's feeling of relief is caused solely by an external punishment. Not surprisingly, he bursts into tears again: "No sooner had papa let go my ear that I seized his hand again and covered it with tears and kisses: 'hurt me again,' I said through my tears, 'do it harder, make it hurt more, I am a good-for-nothing horrid miserable wretch!'" (*ibid.*). In other words, Nikolenka's self-search does not last. Once again he relapses into the vicious cycle of self-pity and hostility; he becomes hysterical and pronounces, choked with tears, that nobody loves him. The boy is finally pitied, taken to bed, and it seems that the crisis is over, Yet, nothing is resolved, so that the next and last chapter of our sequence, which is entitled "Hatred" begins with a description of the feelings of disgust and repulsion toward any action feature, or gesture of the object of his hatred, St. Jerome. Nikolenka hates him and fears him, foreshadowing Anna's attitude toward her husband: "I am afraid of you, and I hate you ... do what you like to me" (Part II, ch. xxix). This hatred poisons Nikolenka's future relationships with the teacher:

> I could not forget all that I had suffered during those two days—
> the despair, the shame, the fear and the hatred. Although after
> that St. Jerome ... hardly concerned himself with me at all, I could

not get into the way of regarding him with indifference. Every time our eyes happened to meet I felt that my look too plainly expressed my animosity ... in short, it was a terrible trial to me to have anything to do with him. (150)

Whatever the teacher's faults are, it is clear that the combination of fear, despair, self-pity, and hatred cannot lead to any resolution. Separation and alienation are inevitable, and the next chapter opens with the following line: "I began to feel more and more lonely" (*ibid.*).

The dynamics of the boy's behaviour—his complete surrender to passions and impulses, his confused passage through the maze of the unresolved questions, his refusal to recognize his own guilt and consequent graduation into the terrifying sequence of hatred, loneliness, and alienation—will be replayed with chilling precision by Tolstoy's grown-up protagonists, be it Pozdnyshev, Evgenii Irtenev, or Anna Karenina. In their case, the stakes are higher, however, and the results are tragic. Similar to Nikolenka, those grown-up characters know the difference between good and evil. They are aware of the wrongs they have inflicted. Yet they avoid dealing with their guilt by trying to ignore it, or when this does not work, by inflicting pain upon themselves (*Anna Karenina* and one ending of *The Devil*) or upon others (*The Kreutzer Sonata* and the second ending of *The Devil*).

But let us return to the parallel between Anna and Nikolenka. We remember that Nikolenka experiences a pleasant moral feeling when his father pulls his ear. It stems, primarily, from the fact that the physical pain enables the boy to forget temporarily about his guilt and St. Jerome; that is why he even insists that his father hurt him more. I believe that similar dynamics underlie Anna's refusal to accept divorce when offered to her by her husband. Instead of correcting the mistake she prefers to annihilate it with another mistake—this time by the evil that she does to herself. Ignoring the linear paradigm of growth, she resorts to the circular rhythm which she describes as: "I hurt him, but I am also suffering" (Part IV, ch. x) or as she puts it later: "I was the inevitable cause of unhappiness to him ... but I don't wish to profit by his calamity. I too am suffering and must suffer" (Part V, ch. viii). This solipsistic and immature method of dealing with the evil done to others becomes Anna's key strategy. By inflicting pain on herself (including her violent suicide) she obviously suffers, and her suffering indeed makes her pathetic. But the pity and sympathy that Tolstoy feels for Anna and with which he obviously infects us, should not blind us to the essentially child-like nature of her responses to her moral predicament. And the fact that they are childlike is underscored by Tolstoy, as he makes Anna replay Nikolenka's helpless wandering through the moral maze.

It is illuminating in this respect to consider Anna's behaviour toward her own son's transgression. Tormented by uncertainty and the feeling of doubleness that began to haunt her after her confession to her husband, Anna learns that Serezha has been punished for stealing a peach from a room to which he was not supposed to go. Yet rather than suggesting a way for Serezha to correct this mistake and thus grow and learn from experience, Anna embraces him, dismisses the governess, and begins to cuddle, caress, and shower him with words of love: "she looked at him not with a severe but with a timid expression which confused and gladdened the boy" (Part III, ch. xv). That is obviously how she wants to be treated for her own transgressions—she wants to be embraced, caressed, and loved.

Anna, thus, prevents herself from growing, she seems to be stuck in adolescence, forever oscillating between mature and childish ways. Critics have observed that Anna is associated with the motif of a downward movement: she experiences a sensation of falling down on her ride back home; she lowers her head; she slips down in the scene of her first love-making with Vronsky; she falls down under the wheels (cf. Vetlovskaia 25–30). Besides its obvious moral undertones, this motif also suggests a reverse development—back to adolescence and its tendency to apply childhood thought patterns to situations far removed from the concerns of childhood. And that is what Anna does as she slowly disintegrates from the height of moral equilibrium at which we first observe her. By the middle of the novel, as she rejects both her husband's forgiveness as well as his magnanimity, Anna's collapse becomes inevitable. Anna knows it herself: "I feel that I am flying headlong over some precipice but must not even try to save myself. And I can't" (Part IV, ch. xxi). Her childish helplessness is underlined at that moment by the fact that she allows Stiva (of all people) to solve her family problems and it is made explicit by Vronsky's observation that Anna now looks like a little boy (Part IV, ch. xxiii). It is thus hardly surprising that before her suicide, Anna describes the complexity of life in the imagery of a child: "We all want something sweet, if not a bon-bon, then a dirty ice cream" (Part VII, ch. xxix). This uncanny relapse into the language of childhood (candies and ice cream) underscores the tragedy of suicide, which is nothing but a radical attempt to arrest one's development.

Tolstoy's presentation of Nikolenka's childlike responses to the complexities of moral life reveals how concerned he is that childhood thinking be confined to childhood. In his 1875 letter to Strakhov, written during his composition of *Anna Karenina*, Tolstoy observes:

In our childhood we desire for ourselves, live within ourselves, love ourselves. But in old age we live outside ourselves, desire outside ourselves, love outside ourselves ... Life is nothing but transition from the love of ourselves, that is from personal life, to love outside ourselves, that is, to communal life. And therefore, being asked the question of what am I to do, I would answer it in the following way: love not yourself; that is, I would have resolved every moment of doubt by choosing not to satisfy the demands of self-love. (*PSS* 62: 226)

Regardless of his fascination with children, Tolstoy follows here St. Paul, rather than his usual guru, Rousseau. Indeed, as Donna Orwin's *Tolstoy's Art and Thought 1847–1880* (1993) convincingly demonstrates, by the time Tolstoy wrote *Anna Karenina*, his Rousseauism was sufficiently tamed by both Schopenhauer and Kant. Hence, Tolstoy's concentration on the second horns of his perennial dilemmas: nature vs. culture; self-assertion and self-centredness vs. self-restraint and altruism. No longer does he doubt that what is good and natural in the case of children becomes counterproductive in the case of grown-ups. A mature way of resolving doubt when it arises (and it should be recognized that for such characters, as Stiva, Betsy, or Liza Merkalova doubt never arises), is to move toward self-restraint, to choose the path of love for one's neighbour. Such was in fact the choice of Karenin at the end of Part Four when he forgave Anna and was ready to sacrifice his pride for the sake of her happiness. Anna, on the other hand, rejects the answer advocated by Tolstoy and sticks to her adolescent self-centredness and self-indulgence.[9]

* * *

In a paradoxical yet profound insight Tolstoy posits the connection between the failure to recognize and correct one's mistakes with the youthful quest for maximalism, sincerity, and integrity. Having learned that not every one of her desires or whims is necessarily a benevolent one, Natasha Rostova modifies her behaviour and grows.[10] In the case of certain other characters in Tolstoy, the refusal to correct one's mistakes or resolve inner tensions caused by sexual passion leads to disaster. The fact that the combination of immaturity, inner blindness, and external sincerity is destructive is made explicit when we compare Anna Karenina not only to the young boy, Nikolenka Irtenev, but to another Irtenev, this time a young man, Evgenii Irtenev, the protagonist of Tolstoy's unfinished short story, *The Devil*. Unable to resolve the inner conflict caused by his simultaneous commitment to his

family and his sexual passion for the attractive Stepanida, Evgenii Irtenev
commits suicide. But this is only one variant of the ending. In another variant
he kills Stepanida.

Anna and Evgenii Irtenev have several key features in common: charm,
vitality, and openness. Their youthful maximalism refuses to recognize values
higher than sincerity or integrity; yet they also share the childish penchant
for self-deception, In their effort to feel honest, sincere, and whole, they
resort to facile and false solutions. Anna deliberately downplays the
significance of her family while proclaiming the power of passion; Evgenii
deliberately downplays the significance of his sexual passion while
proclaiming the sanctity of his family. The terms of the equation might be
different but the dynamics of behaviour are the same. Both characters have a
propensity to disregard the past by claiming that "everything is over," that
things must and will start anew. Both are afflicted with physical
nearsightedness, to which they resort when confronting moral complexities.
In other words, they register the tensions and contradictions of their
situations, yet prefer to find solace in avoidance and self-deception. Anna
travels to Italy in order to forget her commitment to her family, and Irtenev
goes to the Crimea in order to forget his commitment to Stepanida.

Similar to Anna, Evgenii Irtenev is presented as someone who has
higher moral standards than those around him; Irtenev's acquaintances—we
recall—fail to view the affair with a peasant woman as problematic. Yet, when
finding themselves in complex, contradictory, or ambivalent situations and
striving to preserve an integrity impossible in such situations, characters such
as Anna, Irtenev, or Pozdnyshev resort to taking lives, either their own or
someone else's. This is hardly a mature way of solving inner conflicts.

Both in *Anna Karenina* and *Confession* Tolstoy compares those who
muse on suicides to children, and he knows that a youthful yearning for
moral integrity coupled with failure to deal with inner conflict easily leads to
death. Levin, who contemplates suicide as the result of his failure to discover
the meaning of his life, finally finds the solution in fundamental religious
tenets, and having found this meaning, he compares his revolt to the
behaviour of Dolly's children who turn raspberries and milk into an object of
play: "We destroy because we have our fill spiritually. We are children indeed
... I, educated in the conception of God as a Christian, having filled life with
spiritual blessings ... and living by them, I, like a child, not understanding
them, destroy them—that is, I wish to destroy that by which I live" (Part
VIII, ch. xiii).

ANNA AND THE YOUNG WERTHER

In fact, the connection between youth and suicide, or rather between youthful adherence to one's ideals and the realities of choices and sacrifices, was first explored in the paradigmatic modern text of suicide, Goethe's novel, *The Suffering of the Young Werther* (1774), a text which is mentioned in *Anna Karenina* in connection with Anna and Vronsky's highly dramatic passion (Part II, ch. xviii). Tolstoy is explicit about Anna's antecedent.

In his discussion of the explosive and frequently destructive value of integrity, Lionel Trilling interprets the conflict of Goethe's novel as one between compromise and integrity. Suicide is the young Werther's solution to the irresolvable tension between his idea of truth and a complicated reality: "to the end and even in his defeat he held fast to the image of a one true self. This tenacity was what had destroyed him. A disintegrated consciousness, he had persisted in clinging to the simplicity of the honest soul" (Trilling 52). The reason behind Werther's failure to resolve the tension between a disintegrating reality and the insistence on inner sincerity is clear: he is young, after all.

By mentioning Werther, Tolstoy alerts us to the fact that Anna's suicide echoes the same pattern; she also persists, shows tenacity, and holds fast to some imaginary view of the ideal human relationship, as a result of which actuality cannot but repulse her. She follows Werther in his militant refusal to grow up, in his preference for some inner core. Both Tolstoy and Goethe know and sympathize with the predicament of their protagonists, yet they obviously know that a suicide, even if committed for sublime reasons, is hardly a solution to the problems of adulthood.[11] Like Goethe, Tolstoy knew that the only way to solve such problems was through time, through the process of maturity and growth. It is this process that ensures the transition from childish integrity to the complex and contradictory commitments of adult life. Natasha Rostova, true to her name (*rost*—growth) has indeed grown from one extreme to another; Anna Karenina, however, persists in her adolescent ways.

No one who knows Tolstoy would question his commitment to the Rousseauian values of integrity, spontaneity, and authenticity. Yet, Tolstoy's commitments to the integrity of family life, to the poetics of restraint, duty, and sacrifice, do not need articulation either. Tolstoy might be sympathetic and lenient toward the reckless spontaneity of children or adolescents, yet he knows that any unbridled passion carries a destructive potential with it.[12] Already in *Boyhood*, Tolstoy muses on the capability of a child or "a peasant lad of seventeen" to set a house on fire, kill, and destroy in "the absence of reflection [or] reasoning" (43). Petia Rostov's death in *War and Peace* is a case in point. He rides into the line of fire and dies, neglecting Dolokhov's command to wait, that is, to restrain his energy. Referring to this mindless and irresponsible behaviour that results in death and misery, Orwin observes that "we love the vitality in [Petia] as we love it in ourselves" and adds that "Tolstoy's attitude toward vitality was more, critical in *Anna Karenina*" (Orwin 145). I believe, however, that Tolstoy was always wary of reckless vitality, whether it was exhibited by Natasha Rostova, Petia Rostov, or Anna Karenina. The only difference is that Anna is older and has a wider net of responsibilities; her need to use the reins of culture and reason is thus more urgent than that of her younger counterparts.

The description of Petia's death, in fact, utilizes an extremely suggestive image of failing to use the reins properly: "Petia was galloping around in the courtyard, but instead of holding the reins, he was waving his arms around in a queer, jerky way and slipping farther and farther to one side in his saddle" (Book IV, Part III, ch. xi). It is important to recall in this respect that one of Tolstoy's key philosophical concepts in *War and Peace*, that of *sopriagat'*, occurs in Pierre's dream when he overhears the word, *zapriagat'*—to harness. Indeed, throughout his oeuvre, and not just in *Anna Karenina*, it is harnessed energy that Tolstoy seems to value the most.[13] Natasha's singing and dancing, Rostovs' hunting, Levin's mowing—these unmistakably Tolstoyan moments are experienced when power and control act in unison, when energy is harnessed and put to use.

It is worth in this context to revisit the over-interpreted, yet still suggestive, scene of the horse races in *Anna Karenina*. I would argue that it is more accurate to compare Anna not just to Frou-Frou, but to Frou-Frou and her rider together. It is the rider who uses the reins to control and direct the animal's energy. This image is, of course, as old as Plato's *Phaedrus*; Plato, however, is a frequent point of departure for Tolstoy.[14]

Vronsky fails to harness Frou-Frou, to synchronize her energy and his control. "Having fallen behind the movement of the horse" (*ne pospev za dvizheniem loshadi*), he drops back in his saddle at the wrong moment and breaks the horse's back (Part II, ch. xxv). To highlight this crucial failure Tolstoy prefigures Vronsky's fall with that of Prince Kuzovlev, who also fails to control his powerful horse, Diana: "Kuzovlev had let go of the reins at the jump and the horse fell, throwing him over her head" (*ibid.*). Similar to these riders, Anna—as the novel progresses—falls behind her impulses and instincts, she "lets go of the reins," which leads to disastrous consequences both for herself and for others.

* * *

Anna's behaviour fits well with Tolstoy's design to "Portray a woman married and in high society who has strayed ... and to present that woman not as guilty but as merely pathetic" (Tolstaia 32). Anna's childlike qualities not only make her pathetic, but explain, in fact, the tremendous ambiguity that hovers over Tolstoy's portrayal of his heroine. By attributing to Anna elements of childlike behaviour, Tolstoy must have created a trap even for himself. While trying to criticize her violation of family, her irresponsibility, and selfishness, he nevertheless falls in love with the charming child he recognizes in her: hence his ambiguity. Similar to Anna, who during her birth fever pulls Karenin toward her with one hand and pushes him away with another, Tolstoy, perhaps not unlike the reader, is both attracted to Anna's childlike spontaneity, sincerity, integrity, and repulsed by her childish refusal to change and face up to the circumstances.

Authors who question the value of sincerity, whether Molière, Goethe, or Hawthorne, all reveal the profound awareness that the medicine with which one attempts to cure society's hypocrisy and philistinism is frequently more dangerous and destructive than the illness itself. They are correct in associating such a tragic predicament with youth and inexperience: hence such titles as *Young Goodman Brown*, or *The Suffering of the Young Werther*. Tolstoy's attitude toward sincerity appears equally complex and ambivalent. It may even be said that Tolstoy, deemed by many to be Rousseau's greatest follower, challenged his master's belief that sincerity and spontaneity are the hallmarks of human authenticity.

In his study, *The Battle for Childhood: Creation of a Russian Myth* (1990), Andrew Wachtel suggested that Tolstoy has taught generations of Russians to view childhood as some sort of a golden age. Yet it is worth stressing that the epithet "childlike" (*detskii*) does not automatically suggest something positive in Tolstoy's vocabulary. It is indeed positive when it is applied to children; once grown-ups are characterized by it, it frequently becomes a mark of condemnation. Thus he refers to Vladimir Solov'ev's lectures on God-humankind" as "detskii vzdor" (childish gibberish) or dismisses Renan's *Life of Jesus* as "detskaia, poshlaia i podlaia shalost'" (a childish, trivial, and mean-spirited prank) (*PSS* 62; 413–414).

The readers who criticize Tolstoy's transformation of *War and Peace*'s Natasha Rostova from a spontaneous child into a mature wife and mother succumb, I believe, to the nostalgia for childhood and for moral life that accompany it. In his book, *The Cult of Childhood*, George Boas points to the reasons behind such a nostalgia: "it cannot be denied that childhood has few, if any, responsibilities, and the assumption of duties toward others is as painful as it is unavoidable."[15] Tolstoy, as opposed to his' near-sighted critics, knew that childhood was a golden age, but he also knew that in order to become a grown-up one has "to put away childish ways," one has to move forward, not backward.

Boas observes: "If adults are urged to retain their youth, to 'think young,' to act and dress like youngsters, it is because the Child has been held up to them as a paradigm of the ideal man" (Boas 9). Boas describes the cult of childhood as the association of children with "intuitive wisdom ... as contrasted with learning, [with] a keener appreciation of beauty, not of course the beauties of the academy but of something called Nature ... [with] and a greater sensitivity to moral values" (Boas 8). It appears, though, that this phenomenon found in Tolstoy an opponent rather than an ally. Tolstoy knew that one should not only register intellectual, moral, or aesthetic nuances—one has to respond to them as a grown-up person capable of making hard choices. Beginning with her affair with Vronsky, Anna refuses to do so: "Every time the thought of what she had done ... and of what she should do, came to her mind, she was seized with horror and drove these thoughts away" (Part II, ch. xi). Tolstoy, therefore, never lets us forget that Anna—the heroine who prides herself on her truthfulness, who exhibits, in fact, "a greater sensitivity toward moral values" than others, yet refuses to correct mistakes and incorporate these corrections into her behaviour—is bound to wander in the maze of self-righteousness, alienation, hatred, and violence. Surrender to one's impulses may be an authentic, yet it is inevitably a childish way of dealing with grown-up problems.

NOTES

* Quotations from *Anna Karenina* are taken from Leo Tolstoy's *Anna Karenina*, translated by Aylmer Maude (W.W. Norton, 1995). Part and chapter are indicated in parentheses. Quotations from *War and Peace* are taken from Leo Tolstoy's *War and Peace*, translated by Ann Dunnigan (Signet, 1968). Book, part, and chapter are indicated in parentheses. Quotations from *Boyhood* are taken from Leo Tolstoy, *Childhood, Boyhood, Youth*, translated by Rosemary Edmonds (Penguin, 1985). Page number is indicated in parentheses, The rest of the Tolstoy quotations (translations are mine) come from the Jubilee Edition of Tolstoy's *Collected Works*. The volume and page number are indicated in parentheses.

I am most grateful to Thomas Epstein, Svetlana Evdokimova, Richard F. Gustafson, Robert L. Jackson, Robin Feuer Miller, Donna Orwin, as well as to the two anonymous reviewers of TV for their valuable comments; and suggestions.

1. There is a similar comment in the drafts to *The Kreutzer Sonata*. Discussing his deteriorating family life, Pozdnyshev observes: "This summer I lived as usual, but one never lives as usual, one either grows or rots. I was rotting ... Everything was the same, and had been repeating itself for twelve years already" (*PSS* 27: 401). This observation can also be said to describe the pattern of Anna's development in the second half of the novel.

2. Scholars might disagree about the exact sequence of Tolstoy's drafts, but there seems to be a general agreement that the scene corresponding to the gathering at Betsy's was the first one which Tolstoy wrote. *Cf.* C. J. G. Turner's summary of the views of the previous editors, such as N. Gudzii or V. Zhdanov (Turner 1316).

3. Anna's response is, in fact, as irrelevant and untimely as the remark of Society's "*enfant terrible*," Princess Miagkaia, about her childhood infatuation with a deacon. One is not surprised, therefore, when on a different occasion Betsy calls Anna "*uzhasnyi rebenok*." This literal translation of the French expression enables Betsy to comment on the childishness of Anna's responses.

4. In fact, Anna is associated with circles and circular movement from the moment she appears in the novel. We remember how she goes along the car in order to disembark from the train, then returns as she cannot find her brother, then, leaves again and finds Stiva, then returns to her seat due to the commotion connected with a tragic accident, and then moves out again. Significantly, in early drafts Anna ends up on the platform immediately. The changes Tolstoy introduced in the final version indicate his decision to make Anna's circularity her leitmotiv. It is therefore hardly surprising that Anna is haunted by recurrent dreams. The circularity of one such dream, in which an old disheveled peasant does something with a piece of iron, is highlighted even further by the fact that this old an is described as "muzhik-obkladchik," a term that, according to Dahl's *Dictionary of the Russian Language*, describes a hunter who moves in circles around a bear's den: "The bear beater (*obkladchik*), is one who *walks around* the bear, finds its den and makes sure that the animal is there" (emphasis mine).

The dominant impression of Anna's nightmare is her feeling that the peasant is doing something to her while preoccupied with something else. The nightmare reveals to Anna the dynamics of her life: a circle that tightens or narrows around her, caused by forces beyond her control. Furthermore, the narrator informs us that Anna has had this nightmare prior to her acquaintance with Vronsky. It thus reveals an organic part of her nature: her refusal to take charge and change the situation, her awareness that she allows external events to shape her life.

5. This association of circularity with the material life of the body and death seems to be a permanent feature of Tolstoy's poetics. The circular movement of Ivan Ilich's musings immediately comes to mind, and so does the circular movement of Brekhunov, the protagonist of Tolstoy's later story, *Master and Man*. Likewise, the protagonist of *How Much Land does a Man Need* dies trying to come into possession of as much land as he could encircle in one day.

6. The symptoms and causes of the socio-psychological predicament that Kiley describes are gender-neutral; that is why I think it is legitimate to apply his observations to Anna Karenina. It should be noted, however, that the cases that Kiley considers, starting with that of Peter Pan of James Barie story, refer solely to males.

7. It is important to stress the ambivalent nature of Anna's sincerity and to place it within a wider cultural context, since Anna's self-proclaimed sincerity, rather than being a sign of her superiority over hypocritical society, points in fact to her self-destructive immaturity.

Commenting on the cult of sincerity ushered in by the efforts of such thinkers as Rousseau, Lionel Trilling observes: "At a certain point in its history the moral life of Europe added to itself a new element, the state or quality of the self which we call sincerity" (Trilling 2). In other words, the association of such categories as sincerity, authenticity, and youth with moral truth and goodness is a rather recent phenomenon. Trilling also reminded his readers that the Greek term "authentes" means not only "a master or a doer, but also a perpetrator, a murderer, even a self-murderer" (Trilling 131).

Discussing Rousseau's criticism of Molière's portrayal of Alceste, the protagonist of *The Misanthrope* and one of the first champions of limitless sincerity, Trilling observes that "the root of his quarrel with Molière is that the radical moral absolutism of Alceste is not celebrated but questioned and teased" and points out that Rousseau's misreading is indicative of the change that has occurred in European moral attitudes (Trilling 17). This change not only enabled later readers to misunderstand Molière's program of promoting sensible conduct and pragmatic accommodations to society, but also encouraged them to view Alceste's behaviour as an absolute moral ideal. It is my contention that the contemporary embrace of "anti-hypocrisy" is questioned not only by such recent thinkers as Trilling or Judith Shklar (*cf.* her essay "Let's not be Hypocritical" [Shklar 45–86]), but also by such seemingly obvious champions of sincerity as Leo Tolstoy.

8. I recognize that Anna's self-destructive behaviour is bound to elicit numerous explanations, some of them couched in terminology that Tolstoy would find puzzling, to say the least. Thus, for example, Daniel Rancour-Laferriere explains the dynamics of Anna's behaviour in terms of Anna's narcissism and masochism (Rancour-Laferriere 41–44). Likewise, the Peter Pan syndrome is hardly a concept that Tolstoy would immediately recognize. Yet, what he would clearly recognize is the explosive situation of what might be called "psychological adolescence," that is, the tendency to resolve one's already grown-up predicaments through childish means. This situation was sufficiently important for Tolstoy to become the subject of several of his key texts.

9. Anna's irresponsible and self-indulgent behaviour has been examined before. The recent criticism that shaped my own view of Anna includes Richard Gustafson's *Leo Tolstoy: Resident and Stranger* (Gustafson 118–132) and Gary Saul Morson's *Narrative and Freedom: The Shadows of Time* (Morson 71–81).

10. On Natasha's growth see the illuminating essay by Svetlana Evdokimova, "Tolstoj's Challenge to the Concept of Romantic Love: Natasha as Hero" (Evdokimova 23–36).

11. Tolstoy's earliest reference to Werther dates from 1851, his last from 1905. In each case, Werther serves as an emblem of either passionate romantic love (*cf.* his 1856 letters to V. Arsen'eva (60: 100 and 127) and his diary entry of 1905 (*PSS* 55: 151), or of a sublime suicide. Thus in his 1873 letter to N. Strakhov, Tolstoy refers to the scandalous murder-suicide that involved A. Suvorin's wife, and explicitly juxtaposes the Romantic and sublime suicide of Werther with the series of pathetic suicides that were then haunting Russia: "Werther shot himself and so did Komarov, the student who finds Latin homework difficult. One [suicide] is significant and sublime, the other pathetic and disgusting" (*PSS* 62: 50).

12. In this sense David Herman's recent attempt to extrapolate on the basis of Tolstoy's novel the so-called "allowable passions" appears to me rather futile (Herman 5–33).

13. Cf. Robert Jackson's discussion of Anna's initial equilibrium between the forces of animation and restraint (Jackson 317).

14. Those who lack energy and vitality (like Karenin) are not in the races. In terms of Tolstoy these characters are pushed off stage, they serve as spectators, or chorus at best. Purely physical characters, who, like Stiva, lack the controlling element of their drives, do not qualify for the races either. It should be noted, though, that Tolstoy is more interested in this group (which explains the persistence of "Tolstoy-as-the-seer-of-flesh" point of view).

That is why, in terms of the races, Stiva goes down to the field, mingles with the riders, and is closer to the central stage, than is Karenin. And finally the third group consists of those whom Tolstoy endows with both drives and the driver, so to speak, and then puts into the limelight and scrutinizes in his fiction.

15. Boas continues his observation in a way relevant to our understanding of Anna Karenina: "Perhaps that is why writers, even those with a certain intelligence ... will write children's jingles and songs as if writing were a liberation from the burden of maturity" (Boas 76). Writing such books clearly provides a liberation for Anna, who—we learn—was a successful author of a children's book (Part VII, ch. x).

WORKS CITED

Boas, George. *The Cult of Childhood*. London: Warburg Institute, 1966.

Gustafson, Richard F. *Leo Tolstoy: Resident and Stranger*. Princeton, NJ: Princeton University Press, 1986.

Evdokimova, Svetlana, "Tolstoj's Challenge to the Concept of Romantic Love: Natasha as Hero." *Scando-Slavica* 39 (1993): 23–36.

Herman, David. "Allowable Passions in *Anna Karenina*." *Tolstoy Studies Journal* VIII (1995–96): 5–33.

Jackson, Robert. "Chance and Design in *Anna Karenina*." *The Disciplines of Criticism: Essays in Literary Theory, Interpretation and History*. New Haven, CT: Yale University Press, 1968. 315–329.

Kiley, Dan. *The Peter Pan Syndrome: Men Who Have Never Grown Up*. New York: Avon, 1983.

Morson, Gary Saul. *Narrative and Freedom: The Shadows of Time*. New Haven, CT: Yale University Press, 1994.

Orwin, Donna Tussing. *Tolstoy's Art and Thought 1847–1880*. Princeton, NJ: Princeton University Press, 1993.

Rancour-Laferriere, Daniel. "Anna's Adultery: Distal Sociobiology vs. Proximate Psychoanalysis." *Tolstoy Studies Journal* VI (1993): 33–46,

Shklar, Judith N. "Let's not be Hypocritical." *Ordinary Vices*. Cambridge, MA: Harvard University Press, 1984. 45–86.

Tolstaia, S. A. *Dnevniki 1860–1891*. Moscow, 1928.

Trilling, Lionel, *Sincerity and Authenticity*. Cambridge, MA: Harvard University Press, 1972.

Turner, C. J. G. *A Karenina Companion*. Waterloo, ON: Wilfried Lauirier University Press, 1993.

Vetlovskaia, V. E. "Poetika 'Anny Kareninoi'. (Sistema neodnoznachnykh motivov)." *Russkaia literatura* 4 (1979): 17–37.

Wachtel, Andrew. *The Battle for Childhood*. Stanford, CA: Stanford University Press, 1990.

CARYL EMERSON

Pushkin, Tolstoy, and the Possibility of an Ethics of History

In a 1992 essay on new developments in historiography, Sidney Monas addressed the ancient struggle between poets and historians to depict the world.[1] Those two poles—objectivity and free imagination, *Wahrheit* und *Dichtung*—have been "staring at each other, sitting together and spitting at each other, for many centuries now ..." Yet the feud is impure and in many ways still poorly defined. After all, Monas notes, "writers of fiction and poetry tend to speak not of a free but a 'disciplined' imagination" ... [and] "Tolstoy did not simply 'make up' *War and Peace*, though his 'sources' differed from those used by the historians ... When Stephen Dedalus in James Joyce's *Ulysses* says 'History is a nightmare from which I am trying to awake,' he means the process of history (conceived as 'battles and great men'), not, directly, the writing of it. In short, it seems to me that novelists and poets have on the whole shown more respect for history and the writing of it than historians have for 'Dichtung.'" Monas concludes: "And this is a pity."

Keeping Monas's comment in mind, I would like to reconsider the attitude toward history held by Russia's greatest poet, Alexander Pushkin, and by her greatest novelist, Leo Tolstoy. My larger purpose is to raise again the issue that confounds so many in our field, from the literary scholar turned New Historicist to the practicing historical novelist: namely, those

From *Resonant Themes: Literature, History, and the Arts in Nineteenth- and Twentieth-Century Europe: Essays in Honor of Victor Brombert*, edited by Stirling Haig. © 1999 by the Department of Romance Languages, UNC-Chapel Hill.

minimal increments of literary form or literary device that are unavoidable in any historical narrative. Can this inevitability be turned to advantage? A more compact focus is that narrower boundary between "poetry proper" and prose, and it is, I fear, more devious. For it is my suspicion that poetry—which, if it is to persuade at all, must believe absolutely in the tools of its trade—not only exempts its supreme craftsmen from certain epistemological doubts when they begin to practice history, but even prompts them toward a honorable and true method for transcribing historical events. As corollary to this thesis, I suggest that the psychological novel, Tolstoy's proud terrain and the triumph of nineteenth-century Russian prose, is a less successful school for would-be historians. For it goes both too far, and not far enough, in preparing its pupils to register an agreed-upon historical reality, generating a tension that might well prompt a complete rejection of all written texts of history. The latter occurred with Leo Tolstoy.

Certain factors in the biographies of these two great writers encourage comparison. Each contemplated his first historical project at a time of political crisis for Russia. Pushkin, already a famous poet, was attracted by historical drama and ballad, in the mid-1820s, after his Southern exile and during the growing ferment of the Decembrist movement; he then more seriously committed himself to archival research and historical writing after the Polish Rebellion of 1831. For Tolstoy, the sequence is reversed. Virtually unknown as a writer in his mid-twenties, still an army officer on site during the disastrous Crimean War of 1854, Tolstoy considered writing a serious history text—but never did, settling instead for a critique and deconstruction of history from within the novelistic genre only later in his career, after the first of his unsuccessful attempts to exit from literature altogether. Both Pushkin and Tolstoy had been enthralled with Nikolai Karamzin's *History of the Russian State*, the nation's first rigorous, readable, colorful, fully scholarly historical narrative, written by a master of Sentimentalist prose, whose final posthumous volume was in print by 1829. And yet each had problems with the historical profession as it was practiced in their time, in Russia and in Western Europe, and each hoped that his own writings would function as a corrective. Finally, both were drawn to illustrate their methodology with a period of profound military crisis, national risk and ultimate heroism in *Russian* (not world) history. Pushkin's most extended historical exercise is his *History of Pugachev*, 1834, an account of the fantastically destructive Cossack-led rebellion in the early 1770s, midway through Catherine the Great's reign; thirty years later, Tolstoy embedded his comments on history-writing in the Epilogue of his novelistic epic on the Napoleonic campaigns and the 1812 invasion of Russia, *War and Peace* (1860s).[2]

To be sure, the parallel alignment of these two texts is not entirely just. Tolstoy, after all, set out in *War and Peace* to debunk, all official histories, whereas Pushkin—granted official access to government archives in the last five years of his life, and grateful for it sincerely attempted to create a true (if of necessity only a partial) one. But the issues they raised en route to their mature historiographical positions are quite similar. The best work on Pushkin as historian is currently being done by David Bethea; and although Bethea does not encumber his image of the poet with anachronistic comparisons to later masters, the questions he attributes to Pushkin are precisely the ones that will subsequently cause Tolstoy such anguish: "What forces ... exist 'out there' in phenomenal reality to give shape to a uniquely Russian peasant revolt before the historian actually puts pen to paper and shapes his version into narrative? Are these forces recuperable? Is there such a thing as an historical 'plot' ... which the historian does not create but finds in the materials, and if so, is it tellable in a coherent fashion?"[3] Or, to put a Tolstoyan spin on these matters, what is the appropriate way to describe those whom history remembers as prime movers and "great men"—either as villains or as heroes? What is the proper ratio of general laws to historical particularity and (even more contested) the relation of general laws to "chance"? And finally, how might these factors best be fit into a maximally truth-bearing narrative that grants its narrator sufficient authority and, as it were, "light" (or enlightenment) to be worth the candle? In considering these issues, my focus will be less the theory of history that each writer espoused—which would entail in each case complex, disputed hypotheses on causality, fate, human agency, chance and free will, unmanageable in a brief essay—as their ideas, or better their intuitive grasp, of the ways history might be *written up*, that is, their thoughts on the very possibility of an ethical, accurate, responsible recording of an historical event.

Here Tolstoy, that prosiest of writers and a man who disliked and distrusted poetry, is by far the more famous and (I believe) cruder polemicist. This should not surprise us, since Tolstoy's preferred route—saying "no" to all received models—is easier than designing one's own sort of "yes." Thus the weight of my commentary will fall on the remarkable Pushkin, the born poet turned historian who, without ceasing to be a poet, devised an approach to history that was, I will argue, more affirmative, more scrupulously objective, and less sentimental than Tolstoy's. It was also, for its time, far more radical. And thus I hope to demonstrate, in the narrow sense and with these two players only, the wisdom of Monas's perhaps whimsical judgment, that the poetic in temperament have tended to show more respect for history than the historians have shown for *Dichtung*.

Two provocative synthesizing works by American scholars might provide a starting-point. In his 1987 interpretation of *War and Peace* entitled *Hidden in Plain View*, Gary Saul Morson argues the nay-sayer's case: that Tolstoy's positive agenda was exceptionally thin.[4] It consisted, in fact, of a single integrated impulse: systematically to discredit any authority or hierarchy that could be grasped by consciousness and "heroicized" as an explanatory or causal principle in history. Morson buttresses his argument with parallels, dear to Tolstoy, between histories for nations and war stories for soldiers on the battlefield. Amid the most chaotic conditions, Morson argues on Tolstoy's behalf, our minds will construct sequences that "hang together"—and for that reason alone are they remembered; the very structure of human memory is already false to the fullness of an event, and thus all honest attempts at recuperation are doomed to be fraudulent. Somewhat more optimistically, in his 1994 book *An Obsession with History*, Andrew Wachtel reminds us that Russians who write histories have tended to stress Russia's uniqueness among nations and thus her exemption from the usual pan-European measurements and chronologies.[5] Russia's ability to "jump out of time," to fit nowhere, to be (as one of her first philosophers, Pyotr Chaadaev, put it) both nothing and everything at once, both empty of significance and full of the purest, most exciting potential, marked out for her a fate unavailable to other European states. Feeding this exceptionalism was a remarkable tolerance for combining history and literature, for creating "intergeneric dialogues" between the two disciplines, at precisely the time that Western Europe was professionalizing and separating them out. "It is not exactly that Russians do not believe in the importance of historical narrative," Wachtel writes; "it is simply that they have not trusted historians to provide it" (16). What, then, might neophytes (like Pushkin) and non-professionals (like Tolstoy) provide in its stead?

Each writer, in his respective decade, formulated an efficient credo for himself while criticizing (often quite severely) important rival historians or historiographical schools. To take the better-known Tolstoyan position first. In *War and Peace*, Tolstoy found almost nothing to endorse in the famous—mostly French—authorities whom he had consulted on the so-called "facts" of Napoleon's invasion. His reproach to the professional historians is as follows. Of the many false laws to which the human mind is prone and which lead to the writing of faulty histories, the "law of retrospection" is among the worst. Based on the groundless assumption that humanity is progressing toward some more perfect state, it presumes that the results, wisdoms and values of the historian's present day were in place and available for the inhabitants of an other earlier time. Since, however, we in our own present day could not abide such judgment from future "transcribers" of our reality since, that is, we insist upon conceiving of ourselves as conscious and free—and since historical events are so manifestly bloody, wasteful and unprogressive, the only way we can "explain" these events in any orderly way is to resort to two highly suspicious categories, *chance* and *genius*. Tolstoy wholly disbelieves in chance, which he considers nothing more than a covering term for our ignorance of the multiplicity of causes; the honest historian of a secular age should humbly renounce any claim to know ultimate purpose. Tolstoy is also wholly against "genius," which, in his view, utterly misrepresents the way power works in the world. Power—that which moves nations—is cumulative and accretive; it cannot be reduced to the will of a single "great personage" at the top of a power-pyramid. In fact, by virtue of being the most distanced from direct action, the ones trapped at the top are the least free and the least effective. And if historians cannot answer what force it is that moves nations, Tolstoy insists, they cannot be relied upon to answer anything at all.

Worth noting at the outset is the fact that Tolstoy's stock cast of characters in an "historical event"—and his preferred hunting-ground for "historical cause," which he then ridicules and depersonalizes—is an autocratic government mobilized for total war. "History" is either the marionette-like maneuverings of an imperial bureaucracy hopelessly out of touch or the random escapes and savageries of a battlefield. Tolstoy's model for the exercise of power is a military hierarchy. And his illustration of human agency is of the most primitively simple sort, a caricature of human intelligence: it is either a unit of manual labor—a peasant behind a plow or pushing a log—or, more frequently, a man with a gun (this represents power) as opposed to a commander-in-chief who orders others to kill but does not physically do so himself (this represents impotence). What Tolstoy specifically avoids in his historical ruminations are traces of situations where one would think the psychological novel had equipped him superbly to examine: the subtle interaction of public personalities, delicately timed and honorably intentioned; the passing exaltation that yields up—if only for a moment—an insight into large or coordinated movements of minds or bodies, and perhaps serves as inspiration for them; the interplay between public reputation and its beneficial private effects. In short, he will not attend to that middle layer which would seem to offer so much to the open-minded and curious student of human affairs, namely: what did these historical personages themselves, without cynicism, in all sincerity, even if conflicted and inconsistent, think they were doing; how are they revealed in terms of their own beliefs? But no: precision, humility and psychological acumen are reserved for the private or fictional sphere, which Tolstoy fills with coincidence, happenstance and true love after the manner of all good novels. In *War and Peace*, those who feel at home in history—that is, who admit the possibility of serving the whole, and who believe they know why and whom they serve—are usually exposed as deluded fools. Historical understanding becomes possible, in Tolstoy's view, only when we acknowledge our helplessness before "the infinitesimally small units" into which life breaks down. "There can be no cause of an historical event except the one cause of all causes," Tolstoy writes. "But there are laws ..."[6]

"To study the laws of history," Tolstoy continues, "we must entirely change the subject of our observation, must leave aside kings, ministers and generals, and study the common, infinitesimally small elements that influence the masses" (988). But leaving out kings and generals is not, one could argue, the problem. The problem is Tolstoy's apparently untroubled move from human material at the top—which is denied any dignity—to mere mechanical "elements" at the bottom, which can only act bluntly and blindly, out of a sort of animal or clan self-interest. This is the reduction that appears to provide Tolstoy with his ethics of history: by definition, historical activity cannot be ethical at the higher levels and it cannot be conscious at the lower levels. How much of this vast militarization and depersonalization of metaphors for the working of history is an accidental byproduct of his subject matter (Napoleon's invasion and the cost it exacted), and how much is organically crucial to Tolstoy's theory, is not easy to say. Military historians certainly called him on this matter in the 1860s. To them and to other astonished reviewers, Tolstoy saw inevitability, collective dehumanization, violence, fraudulent loyalty mixed with blind chance—in short, a debased battlefield—in all events of abstract historical scope; and individuals in "non-historical" life, that is, individuals living and planning for life in an orderly, free, and conscious state, lived by wholly other standards. Or put another way: War and Peace are run by wholly different rules. To drop out of one is to drop in to the other. Real life is the life of the bees and the swarm and in that context, individual flying insects are not counted (indeed, not even clearly seen); and what we do see and do count, the generals and kings, we are encouraged to dismiss as fraudulent. All this is unmistakably the voice of Tolstoy himself, hollowing out the middle realms of meaning, denying the reality of transitional states—and, although the ethical life is its goal, it is marked by Tolstoy's characteristic unkindness toward institutions, social conventions, and isolated products of the intellect.

Let us now consider Pushkin's *History of Pugachev*.[7] Pushkin chose as his subject matter a military adventure that was, if anything, more savage, senseless and destabilizing than Russia's experience in 1812 (he called the Pugachev Rebellion just that, "merciless and senseless"). Like Tolstoy, Pushkin too was extraordinarily alert to the pressure of popular discontent on so-called "political leaders," and he emphasized that Pugachev—like Tolstoy's later image of Napoleon—was no initiator of a master plan, was not in control, but once his region had become a powderkeg "only a leader was missing," and "a leader was soon found" (368). Both Pushkin and Tolstoy treated this mortal threat to the legitimate government in terms of waves that rose up and then subsided; and at the peak of this bloody wave, the Battle of Borodino during the War of 1812 and the defense of Tatishcheva during the Pugachev Rebellion, neither the government nor the enemy knew who had been the winner until long after the event. Pushkin's tale of the modest, honorable General Bibikov, recalled by the Empress Catherine to defend Kazan', whose firm leadership amid demoralization and chaos turned the tide against Pugachev's rebel army (although the man himself did not survive to celebrate the victory), reminds one of Tolstoy's magisterial, mystical portrait of Fieldmarshal Kutuzov.

And yet the contrasts between the two writers are even more instructive. Unlike Tolstoy, Pushkin had a basically positive attitude toward the explanatory potential contained in chance, in genius, and in "great men"—an outgrowth, surely, of Pushkin's unembarrassed aristocratism and absolute freedom from class guilt. Although both writers found fault with many of the same positivist, "progressive" French historians, Pushkin, unlike Tolstoy, was suspicious of depersonalization for ideological purposes. This is not to say that Pushkin, in trying to understand the rebellion, embroidered his account with poetry. Quite the contrary; being a master poet, he knew what poetry could do; and he was extremely careful in his handling of rumors and legends. He specifically disdained any didactic or poetic digressions from the historian's pen. Indeed, in his rebuttals to a (largely unfriendly) 1835 review, Pushkin remarked with special irritation that although the reviewer, a minor historian of the Don Cossack region named I. P. Bronevsky, "regretted that the *History of the Pugachev Rebellion* was written so palely, coldly, drily, without the flaming brush of Byron, etc."—in fact, a precise use of facts and strict authorial restraint was what made his account of this terrible event unique, not an illustration of his own feelings or (perhaps more culpable) of universal laws. "The political and moralizing ruminations with which Mr. Bronevsky embellished his narrative are weak and vulgar,"

Pushkin wrote in a counter-review of his opponent's work. "They do not compensate readers for an insufficiency of facts, precise information and a clear exposition of events."[8]

How are we to understand Pushkin's irritation here? For his era, the poet espoused radical ideas about the particularity (that is, the "non-generalizability") of historical conditions, historical agents, and cultures. He would have resisted instinctively any attempt to frivolize the exercise of power, or the miraculousness of chance, by replacing those realities with something as presumptuous as a search for universal laws. A neoclassicist by temperament in Russia's Romantic Age, belonging to a generation that had built up meticulous personal identities by working with conventions, parodic masks and social codes, Pushkin accorded those structures considerable respect (they constituted part of a man's honor). Tolstoy, in contrast, was the first major Russian writer not to pass through the Romantic school. Very early on, he felt that "honor" could only be had *outside* a societal network: each individual was obliged to define it for himself, for it depended more upon one's autonomy, discipline, and attitude toward work than upon social codes; and if humanity was to be united at all, Tolstoy felt, it would have to be through universalizing virtues that override particularities. Peasants or manual workers everywhere would understand one another, and everywhere a person in Napoleon's position would be a fool.

Pushkin was not an essentialist, and he was far less insulted by the reality of social constraint. His purpose was to register, as fully and conscientiously as his sources permitted, the multiple perspectives and rumor-laden reality of the (still fresh) cataclysm. Since Pushkin brought so many points of view to bear on the events he depicted and recorded so little of his own, his history has been considered by many tedious and dimly motivated. He does not psychologize the participants, but rather announces the atrocities coolly. His perspective is almost entirely external; it examines, as it were, the working-out of three words in the Epigraph to his *History* that refer to the career of the rebel Pugachev: *derzost'*, *sluchai*, *udacha*—daring, chance, luck.[9] It was the proper interaction of those three factors, and not a passionately intrusive narrator of the Tolstoyan sort who denies retrievable causes while pursuing mathematical laws, that was, in Pushkin's view, a surer route to an ethical history. How, then, might the reality of "daring, chance, and luck" be communicated in a history text?

In answer to this question, David Bethea has offered the intriguing hypothesis that Pushkin's "metaphorical" instincts as a poet made it easier for him to work in categories of *simultaneity*, even while composing a necessarily linear historical narrative.[10] This gift for feeling "at home" with multiple, simultaneous pressures on an event (such as, indeed, are registered on a poetic word) served both to bind Pushkin to the present-tense of whatever he was depicting—one of his criteria for historical honesty—as well as to release him from the need to pass judgment. As an added benefit, Pushkin could honor the audience of his *History* by treating it not as a recalcitrant or gullible pupil being fed a lesson but by expecting from it the patience, subtlety, and adult interpretive gifts required by the reader of a poem. Here, perhaps, we can see Pushkin's "poetic" advantage as an historian over the fiercely metonymic prose-writer Tolstoy, who had to solve everything cognitively, linearly, logically on the level—or declare it unsolvable.

* * *

We may now sum up Tolstoy and Pushkin on the writing of history by introducing one more final document. Perhaps the most famous statement Pushkin made on the topic of "proper histories" is contained in his 1830 review of Nikolai Polevoi's *History of the Russian People*—a second-rate project that was itself a rebuttal and attempt to modernize, in the spirit of the popular French Romantic historians Guizot, Cousin, and Thierry, the work of Polevoi's (and Pushkin's) great predecessor, Nikolai Karamzin.[11] The French historians whom Polevoi admired were not mere factographers: they believed that history was progressive, moral, "scientific," and that the duty of the historian was to discover historical laws beneath chaotic particulars. The bloodiest conflict could release energy, or fuel, for historical progress—and thus was meaningful, if not inevitable. In his review of Polevoi, taking just this aspect of Guizot to task, Pushkin writes:

> Remember that Russia has never had anything in common with the rest of Europe; her history requires another formula than the thoughts and formulas deduced by Guizot from the history of the Christian West. Don't say: *It could not have been otherwise.* If that were true, then the historian would be an astronomer and events in the life of humanity could be predicted in calendars, like eclipses of the sun. But Providence is not algebra. The human mind ... is not a prophet but a conjecturor, it sees the general course of things and can deduce from it profound suppositions, often justified by time, but it is impossible to predict *chance*—that powerful and instantaneous tool of Providence.[12]

Let us consider the several parts of this statement, which resonate so suggestively with Tolstoy's later judgments. First there is Pushkin's conviction that Russia is not like the West and that the dynamics of Russian history therefore cannot be explained by Western models—or, by implication, by any universal laws. We know that in Pushkin's day the French phrase 'l'histoire universelle," "universal history," was translated into Russian two different ways. At times it was rendered in a Hegelian spirit as *vseobshchaia istoriia* (history that is "common to all"), which tended to foster those heartless paradigms where Russians were always the losers, lagging behind, left out, unable to compete with Europe in the linear progress toward "Geist." But it was also translated more in the spirit of Herder as *vsemirnaia istoriia*, history that contained a multiplicity of unranked, highly various and coexisting worlds.[13] Pushkin, with his commitment to differentiation and particularity both personal and national, sympathized with the Herderian model. Russia was not an autonomous or sealed-off world, but neither did her path necessarily lead in the same direction as any other nation in Europe; to participate in *vsemirnost'*, then, meant that one's own country could help fill out a picture of the world that was rich in its complexities and unpredictable interconnections. But if history did not detect patterns and predict, what was the task of the historian, as Pushkin saw it?

Following Pushkin's own programmatic statement, this task was, first, to understand how *chance* worked in a given national culture over time. As the Pushkinist Svetlana Evdokimova has elaborated on this idea, in cultures like the Russian, where power was highly centralized and an individual's personal initiative (as well as legal rights) were severely circumscribed, "chance" played a proportionately larger role than in more democratically inclined societies. Thus Pushkin's fascination with Napoleon and Peter the Great, and his great interest in de Tocqueville's *Democracy in America*—the North American states being a nation where, for all its unattractive republicanism, Pushkin felt that the effectiveness of chance or arbitrary initiative was diffused throughout the population and thus potentially less disruptive.[14] In Russia, both chance and genius mattered, profoundly, if they occurred at the top. Chance events could not be predicted or prepared for exhaustively, of course, but genius is precisely that which moves fast and forcefully enough to take advantage of such events when they occur. The historian in such cultures must, in all humility, study this interaction—not as an astronomer, but as a "conjecturor." At any point, and apparently for the most arbitrary and trivial of reasons, everything "could have been otherwise." But this does not mean that power in history is unreal. Or as David Bethea has formulated Pushkin's position, history may not be "straightforwardly transcribable," but that need not imply that historical meaning is an illusion. To which I would add: in Pushkin's view, it would appear, historical meaning *is as competent as language ever is* to create value and to communicate realities. And here we arrive at my tentative conclusions for this whole tangled juxtaposition. For Pushkin and Tolstoy, undisputedly great literary masters, the ethics of history ultimately came down to an *aesthetic* criterion: the durability and trustworthiness of words.

For the act of writing history is equal parts the experienced event and the words used to transcribe that event. Tolstoy's well-advertised, almost routine crises where he resolved to "leave literature behind" and "write no more" are symptomatic of his difficulties with transcription, even (or perhaps especially) in the medium of which he was a master. He pursued "the event itself." Suspiciously, Tolstoy relegated "ideas," "convictions," and delight in verbal inventiveness to a secondary or service role, assuming that words were always in thrall to something greedier and more immediate. Unless the author tied that poetic energy down to an ethical end, it risked to seduce and pollute. Much of Tolstoy's animus against Shakespeare, it appears, was rooted in his suspicion—as he said of *King Lear*—that only wit and wordplay were at stake in the great dramas; and if that were a writer's primary aim, no moral progress could ensue. Added to this anxiety about language were the traditions and expectations of the psychological novel as Tolstoy practiced it, where access to inner states had become so unproblematic that "how something looked from the outside" was never adequate, was always false. And since history leaves largely external traces, verbal or otherwise, it could not be represented honestly: honest things, as Saul Morson has memorably remarked in his study of *War and Peace*, are "hidden in plain view." They need not be teased out by words.

Pushkin put up with a great deal in his brief life, but he did not, I submit, experience a "Tolstoyan" anxiety about words and their relationship to reality. A consummate craftsman, he simply trusted them as the tools of his trade: and it was up to the poet to produce beauty, to inspire himself and others, to nourish, quite simply, a Muse. (Why is it that we cannot imagine Tolstoy ever tolerating a Muse?) For Pushkin, words properly employed had almost incantational powers and could cohere as primary realities. Language could create order, and—as in the case of his delicately constructed and highly disciplined *History of Pugachev*, which ends on intimations of Easter Week—it could probe down to order, thus revealing a unique cohesion of a particular time and a particular personality. But to make such cohesion persuasive, one had to accept the fact that the world was indeed a stage, that those who come later must view the performance from "out there," and that the fragile verbal texts we generate or recuperate on that stage are nevertheless, after their own fashion, "real." Pushkin was as devoted to Shakespeare as Tolstoy was resistant to him.

* * *

In sum: Pushkin, it seems, was more comfortable than Tolstoy with what words could hope to accomplish. His instincts as an historian were his instincts as a poet: trust the trace of a thing, trust your ability to create a structure for it, be grateful for the power and grace of that construct. And, as an historian, cultivate in yourself the disinterested curiosity required to pursue as many traces as possible. With good reason did Pushkin write in 1825 to his friend Nikolai Gnedich, Russian translator of the *Iliad*, that "The history of a people belongs to the poet."[15] And to whom would Tolstoy say that history belonged? Leo Tolstoy was very possibly Russia's least grateful writer of genius: he had everything, too much of everything, and yet again and again he asks, in confession after confession: *A chto potom?*, "What next?" As a corollary to this ingratitude, I suggest that Tolstoy, in the largeness and restlessness of his spirit, feared that curiosity itself was at some level incompatible with an ethical presence or trace in the world. As Tolstoy would have it, the right sort of human history belonged to Gerasim, house serf to the dying Ivan Ilych, or to holy fools, or to Pierre Bezukhov's mentor in captivity, the peasant Platon Karataev—in short, to all those innumerable simple and innocent folk who, so very unlike Tolstoy himself and so unknown by him, spoke in timeless proverbs and could not read at all.

NOTES

1. Sidney Monas, "Introduction: Contemporary Historiography: Some Kicks in the Old Coffin," in H. Kozicki, ed., *Developments in Modern Historiography*. New York: St. Martin's, 1992: 1–16, esp. 2.

2. See, for these parallels, Yakov Gordin, *Lev Tolstoi i russkaia istoriia*. Tenafly, NJ: Ermitazh, 1992: 28–29, 41.

3. David M. Bethea, *"The History of Pugachev*: Pushkin and Post-Karamzinian Historiography," in David M. Bethea and Sergei Davydov, *The Poet Descends to Despised Prose: History and Fiction in the Later Pushkin* (U of Wisconsin P, forthcoming). For related ideas, see David M. Bethea, "Pushkin's Pretenders: From the Poet in Society to the Poet in History," in Peter Rollberg, ed., *And Meaning for a Life Entire: Festschrift for Charles A. Mose*. Columbus, OH: Slavica, 1997: 61–74.

4. Gary Saul Morson, *Hidden in Plain View: Narrative and Creative Potentials in Tolstoy's "War and Peace."* Stanford: Stanford UP, 1987.

5. Andrew Baruch Wachtel, *An Obsession with History: Russian Writers Confront the Past*, Stanford: Stanford UP, 1994.

6. Reference is to the Ann Dunnigan translation of Leo Tolstoy, *War and Peace*. New York: Signet Classic, 1968: 986, 1178–79; further page references included in text.

7. References here, and elsewhere in the footnotes or text, to "A History of Pugachev" in *Alexander Pushkin: Complete Prose Fiction*, trans., with an Introduction and Notes, by Paul Debreczeny. Stanford: Stanford UP, 1983: 359–438.

8. I. P. Bronevskii, "Ob 'Istorii pugachevskogo bunta' (Razbor stat'i, napechatannoi v 'Syne otechestva' v ianvare 1835 goda)," in A. S. Pushkin, *Sobranie sochinenii v desiati tomakh*. Moscow: Khudozhestvennaia literatura, 1976: VII 130–45, esp. 144.

9. Pushkin chose as epigraph a passage from the account of Pugachev's atrocities by the Archimandrite Platon Liubarskii, spiritual leader of the Kazan' Monastery of the Savior at the time of the Rebellion. It opens with this sentence: "To render a proper account of all the designs and adventures of this imposter would, it seems, be almost impossible not only for a historian of average abilities but even for the most excellent one, because all of this imposter's undertakings depended, not on rational considerations or military precepts, but on daring, happenstance, and luck" (362).

10. Cf. n. 3, Bethea, "*The History of Pugachev: Pushkin and post-Karamzinian Historiography*."

11. Discussion of this review and its place in Pushkin's thought is central to most considerations of Pushkin as historian, but for our purposes among the best recent interpretations is Alexander A. Dolinin, "Historicism or Providentialism? Pushkin's *History of the Pugachev Rebellion* in the Context of Romantic Historiography," forthcoming in *Slavic Review* Fall 1999, Special Pushkin Bicentennial Issue, guest editor Stephanie Sandler.

12. "Istoriia Russkogo naroda, sochinenie Nikolaia Polevogo," in A. S. Pushkin, *Polnoe sobranie sochinenii*, ed. B. V. Tomashevskii, in 10 vv., VII 144.

13. See Igor' Shaitanov, "Geograficheskie trudnosti russkoi istorii (Chaadaev i Pushkin v spore o vsemirnosti)," in *Voprosy literatury* 6 (1995): 160–202.

14. See Svetlana Evdokimova, *Pushkin's Historical Imagination* (New Haven: Yale UP, 1999), esp. ch. 2, "Chance and Historical Necessity."

15. Pushkin to Nikolai Ivanovich Gnedich, 23 February 1825, in *The Letters of Alexander Pushkin*, ed. J. Thomas Shaw. Madison: U of Wisconsin P, 1967: 204.

Chronology

1828	Lev Nikolayevich Tolstoy is born on August 28, at Yasnaya Polyana, his father's estate 80 miles south of Moscow, to Nikolay Ilich Tolstoy and Maria Nikolayevna Tolstaya. Tolstoy has three older brothers and, later, a younger sister. Tolstoy's family belonged to the oldest Russian nobility: he was related on his mother's side to the aristocratic Trubetskoy, Golitsyn and Odoevsky families. On his father's side, Tolstoy is descended from one of the first Russians to receive the title of (*graf*) count. His father had fought in the war of 1812.
1830	Tolstoy's mother dies on August 4.
1837	Tolstoy's father dies on June 20. He and his siblings move to Kazan', where they are brought up by their father's distant relative, "Auntie" T.A. Ergol'skaia, to whom Tolstoy is devoted.
1844-47	Tolstoy attends the University of Kazan. He enters in the Department of Turkish-Arabic studies, but transfers to the law faculty in 1845. His professors recognized his linguistic talent, becoming proficient in more than a dozen languages, among them English, German and French. However, Tolstoy's pursuit of pleasure while at the university comes into conflict with a rigorous morality. He leaves the University without having graduated, and returns

	to Yasnaya Polyana, where he attempts to initiate social reform among the peasants.
1848	Enjoys the aristocratic life in Moscow.
1849	Studies law in St. Petersburg.
1850	At the end of the year, he begins his writing career with a story about gypsies and "Istoriia vcherashnego dnia" ("History of Yesterday"), both of which are now lost. The 1850s, the decade when Tolstoy is establishing his literary career, is a time of intense political debate about the freeing of serfs. Many contemporary writers belong to a new generation and social class, not landowners, but a majority of whom are university trained and strong advocates for radical reform. For his part, Tolstoy appears to be indifferent to the political realities of his day, focusing instead on such themes as the consciousness of a child and how to make a successful marriage.
1851	On May 2 Tolstoy leaves for the Caucasus with Nikolay, his oldest brother, and participates in the Caucasian campaign. His military experiences are described in such stories as "Nabeg" ("The Raid," 1853) and "Rubka lesa" ("The Wood Felling," 1855), both published in the journal Sovremennik (*The Contemporary*).
1852	Tolstoy officially joins the army.
1853	Tolstoy sends the manuscript of *Childhood* to Nekrasov, editor of *The Contemporary*, on July 3. *Childhood* is published on September 6. Turgenev praises *Childhood* in a letter to Nekrasov.
1854	Tolstoy becomes a commissioned officer and goes on to serve on the Danube and then in the Crimea, participating in the siege of Sevastopol during the Crimean War. Tolstoy is decorated for his bravery.
1855	Tolstoy comes to St. Petersburg and develops friendships with various prominent literary figures, among them Turgenev, Goncharov, Ostrovsky and Chernyshevsky.
1856	Tolstoy retires from the military, noting in his diary that a military career was not the right choice.
1854–57	Tolstoy is a frequent contributor to *The Contemporary*, publishing several stories and short novels, including

	Boyhood (1854), "Sevastopol in August, 1855" (1856), *The Two Hussars* (1856) and *Youth* (1857). The critical reception of his work is enthusiastic.
1858	Tolstoy finishes *Three Deaths* and works on *The Cossacks*, then stops writing and devotes himself to farm work during the summer.
1859	Tolstoy publishes *Three Deaths* and *Family Happiness*; the critical response is less enthusiastic. In October, he founds an experimental school for the peasant children of Yasnaya Polyana.
1860	Tolstoy continues teaching at Yasnaya Polyana until he leaves for Western Europe on June 25, traveling to France, Germany, Italy and England to visit schools and survey educational practices. He sets up a school in the manor house on his estate, urging complete liberty for studies where even the content of what is taught comes from individual needs rather than any general curriculum. His brother Nikolay dies on September 20.
1861	Tolstoy returns to Russia on April 12. He publishes *Yasnaya Polyana*, an educational journal. On May 27, he quarrels with Turgenev and challenges him to a duel.
1862	Tolstoy proposes to Sofia Andreyevna Bers, the daughter of a Moscow doctor, on September 14; they are married on September 23. Having given her his diaries to read before their marriage, the innocent Sofia is shocked to learn of his previous sexual escapades, including a relationship with a peasant woman that resulted in an illegitimate child. Their marriage begins very happily, but grows increasingly difficult over the years. Sofia will bear thirteen children.
1863	Tolstoy publishes *The Cossacks*. On August 3, his first son is born.
1864-69	Tolstoy writes and publishes *War and Peace*. The work provokes heated critical debate.
1863-76	Tolstoy writes *Anna Karenina*. The novel is published in serial form in the Russian. Tolstoy does not enjoy writing it, and struggles to produce each installment. The novel is very popular and the critical reaction is generally favorable.
1877	Tolstoy has an increased interest in religion and spirituality.

1878	Tolstoy and Turgenev are reconciled.
1882	Tolstoy learns Hebrew and reads the *Old Testament*. He publishes *Confession*.
1883	Turgenev writes to Tolstoy from his deathbed, urging him to continue writing fiction.
1884–86	Tolstoy writes and publishes *The Death of Ivan Ilych*, to positive critical response.
1887	Tolstoy publishes *The Power of Darkness*, a play which seriously offends the Tsar.
1889	Tolstoy publishes *The Kreutzer Sonata*.
1895	Tolstoy publishes *Master and Man*. Chekhov makes his first visit to Yasnaya Polyana on August 8.
1899	Tolstoy publishes a final version of *Resurrection*, which he has been writing for more than ten years.
1902	Tolstoy finishes *Hadji Murad*.
1902–10	Tolstoy's relations with his wife are increasingly bad. On the night of October 27, 1910, he decides to leave her. He falls ill on the train and is taken off at Astapovo, where he dies on November 7.

Contributors

HAROLD BLOOM is Sterling Professor of the Humanities at Yale University and Henry W. and Albert A. Berg Professor of English at the New York University Graduate School. He is the author of over 20 books, including *Shelley's Mythmaking* (1959), *The Visionary Company* (1961), *Blake's Apocalypse* (1963), *Yeats* (1970), *A Map of Misreading* (1975), *Kabbalah and Criticism* (1975), *Agon: Toward a Theory of Revisionism* (1982), *The American Religion* (1992), *The Western Canon* (1994), and *Omens of Millennium: The Gnosis of Angels, Dreams, and Resurrection* (1996). *The Anxiety of Influence* (1973) sets forth Professor Bloom's provocative theory of the literary relationships between the great writers and their predecessors. His most recent books include *Shakespeare: The Invention of the Human* (1998), a 1998 National Book Award finalist, *How to Read and Why* (2000), and *Genius: A Mosaic of One Hundred Exemplary Creative Minds* (2002). In 1999, Professor Bloom received the prestigious American Academy of Arts and Letters Gold Medal for Criticism, and in 2002 he received the Catalonia International Prize.

R. P. BLACKMUR was Professor of English and Chairman of the Gauss Seminars at Princeton University. He is the author of "The Lord of Small Counterpositions: Mann's *The Magic Mountain*" (1998) and *Language as Gesture: Essays in Poetry* (1981).

SIR ISAIAH BERLIN, O.M. is former Master of Wolfson College at Oxford. He is the author of *The Roots of Romanticism* (1999) and "Edmund Wilson at Oxford" (1987).

JOHN BAYLEY has been Warton Professor of English Literature at Oxford University. He is the author of *Housman's Poems* (1992), *Elegy for Iris* (1999) and "Lewis Caroll in Shropshire" (2000).

ANNA A. TAVIS is a Russian and Eastern European Studies Scholar at Fairfield University. She is the author of "Marie Bashkirtseva" (1999) and "Russia in Rilke: Rainer Maria Rilke's Correspondence with Marina Tsvetaeva" (1993).

AMY MANDELKER has been a Professor of Comparative Literature at the Graduate Center of the City University of New York. She is the author of "The Judgment of Anna Karenina" (1995) and co-editor of *Bakhtin in Contexts: Across the Disciplines* (1995).

CARYL EMERSON has been Professor of Slavic Languages and Literatures and of Comparative Literature at Princeton University. She is the author of *Boris Godunov: Transpositions of a Russian Theme* (1986), "A Bakhtin for the Twenty-First Century: Double-Voiced, Double-Faced, Face to Face" (1999) and "Coming to Terms with Bakhtin's Carnival: Ancient, Modern, sub Specie Aeternitatis" (2002).

W. GARETH JONES is a Professor of Russian literature at the University of Wales, Bangor. Jones is the author of "Russian Literature in the 18th Century" (1998) and "D. H. Lawrence's *The Rainbow* and Leo Tolstoy's *Anna Karenina*: An Instance of Literary 'Clinamen'" (1995).

MARTIN BIDNEY has been Professor of English and Comparative Literature at the State University of New York at Binghamton. He is the author of "The Secretive-Playful Epiphanies of Robert Frost: Solitude, Companionship, and the Ambivalent Imagination" (2002) and "Virtuoso Translations as Visions of Water and Fire: The Elemental Sublime in Swinburne's Arthurian Tale and Bal'mont's Medieval Georgian Epic" (1998).

FELICIA GORDON teaches at Anglia University, UK. She is the author of *The Integral Feminist: Madeleine Pelletier 1874-1939: Feminism, Socialism and Medicine* (1990) and *A Preface to the Brontës* (1989).

A. GALKIN is the author of "Smert' ili bessmertie? Dostoevskii protiv Tolstogo" (1993) and "Ob odnom simvole v romane M. Iu. Lermontova 'Geroi nashego vremeni'" (1991).

VLADIMIR GOLSTEIN has been affiliated with Yale University. He is the author of *Lermontov's Narratives of Heroism* (1998) and "Narrating the Murder: The Rhetoric of Evasion in 'The Kreutzer Sonata'" (1996).

Bibliography

Anemone, Anthony. "Gender, Genre, and the Discourse of Imperialism in Tolstoy's *The Cossacks*". *Tolstoy Studies Journal* 6 (1993): 47–63.

Any, Carol. "Boris Eikhenbaum's Unfinished Work on Tolstoy: A Dialogue with Soviet History." *PMLA* 105, no. 2 (March 1990): 233–244.

Arnold, Matthew. "Count Leo Tolstoy." *Essays in Criticism, Second Series*. New York: Macmillan, 1906.

Barran, Thomas. "Rousseau's Political Vision and Tolstoy's 'What Is Art?'" *Tolstoy Studies Journal* 5 (1992): 1–13.

Berlin, Isaiah. *The Hedgehog and The Fox: An Essay on Tolstoy's View of History*. New York: Simon and Schuster, 1953.

Bloom, Harold. "Homer, Virgil, Tolstoy: The Epic Hero." *Raritan* 6, no. 1 (Summer 1986): 1–25.

Bulgakov, Valentin. *The Last Year of Leo Tolstoy*. Translated by Ann Dunnigan. New York: Dial Press, 1971.

Carroll, Traci. "Sports/Writing and Tolstoy's Critique of Male Authority in *Anna Karenina*." *Tolstoy Studies Journal* 3 (1990): 21–32.

Clay, George R. "In Defense of Flat Characters: A Discussion of Their Value to Charles Dickens, Jane Austen and Leo Tolstoy." *Italia Francescana* 27, no. 1–2 (2000): 20–36.

Daugherty, Sarah B. "Howells, Tolstoy, and the Limits of Realism: The Case of Annie Kilburn." *American Literary Realism* 19, no. 1 (Fall 1986): 21–41.

241

Diment, Galya. "Tolstoy and Bloomsbury." *Tolstoy Studies Journal* 5 (1992): 39–53.

Dinega, Alyssa W. "Bearing the Standard: Transformative Ritual in Gorky's Mother andthe Legacy of Tolstoy." *Slavic and East European Journal* 42, no. 1 (Spring 1998): 76–101.

Dostoevsky, F.M. *The Diary of a Writer*. Translated and annotated by Boris Brasol. New York: Charles Scribner's Sons, 1949.

Durey, Jill Felicity. "Intermodality in the Novels of George Eliot, Lev Tolstoy and Gustave Flaubert." *Revue de Litterature Comparee* 66, no. 2 (April–June 1992): 173–93.

Edwards, Robert. "Tolstoy and John Dewey: Pragmatism and Prosaics." *Tolstoy Studies Journal* 5 (1992): 15–37.

———. "Tolstoy and Alice B. Stockham: The Influence of 'Tokology' on 'The Kreutzer Sonata.'" *Tolstoy Studies Journal* 6 (1993): 87–106.

Eikhenbaum, Boris. *The Young Tolstoy*. Translation edited by Gary Kern. Ann Arbor, Michigan: Ardis, 1972.

———. *Tolstoy*. 3 vols. Ann Arbor, Michigan: Ardis, 1982.

Emerson, Caryl. "Tolstoy and Dostoevsky: Seductions of the Old Criticism." *Reading George Steiner*, edited by Nathan A. Scott, Jr. and Ronald Sharp. Baltimore: Johns Hopkins University Press (1994): 74–98.

Feuer, Kathryn B., Robin Feuer Miller, and Donna Tussing Orwin, eds. *Tolstoy and the Genesis of War and Peace*. Ithaca, NY: Cornell University Press (1996).

Foertsch, Mary. "Tolstoy and Greek: A Speculation about *Anna Karenina*." *The Cambridge Quarterly* 23, no. 1 (1994): 20–31.

Gibian, George. *Tolstoy and Shakespeare*. The Hague: Mouton, 1957.

———. "Two Kinds of Human Understanding and the Narrator's Voice in *Anna Karenina*." *Orbis Scriptus* 92 (1966): 314–22.

Goldfarb, Clare R. "William Dean Howells: An American Reaction to Tolstoy." *Comparative Literature Studies* 8 (1971): 317–37.

Gorky, Maxim. *Reminiscences*. Translated by S.S. Koteliansky and Leonard Woolf. Richmond, England: Hogarth Press, 1920.

Green, Martin Burgess. *Tolstoy and Gandhi, Men of Peace: A Biography*. New York: Basic Books, 1983.

Hagan, John H. "A Pattern of Character Development in *War and Peace*." *Slavic and East European Journal* 13 (January 1963): 17–49.

Hardy, Barbara. "Form and Freedom: Tolstoy's *Anna Karenina.*" *The Appropriate Form: An Essay on the Novel* by Barbara Hardy. London: The Athlone Press, University of London (1964): 174–211.

Harkins, William E. "Battle Scenes in the Writing of Tolstoy and Stephen Crane." *Russianness: Studies on a Nation's Identity,* edited by Robert L. Belknap. Ann Arbor, Mich.: Ardis, 1990.

Hooper, Cynthia. "Forms of Love: Vladimir Solov'ev and Lev Tolstoy on Eros and Ego." *Russian Review* 60, no. 3 (July 2001): 360–80.

Hruska, Anne. "Ghosts in the Garden: Ann Radcliffe and Tolstoy's Childhood, Boyhood, Youth." *Tolstoy Studies Journal* 9 (1997): 1–10.

Jackson, Robert L. "Chance and Design in *Anna Karenina.*" *The Disciplines of Criticism: Essays in Literary Theory, Interpretation and History,* edited by Peter Demetz, Thomas Greene, and Lowry Nelson. New Haven: Yale University Press, 1968.

James, Henry. *The Art of the Novel.* New York: Charles Scribner's Sons, 1934.

Jones, W. Gareth, ed. Tolstoi and Britain. Oxford University Press (1995).

———. "George Eliot's *Adam Bede* and Tolstoy's Conception of Anna Karenina." *Modern Language Review* 61 (1966): 73–81.

Jones, Malcolm V. "Problems of Communication in *Anna Karenina. New Essays on Tolstoy,* edited by Malcolm Jones. New York: Cambridge University Press, 1978.

Knapp, Liza. "Tolstoy on Musical Mimesis: Platonic Aesthetics and Erotics in 'The Kreutzer Sonata.'" *Tolstoy Studies Journal* 4 (1991): 25–42.

———. "Language and Death in Tolstoy's Childhood and Boyhood: Rousseau and the Holy Fool." *Tolstoy Studies Journal 10* (1998): 50–62.

McLean, Hugh, ed. *In the Shade of the Giant: Essays on Tolstoy.* Berkeley: University of California Press, 1989.

Lawrence, D.H. *Reflections on the Death of a Porcupine and Other Essays.* Philadelphia: The Centaur Press, 1925.

LeBlanc, Ronald. "Unpalatable Pleasures: Tolstoy, Food, and Sex." *Tolstoy Studies Journal* 6 (1993): 1–32.

———. "Levin Visits Anna: The Iconology of Harlotry." *Tolstoy Studies Journal* 3 (1990): 1–20.

Lubbock, Percy. *The Craft of Fiction.* New York: Viking, 1957.

Lucas, Victor. *Tolstoy in London.* London: Evans, 1979.

Lukacs, Gyorgy. *Studies in European Realism,* translated by Edith Bone. New York: Grosset and Dunlap, 1964.

Mandelker, Amy. "Feminist Criticism and Anna Karenina." *Tolstoy Studies Journal* 3 (1990): 82–103.

Mann, Thomas. *"Anna Karenina." Essays of Three Decades*, translated by H. Lowe–Porter. New York: Knopf, 1965.

Matlaw, Ralph, ed. *Tolstoy: A Collection of Critical Essays*. Englewood Cliffs, N.J.: Prentice-Hall, 1967.

Maude, Aylmer. *The Life of Tolstoy*. 2 vols. London: Constable, 1908.

Milivojevic, Dragan. "Tolstoy's Views of Buddhism." *Tolstoy Studies Journal* 3 (1990): 62–75.

Morson, Gary Saul. "Work and the Authentic Life in Tolstoy." *Tolstoy Studies Journal* 9 (1997): 36–48.

Muir, Edwin. *The Structure of the Novel*. New York: Harcourt, Brace and Company, 1929.

Pittock, Malcolm. "Wilfred Owen, Tailhade, Tolstoy, and Pacifism." *Review of English Studies* 49, no. 194 (May 1998 May): 154–66.

Poggioli, Renato. "A Portrait of Tolstoy at Alceste." *The Phoenix and the Spider*. Cambridge, MA: Harvard University Press, 1957.

Redston, David. "Tolstoy and the Greek Gospel." *Journal of Russian Studies* 54 (1988): 21–33.

Rogers, Philip. "Tolstoy's Hamlet." *Tolstoy Studies Journal* 5 (1992): 55–65.

Rojas, Carlos. "Picasso and Tolstoy: On Life, Love, and Death." *The Comparatist* 17 (May 1993): 1–17.

Rolland, Romain. *Tolstoy*. Translated by Bernard Miall. London: T.F. Unwin, 1911.

Sankovitch, Natasha. *Creating and Recovering Experience: Repetition in Tolstoy*. Stanford, California: Stanford University Press (1998).

Seifrid, Thomas. "Gazing on Life's Page: Perspectival Vision in Tolstoy." *PMLA* 113, no. 3 (May 1998): 436–48.

Shestov, L. *Dostoevsky, Tolstoy, and Nietzsche*. Athens, Ohio: Ohio University Press, 1969.

Simmons, Ernest J. *Leo Tolstoy*. New York: Vintage Books, 1960.

———. *Introduction to Tolstoy's Writings*. Chicago: The University of Chicago Press, 1968.

Spence, Gordon William. *Tolstoy the Ascetic*. Edinburgh, London: Oliver & Boyd, 1967.

States, Bert O. "The Hero and the World: Our Sense of Space in *War and Peace*." *Modern Fiction Studies* 11 (1965): 153–64.

Steiner, George. *Tolstoy or Dostoevsky: An Essay in the Old Criticism*. New York: Knopf, 1959.

Steward, David D. "*Anna Karenina*: The Dialectic of Prophecy." *PMLA* 79 (June 1940): 266–82.

Syrkin, A. "The 'Indian' in Tolstoy, II." *Leo Tolstoy*. Dragan Milivojevic, editor. New York: East European Monographs (1998).

Thompson, Ewa M. "Henryk Sienkiewicz and Alexey Konstantinovich Tolstoy: A Case of Creative Borrowing. *The Polish Review* 17, no. 3 (1972): 52–66.

Trahan, Elizabeth W. "'The Divine and the Human: Or Three More Deaths': A Late Chapter in Leo Tolstoy's Dialogue with Death." *Tolstoy Studies Journal* 3 (1990): 33–48.

Troyat, Henri. *Tolstoy*. Translated by Nancy Amphoux. New York: Doubleday, 1967.

Vogue, E. M. de. *The Russian Novel*. Translated by H. A. Sawyer. New York: Doran, 1914.

Wasiolek, Edward. *Tolstoy's Major Fiction*. Chicago: The University of Chicago Press, 1978.

———. "The Theory of History in *War and Peace*." *Midway* 2, vol. 9 (1968): 117–35.

White, Duffield. "An Evolutionary Study of Tolstoy's First Story, 'The Raid.'" *Tolstoy Studies Journal* 4 (1991): 43–72.

Woolf, Virginia. "The Russian Point of View." *The Common Reader*. New York: Harcourt, Brace and Company, 1925.

Zweers, Alexlander. *Grown–up Narrator and Childlike Hero: An Analysis of the Literary Devices Employed in Tolstoy's Trilogy, "Childhood," "Boyhood," and "Youth."* The Hague: Mouton, 1971.

Acknowledgments

"The Dialectic of Incarnation: Tolstoi's *Anna Karenina*" by R. P. Blackmur. From *Eleven Essays in the European Novel* by R. P. Blackmur. © 1964 by R. P. Blackmur. Reprinted by permission.

"Tolstoy and Enlightenment" by Isaiah Berlin. From *Mightier Than the Sword* by Charles Morgan, J.B. Priestley, et al. © 1964 by The English Centre. Reprinted by permission.

"*Anna Karenina* and *What is Art?*" by John Bayley. From *Tolstoy and the Novel* by John Bayley. © 1966 by Chatto & Windus Ltd. Reprinted by permission.

"Authority and Its Discontents in Tolstoy and Joyce" by Anna A. Tavis. From *Irish Slavonic Studies* 12. © 1991 by *Irish Slavonic Studies*. Reprinted by permission.

"A Painted Lady: The Poetics of *Ekphrasis*" by Amy Mandelker. From *Framing Anna Karenina: Tolstoy, the Woman Question, and the Victorian Novel*. © 1993 by Ohio State University Press. Reprinted by permission.

"Tolstoy and Dostoevsky: Seductions of the Old Criticism" by Caryl Emerson. From *Reading George Steiner*, edited by Nathan A. Scott, Jr. and Ronald A. Sharp. © 1994 by The Johns Hopkins University Press. Reprinted with permission of the Johns Hopkins University Press.

"A Man Speaking to Men: The Narratives of *War and Peace*" by W. Gareth Jones. From *New Essays on Tolstoy*, edited by Malcolm Jones. © 1978 by Cambridge University Press. Reprinted with the permission of Cambridge University Press.

"Water, Movement, Roundness: *Epiphanies and History in Tolstoy's* War and Peace" by Martin Bidney. From *Patterns of Epiphany: From Wordsworth to Tolstoy, Pater, and Barrett Browning* by Martin Bidney. © 1997 by Southern Illinois University Press. Reprinted by permission.

"Legitimation and Irony in Tolstoy and Fontane" by Felicia Gordon. From *Scarlett Letteres: Fictions of Adultery from Antiquity to the 1990s*, edited by Nicholas White and Naomi Segal. © by Nicholas White and Naomi Segal. Reprinted with permission of Palgrave MacMillan.

"Death or Immortality? Dostoevsky versus Tolstoy" by A. Galkin. English-language translation copyright © by M. E. Sharpe, Inc. From *Russian Studies in Literature* 34, no. 4 (Fall 1998) pp. 4–18. Reprinted by permission.

"Anna Karenina's Peter Pan Syndrome" by Vladimir Golstein. From *Tolstoy Studies Journal* 10. © 1998 by *Tolstoy Studies Journal*. Reprinted by permission.

"Pushkin, Tolstoy, and the Possibility of an Ethics of History" by Caryl Emerson. From *Resonant Themes: Literature, History, and the Arts in Nineteenth- and Twentieth-Century Europe: Essays in Honor of Victor Brombert*, edited by Stirling Haig. © 1999 by the Department of Romance Languages, UNC-Chapel Hill. Used by permission of the publisher.

Index